A POET'S COUNTRY

D1453295

PATRICK KAVANAGH

A Poet's Country
Selected Prose

Edited by Antoinette Quinn

THE LILLIPUT PRESS
DUBLIN

First published 2003 by
THE LILLIPUT PRESS LTD
62–63 Sitric Road, Arbour Hill,
Dublin 7, Ireland
www.lilliputpress.ie

A CIP record for this title is available from
The British Library.

3 5 7 9 10 8 6 4 2

ISBN 1 84351 010 3

*The Lilliput Press receives financial assistance from
An Chomhairle Ealaíon / The Arts Council of Ireland.*

Set in Adobe Garamond
Printed in Ireland by Betaprint of Clonshaugh, Dublin

Contents

Part II

Part III

Part IV

Introduction

'A man should avoid the daily press; it falsifies his sense of values.'
(*Kavanagh's Weekly*, 28 June 1952)

I

On 24 July 1943, towards the beginning of his career in journalism, Patrick Kavanagh was among the press corps invited to attend a presidential garden party for the Irish Red Cross Society at Áras an Uachtaráin. The President was Douglas Hyde, former leader of the Gaelic Revival, poet, dramatist and folklore collector. Kavanagh, who was given to seeking the patronage of powerful men with an interest in the arts, had requested an audience with him three years previously. 'I am vain enough to hope that you are acquainted with my name, Patrick Kavanagh poet,' he wrote. Hyde underlined the sentence and scribbled 'No' in the margin; no meeting took place.[1]

Kavanagh's account of the garden party appeared in 'City Commentary', the twice-weekly social column he contributed to the *Irish Press* under the pen-name Piers Plowman. It is highly complimentary about Hyde and portrays Kavanagh himself hobnobbing with other dignitaries: Gerald Boland, Minister for Justice; Mrs Ryan, wife of Dr James Ryan, Minister for Agriculture; and J.J. McElligott, the formidable Secretary of the Department of Finance.

Kavanagh's rose-tinted view of his own performance at this gala social event was not shared by the President's entourage. A report in the presidential files reveals that he was already regarded with disfavour as 'the author of some very obscene poems in English papers' and that his conduct at the reception further alienated officialdom.[2] The report states that he had abused his press privileges, comporting himself as a guest rather than a journalist and mingling with invited guests in the drawing-room and on the lawn. Other members of the press corps, thinking he had been singled out for special treatment, had expressed their resentment. Minister Boland, whom Kavanagh had engaged in argument, complained of being harassed, and not for the first time; the poet had a reputation for being truculent with ministers, the report adds. Kavanagh also failed to observe the dress code for press representatives, and his appearance among the fashionable throng provoked 'a considerable amount of comment'. He was wearing a green woollen jumper under his jacket instead of the expected shirt and tie; he sported sandals without socks; overall, he 'looked untidy and not altogether clean'. While it was conceded that his scruffiness might be due to his having walked to the reception, it was also in keeping with the well-known fact that he was 'not particular about his appearance'. The report concludes: 'Enter a caveat on his social card.' There would be no further invitations to Áras an Uachtaráin.

The garden party and its aftermath augured ill for Kavanagh's future as a gossip columnist; the 'City Commentary' column was dropped a little over six months later. That he broke ranks with his fellow-journalists is not surprising: though a practising part-time journalist, fitfully aspiring to full-time status, he nevertheless regarded his colleagues as artistic inferiors.

Kavanagh had a profound and lifelong reverence for the idea of the poet, elevating him (never her) to the position of a god surrounded by mere mortals. It was not a view widely shared by the mortals. His flouting of social etiquette was deliberate. (He was well aware that if a farmer wished to be treated with respect in town he had to wear his Sunday suit.) As the author of *The Great Hunger*, he saw no reason to kowtow to government ministers and senior civil servants, expecting to be indulged as a genius, however *outré* his manner or attire. The governing class in the twenty-year-old state was probably less tolerant of mavericks than a long-established and secure political elite would have been. Both sides refused to give way on the inessentials of dress, polite speech and behaviour and, inevitably, Kavanagh was the loser.

His non-conformism was foolhardy for a man still at the start of his journalistic career – and for one as intent as he was on escaping from journalism into a well-salaried position in public relations, advertising or management. He coveted the status and income of the bourgeoisie while refusing to observe its code of manners. In his youth the people of Inniskeen used to say of a drunken and disreputable local bard that he could make a 'tidy' living, 'if he had conduct'. Two years previously Kavanagh had cited this in an *Irish Times* article, 'Old Moore's Poets'. His own lack of 'conduct' would militate against him in the tightly restricted middle-class employment market, condemning him to eke out a livelihood from casual journalism.

II

Patrick Kavanagh (1904–67) regarded himself primarily as a poet and from the mid-1940s as *the* Irish poet, but he devoted most of his working hours to journalism and fiction, and prose bulks far larger than poetry in his published oeuvre. From August 1939, when he turned his back on his small farm in Inniskeen, County Monaghan to become a professional writer, until 30 June 1967, five months before his death, he earned his living as a journalist: by turns freelance, columnist, staff reporter, film critic and book reviewer. Even before he left Inniskeen, he had begun publishing feature articles as well as poems in the *Irish Times* and the *Irish Press*, the first of these being 'Journeymen Shoemakers', which appeared in the *Irish Times* in the same year as his first volume of poetry, *Ploughman and Other Poems* (1936). However, it was not until after he had completed his fictionalized autobiography, *The Green Fool* (1938), that he turned his hand seriously to journalism. Most of his articles of the late 1930s were similar in technique to *The Green Fool*, presenting country men and women as comic characters enacting scenes from small-farm life. He was less concerned to describe or report on seasonal events such as steam threshing, potato planting or harvesting than to construct affectionately humorous playlets, casting himself as both observer and participant. For the rest of his life there would always be a demand for reminiscences of his country days, and had he been content to cater for this market he could probably have earned more from describing farming than from actually working at it.

While doing his utmost to secure a non-journalistic job after he had first settled in Dublin, Kavanagh made a point of cultivating the editor of the *Irish Times*, Bertie Smyllie, in the hope of casual or permanent employment. Although he had not yet acquired a taste for alcohol, he frequented the Palace, the pub where Smyllie and his cronies met every evening and where most of Dublin's literary and artistic types foregathered. Smyllie commissioned a few 'specials', as feature articles in the *Irish Times* were called, and supplied Kavanagh with books to review throughout 1942 and occasionally in 1943.

Frank Geary, editor of the *Irish Independent*, the largest-circulation Irish daily, also put some work his way. Book reviewing was welcome because the ten shillings or so he earned for the actual review was supplemented by selling the book to Greene's of Clare Street at one third the list price.

The life of a freelance journalist was precarious in the extreme, especially during the Second World War, as paper rationing gradually reduced the number of pages in newspapers. In addition, Irish journalists were not as well paid as their English counterparts. Kavanagh had passed three exceedingly lean years in Dublin before acquiring his first regular job as a journalist in September 1942: the 'City Commentary' column in the *Irish Press*. The garden party report is typical of the column: cheerful, lighthearted, much given to name-dropping, and often including a verse jingle. Kavanagh's more serious side was revealed in 'The Literary Scene', a column largely based on book reviews, which he contributed to the Irish Catholic weekly *The Standard* from 26 February to 11 June 1943. Here he launched his first attacks against the Literary Revival, questioning the Irishness of Yeats, Lady Gregory and Synge on grounds of creed and class.

After Kavanagh's *Irish Press* column was wound up in spring 1944 he was unable to obtain work of any kind, despite the frantic efforts to sell his talents alluded to in his poem 'Pegasus', where 'Church and State and meanest trade' all reject him. It was August 1945 before he was back in regular employment, this time as staff journalist with *The Standard*. The following February he also became that paper's film critic. His job at *The Standard*, obtained through the influence of the archbishops of Dublin and Tuam, was safe and undemanding but mentally stultifying. He attended ordination and profession ceremonies, pilgrimages, and the funerals of the great and good, or anonymously recycled bland reports on religious affairs at home and abroad. Looking back on these years of dutiful pious prose in an unpublished novel, he remarked: 'You couldn't work for a so-called Catholic newspaper without being an atheist …'[3]

The film column was a safety valve for his pent-up intellectual frustration, since his chief qualification as film critic was an Olympian disdain for popular cinema. His disgust at the tinsel emotions and moral tawdriness of most films would have pleased his episcopal patrons.

By 1947, when his second volume of verse, *A Soul for Sale and Other Poems*, appeared, Kavanagh was seeking refuge from the role of *Standard* hack by associating himself with *The Bell*, the monthly literary and socio-cultural journal, whose office was at 14 Lower O'Connell Street, near the *Standard* office. The previous year Peadar O'Donnell had taken over as *The Bell*'s editor from Sean O'Faoláin, a former mentor of Kavanagh's whom he now despised as a mere man of letters. *The Bell* printed four excerpts from his forthcoming novel *Tarry Flynn* (1948), and he was publishing so frequently in the magazine and taking such a keen interest in its affairs that towards the end of 1947 O'Donnell appointed him Assistant Editor. At the same time, his connection with *The Standard* was becoming so nominal that its editor, Peadar O'Curry, would have had no option but to sack him by summer 1947, had Kavanagh not beaten him to it in early May by negotiating a deal that allowed him to freelance and continue as film critic.

From 1947 Kavanagh's criticism of fellow writers and of contemporary Irish culture began to display the terse abusiveness for which he came to be dreaded and disliked. A disparaging assessment in *The Bell* of the work of Frank O'Connor, until then a close friend, was followed by an essay on the language revival movement so inflammatory that it had to be presented as a 'letter to the editor' in order to distance the magazine from its heterodox views. Elsewhere, in the new Cork-based journal *Irish Writing*, he ridiculed F.R. Higgins, another former friend, as 'The Gallivanting Poet'. 'Gallivanting' was an early synonym for 'bucklepping', the term he would apply to the antics of writers who under a veneer of folksy charm were making a career out of Irishness. Higgins is accused of adopting the phoney 'Irish' persona of colourful, roistering poet, and accentuating his Irishness by a pretence of Catholicism. This essay was also the first in which Kavanagh inveighed against the significance attributed to place in Irish writing.

When *The Bell*, which had suspended publication in 1948, was succeeded in December 1949 by *Envoy*, a new monthly dedicated to art and literature, the editor John Ryan offered Kavanagh a 'Diary' column and a licence to be outrageous. In the column Kavanagh defined 'a true creative critic' as 'a sweeping critic who violently hates certain things because they are weeds which choke the field against the crop which he wants to sow'.[4] The chief objects of Kavanagh's own hatred were 'the pygmy literature of the so-called Literary Revival' and the contemporary literary obsession with Irishness in theme and technique. Henceforth the label 'Irish', applied to writers or writing as either a descriptive adjective or a term of approbation, would enrage him. One of his shock tactics in *Envoy* was to nominate W.H. Auden and George Barker as Ireland's leading poets. From now on he rarely praised any Irish writer other than William Carleton, George Moore, James Joyce and Samuel Beckett – and he could be quite critical of Carleton and Joyce. About Yeats he was always ambivalent, though he admired the older poet for wielding the kind of moral authority in Irish society towards which he himself aspired. In addition to providing Kavanagh with a critical platform, *Envoy* published some of his finest prose writing on country life, especially the essays 'Some Evocations of No Importance' and 'Ash Wednesday in Inniskeen'.

After the collapse of *Envoy* in July 1951, Kavanagh felt muzzled. By the following April he had persuaded his brother Peter to invest his savings in a new paper, *Kavanagh's Weekly*. In this paper, written in collaboration with Peter, he branched out into political and social as well as cultural criticism. He believed that a poet should be 'dangerous', 'a menace' to society, should 'bother / Ireland with muck and anger'; but it was in prose, and especially in *Kavanagh's Weekly*, that Kavanagh succeeded most in this aim. Fianna Fáil in office was denigrated as 'a great wet blanket' stifling 'the imaginative life of the country'. The post-war Republic was not a democracy but 'a mediocracy' whose patron saint was the Taoiseach, Éamon de Valera. State-sponsored institutions such as Radio Éireann, the Abbey Theatre and the newly formed Arts Council were lambasted. Ireland's materialism and its low artistic standards were repeatedly highlighted by reference to Britain's superior cultural vitality, a most unpopular stance at a time when a Brit-bashing patriotism was common. The closing number of the *Weekly* consisted of a single lengthy editorial in which the crusading editor lamented the lack of audience support, both financial and intellectual. Kavanagh's preoccupation was the role of the artist in society; he longed to be as influential and respected as Yeats and George Russell had been in his youth. But to some observers he appeared a marginal figure, an irresponsible rebel. After a thirteen-week orgy of destructive criticism, he had antagonized so many sectors of the Irish public that he was unemployable as a journalist. Two years would pass before he was offered work again, this time an innocuous and anonymous series of 'Sporting Prints' in the *Irish Press*, rural reminiscences devoid of political content.[5]

In May 1957 Kavanagh was offered a monthly page in a glossy 'Journal of Fashion and Décor', *Creation*. It paid well but was an incongruous publishing base for a thoroughly undomesticated poet. He strove nonetheless to entertain his readers with stories of his holidays and his views on cooking and bachelorhood. His essay on 'The Poetic Spirit' shared the page with an ad for Lancôme moisturizing cream.

A weekly column for the *Irish Farmers' Journal*, begun in June 1958, was more congenial. It was characteristic of him that while he chose his company carefully, refusing to be drawn into literary or philosophical discussion with people he considered cultural inferiors, he was happy to converse about farming, trades, crafts, racing or other sports with enthusiasts and knowledgable folk who had no intellectual pretensions. He once summarized his self-protective attitude towards well-meaning culture-vultures by parodying W.C. Fields: 'Every time I hear the word poetry (or art) I reach for the Form Book.'[6] Predictably, readers of the *Farmers' Journal* were regaled with memories of his farming years, but he also chatted amusingly and unpatronizingly about some of his more recent doings. Such journalism came easily to him. The then deputy editor of the *Farmers' Journal*, Larry Sheedy, recalls that if he were given a subject he was capable of ad-libbing the entire column aloud immediately.[7] With occasional interruptions, some prolonged absences and a great deal of goodwill on the part of the editorial staff, he managed to hold on to this column until March 1963.

Kavanagh's aggressive criticism of Fianna Fáil in office, especially in *Kavanagh's Weekly*, aligned him politically with the Fine Gael party, as did his cultivation of a former adversary, the Fine Gael Taoiseach, John A. Costello, from late 1954. In June 1959 he was recruited as a columnist by the editors of the *National Observer*, a Fine Gael monthly aimed at the thinking and chattering classes. Another outlet for his intellectual ruminations and gripes that October was the new and short-lived *Nonplus*. This literary journal was edited by Patricia Murphy from her home at 1 Wilton Terrace, the house to which Kavanagh had made his way, dripping and shivering, after he fell – or, as he claimed, was pushed – into the Grand Canal in September 1959. Three previously unpublished essays – 'Nationalism and Literature', 'Violence and Literature' and 'Suffering and Literature' – and a sheaf of poems were his thank-you to Patricia Murphy for ministering to him so effectively after one of the most terrifying ordeals of his life. Over the next couple of years he contributed prose as well as poetry to *X*, an avant-garde London-based review of literature and art launched by his friends Patrick Swift and David Wright in November 1959.

Kavanagh was never known to dismiss any literary or journalistic commission. Jim McGuinness was shy about offering him a column in the two-year-old *RTV Guide* in April 1963, knowing it to be unworthy of his talent, but he jumped at the offer and turned in a weekly column, albeit irregularly, until June 1967, five months before his death. As late as spring 1966 he was on the lookout for another column, and welcomed efforts of Welsh literary agent Llewelyn Hughes, a fan, who tried unsuccessfully to find him work with one of the English Sunday newspapers.

In his reflective prose from 1959 onwards Kavanagh was increasingly preoccupied with constructing an autobiographical myth – supremely in his *Self-Portrait*, which originally took the form of a televised address in 1962, representing his poetic career as a journey from simplicity to simplicity. Here, and in 'From Monaghan to the Grand Canal' and the Author's Note to the *Collected Poems*, his convalescence on the bank of the Grand Canal in 1955 after his operation for lung cancer was presented as a rebirth or baptism into a new literary dispensation. It was a time of epiphanic enlightenment when he had suddenly found a new aesthetic in which comedy, celebration, unimportant subject-matter and the use of the vernacular were central.

In his popular journalism he wrote as he talked when relaxing with close companions. His style was humorous and chatty, sometimes detouring off the topic. When he set out to entertain, people from all walks of life were charmed by his conversation. He treated his newspaper or magazine readers as friends and partisans, confiding in them, engaging their interest and sympathy. Whereas in his popular journalism he is often self-deprecating, presenting himself as a comic character, a fall guy, losing out to shrewder, more worldly-wise fellows, in his literary and cultural journalism from *Envoy* onwards he customarily adopts an authoritative, magisterial or sweepingly derisive tone, disposing of opponents or opposing viewpoints with a single devastating assertion rather than a reasoned argument. He made much use of aphorism and often employed a memorable metaphor as a put-down, as when he offered the image of the Irish-language writer Pádraic Ó Conaire as a 'synthetic tramp ... with his goat tethered outside the Bailey'. In his prose reflections on his own career from the late 1950s onwards, on the contrary, he writes as one bemused by his earlier naïveté about the ways of the world and the prevailing literary fashions of his youth, no longer angry and aggressive but wise, smiling and serene.

III

Kavanagh made numerous unsuccessful attempts to publish a prose collection in his lifetime. On the strength of half a dozen reports on pilgrimages, written mainly for *The Standard*, he persuaded the London publishers Hollis and Carter to commission a book on Irish pilgrimages in October 1950. It was possibly a cynical fund-raising exercise – the

£100 advance was very welcome at a time when, apart from a small monthly stipend from *Envoy*, he had no regular income – and he appears to have done no work on the proposed book.

By the following March he was planning a different collection. John Ryan, editor of *Envoy*, was eager to publish the 'Diaries' from the magazine under the *Envoy* imprint. However, Kavanagh envisaged a more diverse gathering of his signed essays and articles, along the lines of Cyril Connolly's *The Condemned Playground*, and hoped to interest an English publisher. He sent a collection to Burns and Oates; this was declined. The proposal to bring out the 'Diaries' in book form also came to nothing because *Envoy* ceased publication in July 1951.

Since the Burns and Oates typescript is lost we can only surmise which of his essays, sketches and 'Diaries' Kavanagh wished to preserve in 1951. It seems that he included some of his 1939 'specials' from the *Irish Times*: Anthony Cronin remembers him riffling through back copies of the newspaper in the National Library and cutting out the pieces he wanted with a razor-blade.[8] To this day some of his 1939 essays are missing from all microfilm copies of the *Irish Times,* among them two items in the present selection, 'Old Moore's Poets' and 'Sentimental Ploughman'.

In September 1955, while he was still quite poorly after his operation for lung cancer the previous spring, Kavanagh made a new collection of his prose. He had this professionally typed and bound and presumably sent a copy to some publisher. It is likely that this collection is the bound prose typescript in the Kavanagh Archive at University College Dublin based on material from 1951 to 1954 and entitled *Some Evocations of No Importance and other pieces*, after the *Envoy* essay of that title. It opens with a three-part sequence in which this essay is combined with two excerpts from his *Envoy* 'Diary', afterwards named 'Ash Wednesday in Inniskeen' and 'Gut Yer Man'. The next five pieces are from *Kavanagh's Weekly*: 'Haste to the Wedding' (originally 'The Marriage Market'); 'School Book Poetry'; 'The Sea' (originally 'My Three Books'); 'George Moore' (originally 'Sex and Christianity'); and 'Fair Day' (originally 'I Went to the Fair'). The typescript concludes with 'The Irish Tradition' (originally 'A Goat Tethered outside the Bailey') from the September 1954 issue of *The Bell*. Comprising only nine pieces, *Some Evocations* is really too short to make up a book, which might explain why it never found a publisher.

Prior to compiling *Some Evocations*, Kavanagh had been in discussion with the Taoiseach, John A. Costello, about the possibility of publishing a book of prose or a long poem under the auspices of the Arts Council. What he proposed was a book about 'the nature of the poetic mind', to take the form of 'a loosely continuous argument under a generic title'.[9] The Taoiseach leaned on the Arts Council to commission such a book and to pay the author £100 on the signing of the contract, and the Council obliged. Kavanagh had told Costello that he owed £100 in rent arrears and would not have the peace of mind to write while the threat of eviction hung over him. Whereas the Taoiseach (and Kavanagh) clearly regarded the payment as a form of cultural almsgiving, the Arts Council was insistent on receiving a publishable typescript by 1 August 1956 (later extended to 1 November), and on having the imprimatur of Dr Michael Tierney, President of University College Dublin, before it paid out the balance of £100. At the end of October Kavanagh submitted *The Forgiven Plough* (recorded by the Council as *The Forgotten Plough*).[10] The title, suggested by Anthony Cronin, was based on a line from William Blake's poem *The Marriage of Heaven and Hell* used as the book's epigraph: 'The cut worm forgives the plough.' As Kavanagh explained elsewhere, the 'cut worm' was his audience.

The Forgiven Plough was an attempt to create the effect of 'a continuous argument', such as he had promised Costello, by stripping previously published essays and reviews of their titles and sometimes amalgamating them within a chapter. Its nine chapters were largely based on a recycling of post-1950 material, especially from *Envoy* and *Kavanagh's Weekly*. From *Envoy* he took the essays on Auden and Joyce, 'Some Evocations of No Importance' (renamed 'The Flying Moment'), 'Ash Wednesday in Inniskeen', 'Literature in the University' and 'Gut Yer Man'; from *Kavanagh's Weekly*, 'My Three Books', 'Sex and Christianity', 'Paris in Aran', 'School Book Poetry' and 'I Went to the Fair'. The first and by far the longest chapter, which incorporated his review of *Waiting for Godot*, began by excerpting sentences and groups of sentences from the *Envoy* 'Diaries', presenting them as a series of aphorisms. *The Forgiven Plough* amounted to eighty-nine typescript pages, quite a short book. Seven of the *Some Evocations* essays were retained, suggesting that these were particular favourites. By August 1959 the Arts Council had failed to find an Irish publisher for *The Forgiven Plough* and returned the typescript.

The Forgiven Plough was Kavanagh's last attempt to compile a selection of prose. When MacGibbon & Kee, who took over as his publishers in the 1960s, decided to commission a collected prose in 1965, the task of collecting and editing the material was assigned to Niall Sheridan, a Dublin man of letters who worked for RTÉ. Kavanagh was by then too worn down by alcoholism and illness to undertake the work and was more interested in the money to be made from the collection than in its contents. When the contract was ready he was broke as usual and wrote to Timothy O'Keeffe, his editor at MacGibbon & Kee, 'Maybe you could send the Agreement and the cheque in the same envelope.'

Kavanagh gave Sheridan the *Some Evocations* typescript and Sheridan took all nine pieces from it. Sheridan was also lent *The Forgiven Plough* from which he took the opening series of aphorisms and one chapter renamed 'The Parish and the Universe'. Sheridan also based the opening pages of his book on the opening pages of *The Forgiven Plough*; the series of aphorisms culled from the 'Diaries' was entitled 'Signposts'. The overall title of the book, *Collected Pruse*, was Kavanagh's choice. It was intended to mimic an affected pronunciation of 'prose' and thus undermine the pretentiousness of the endeavour.

Since the prose collection made for Burns and Oates in 1951 was missing and Sheridan was unfamiliar with Kavanagh's 1930s and 1940s journalism, he mainly relied on extracts from *The Green Fool* and *Tarry Flynn* to represent these decades, despite the fact that *Tarry Flynn* had already been reprinted twice in the 1960s and was widely available. He also bulked out the collection by reprinting *Irish Times* reports of the 1954 libel action the author took against *The Leader*, hardly an example of Kavanagh's prose. Sheridan's approach was unscholarly: he dated none of the essays, sometimes provided the wrong source or no source, and abridged essays without signalling that he was doing so.

IV

For the present collection I have aimed to make a representative selection of Kavanagh's essays and journalism, much of which has languished unread in the back files of newspapers and magazines.

None of Kavanagh's fiction is collected here. *The Green Fool* and *Tarry Flynn* have both been continuously available in paperback for the past twenty-five years, and the two unpublished novels that succeeded *Tarry Flynn* would be better served by being presented in full in a separate edition, together with the short stories that relate to them.

The shape of the present selection is thematic rather than chronological, beginning with a group of pieces on small-farm life. This is followed by a shorter cross-section of miscellaneous journalism, essays on literature, and, finally, a series of self-portraits of the artist. The four divisions are not rigid; it is difficult to compartmentalize Kavanagh's writings because he is so pervasively autobiographical and literary-minded.

Kavanagh can also appear repetitive, especially in the essays on Irish literature, where he loses no opportunity to air his impassioned opinions on the Literary Revival, on such predecessors as William Carleton, and on some of his own contemporaries. Originally these literary essays, dispersed across three decades and various publications, would have addressed different audiences. Collecting them in a single volume emphasizes Kavanagh's obsessiveness. As he reveals in his preface to the *Collected Poems* and elsewhere, he came to dislike the dogmatic, righteous, committed ('sticky with a purpose') aspect of his own temperament, and to believe that the artist should cultivate comic detachment. When he draws on his own experiences as a small farmer in Part I of the present book, or reflects on his life as a writer in Part IV, he writes in this comic mode. Yet, Kavanagh's prose is all of a piece: whether angry, amused or meditative, it exudes personality. As Thomas Blackburn observed of his poetry, the human being is 'present in the work and breathing'.[11]

ANTOINETTE QUINN
Dublin, October 2002

NOTES

1. Letter of 24 September 1940, National Archives, Dublin.
2. Office of Secretary of the President, Report dated 27 July 1943, National Archives; 'obscene poems' alludes to the publication in part of *The Great Hunger* in the London journal *Horizon* in January 1942.
3. Antoinette Quinn, *Patrick Kavanagh: A Biography* (Dublin, 2001), p. 277.
4. *Envoy*, September 1950, p. 82.
5. 'Sporting Prints' was Kavanagh's private name for a series of five articles on country sports and pastimes published between 16 April and 24 September 1954.
6. *RTV Guide*, 25 July 1962.
7. Quinn, op. cit., p. 374.
8. Conversation with Anthony Cronin, 23 January 2002.
9. Letter of 27 May 1955 to J.A. Costello, National Archives.
10. Arts Council papers, 1955–1959, and letter of 2 July 1955 from Kavanagh to J.A. Costello, National Archives.
11. Letter of 20 March 1959 to Cyprian Blagdan, Archives of Longman, Reading University Library.

Editor's Note

Kavanagh occasionally republished essays and articles, sometimes with slight variations or under a different title. In such cases the alternative title and source are given in the source note at the end of the piece.

I have supplied titles for pieces that were originally untitled, notably material reprinted from Kavanagh's monthly 'Diary' in *Envoy*. Three pieces – 'The Turkey Market', 'On Poetry', and 'Parochialism and Provincialism' – are extracts from longer articles that originally appeared under different titles. In these cases, to signal the abridgement and to signpost the content of the extracts, I have supplied new titles, with the originals indicated in the source notes.

A lengthy parenthesis on the contemporary Irish literary scene has been omitted from 'Ash Wednesday in Inniskeen' in keeping with Kavanagh's own editing of the essay for the unpublished prose collection *Some Evocations of No Importance*. Substantial abridgements and a handful of smaller cuts are indicated by ellipses in square brackets.

When quoting his own poetry Kavanagh sometimes gave an early draft of lines he would later revise for book publication; such lines have not been altered. Where he misquotes lines from already published poems, I have silently corrected them, as I have, so far as possible, his misquotations from other writers.

Part I

A Poet's Country

The Mill o' Louth. Smell Bacon. The Stone Trough. I touch these three keys and immediately my native district comes alive in my imagination. The first and third are the names of well-known landmarks. But who would guess that the middle one is a man's nickname? How hopeless are the nicknames that one finds in fiction!

Smell Bacon is a real ballad nickname, flat and surprising like the names in American folk songs. They are never 'poetical', which means that they are poetry.

The Mill o' Louth, which stands off the road from Carrickmacross to Dundalk, occupies a great place in local lore. It is associated with the Prophecies of St Columcille. Something apocalyptical, its wheel was to be driven round with human blood when the Great (never clearly defined) Battle took place. Things of the imagination pass into a penumbra in this way.

Many's the time I heard the story from poor oul' Pether the Bodagh. Those were wonderful stories for a child's imagination. The Stone Trough was – and still is, needless to say – exactly halfway between my native village of Inniskeen and Dundalk. It was an important landmark in the not-so-long-ago days of the horse-drawn vehicle. Going to Dundalk in a cart was a big adventure. The world was an enormous place; it took a good-stepping horse two hours and a half to make the journey. We had three ways of going to Dundalk and there was a dispute as to which was the shortest.

We could go by Ballykelly, or by the Chanonrock road, or the Low Road by Hackballscross. The first two roads brought us past Smell Bacon's shop. I remembered the nickname Smell Bacon, or rather I had my memory awakened to it by a barman in Mooney's in Fleet Street, London, not long ago. This barman was from the same district and if he had presented me with a complete film of our mutually native fields he could not have brought the place more vividly before me than by this nickname.

As he uttered that magic incantation it was a summer Sunday and I was leaning over the handlebars of my bicycle beside Smell's shop, talking to, or at least listening to, a group of young fellows who were tossing ha'pence. And I remember the Sunday years earlier when we all went up to play football in a meadow belonging to the same Smell. Although the excitement of this district for me is mostly subjective and emotional, it has also some more obvious claims on our attention. Very little has been written about it in recent years, yet Farney, in south Monaghan, is one of the few places in Ireland which has an indigenous literature, as anyone can see who reads the Gaelic stories collected by Henry Morris.* There were poets in this area and though they were not great poets they absorbed the little fields and lanes and became authentic through them. For that is the way the poet's mind works.

No poet ever travelled in search of beauty. No poet ever looked at a scene and cried 'Wonderful'. Memorable beauty comes at us obliquely while we are going about our troubled business. W.H. Davies wrote:

> *What is this life if full of care,*
> *We have no time to stand and stare?*

But Davies was wrong:

> *What is this life if NOT full of care*
> *We do not let the cart-tracks stare*
> *Into our hearts with love's despair?*

---

* Henry Morris (Enri Ó Muirgheasa), 1874–1945, an inspector of schools from Co. Monaghan who collected Ulster folklore and encouraged local archaeological studies.

This pursuit of beauty is one of the defects of the tourist's point of view. The tourist is in a hurry; he demands quick returns of the picturesque and the obvious. But for all that, it is possible even when we pursue beauty or happiness to come upon oblique references to it. The job is to recognize them in the hurry. Not everybody can have the fields and lanes stare at him as they stare at a man driving a cow to a fair.

Farney has other claims to fame. I once heard Joseph Hone, the biographer of Yeats and many other famous men, say that the view from the top of Maracloone Hill, south-east of Carrickmacross, was the most exciting view he had ever encountered. But I wasn't thinking of that – Farney has had its history written. The author was Philip Shirley. This history of Farney is a subsidiary of Shirley's larger *History of Monaghan*, which is considered one of the greatest local histories ever written. But Shirley's Farney is an even greater history, for it is the intimate history of fields and lanes and the private lives of rocks. It has that wonderful validity which we find in local newspapers. It is also a history of Ireland in microcosm. This Shirley, who was a landlord, was undoubtedly a remarkable man, and notwithstanding Sir Shane Leslie's efforts, he deserves to be more seriously considered. He was intelligent enough when working on his histories to get the services of the great O'Donovan to look after the Gaelic scholarship side.

Shirley, who lived just over a century ago, rescued from oblivion a valuable part of the native heritage and deserves our profound affection. He tells stories of the McMahons, the chiefs of Farney, who are not as well known as the O'Neills or O'Donnells; but for me, as their deeds filtered through my boyhood imagination, they loom large and mysterious. McMahon and his sixteen sons once rode into the town of Louth on sixteen white horses. They had a residence – or so the story went – up the lane upon which I lived, and I often searched among the rocks hoping I might find some memory of their lives. The tomb of the McMahons is in the village of Inniskeen beside a round tower, and there remained in the legends of their lives something not merely noble but mystical.

And once again it is a summer Sunday afternoon in my imagination and I am on my bicycle passing over the Fane bridge. The Fane river, which runs through this village, is considered one of the best trout streams in Ireland, though the only fishing I ever did there was salmon-poaching. One of my most memorable bicycle tours used to be by the Low Road via Hackballscross or Annavacky. Ahead of me lie the fields of south Armagh with Slieve Gullion in the hollow. To my right is Dundalk and it is that way I go down a tree-lined road to Kilcurry and Faughart and up through Ravensdale. Ravensdale, north of Dundalk, is at least as delightful in the usual picturesque sense as south Dublin and Wicklow. A limestone country full of history, it is one of the pillars of the Gap of the North looking over Cooley and the magic setting of the Táin.

I cycle home through the Plain of Muirthemne, past Smell Bacon's again, down by Ballykelly and the undulating narrow road from the Bohar Bhee – the Yellow Road. Over there on the edge of the Red Bog lived the Bard of Callenberg. The Bard was a great character, though he did me no good when it was first discovered that I was addicted to vers-ing. Everyone thought that I would turn out like the Bard – a rapscal-lion, a scandalmonger making rhymes about the neighbours. Remember the rhyme he made about our local grocer:

> *The welkin was ringing*
> *And off I went singing*
> *For in Inniskeen I'm well pleased for to be,*
> *But in less than an hour*
> *Male, pollard and flour*
> *Was whipped off me cart by consaitey Magee.*

The Bard hadn't the money to pay for the stuff!

(*The Word*, August 1962; also *Ireland of the Welcomes*, March–April 1953, pp. 20–5)

Journeymen Shoemakers

My father was a shoemaker in the happy days when a pair of shop boots were an insult to any decent man's feet.

With porter at twopence a pint and only a day's walk between the workhouses, the journeymen shoemakers flourished. They were surrealists. The Casual Ward – the Black Hole – and the Irish pub were the first schools to teach that altogether delightful cult. Sullivan's geography could teach them nothing of the 'lie' of Ireland: they knew every parish in the four provinces, and they could sing ballads and tell tales of peace and war, for often their thirst had sought and found the Saxon shilling.

Like strange men out of a magic land I remember them coming to my father's place, their cobbler's tools tied up in an ancient apron and a road-weariness in their hearts. If they came without warning, they gave no notice of their going. In the middle of a boot the journeyman shoemaker would suddenly say, 'I'm goin',' and gather up his tools in his apron, stick them under his arm, and walk out. No offer of wages or praise could hold him.

There were no rogues among them; the dishonest one would be exposed by his fellows and pushed out of the trade. They were not exceptional craftsmen; but they knew the tricks of the trade, and could disguise a flaw in an upper or a slip of the knife.

On Monday, the cobblers' holiday, they would go to the nearest pub and drink their week's wages. I remember a little fellow called Jem Fagan, who used to come home across the hills, shouting with terrific voice the incoherencies of Bacchus. Jem's Monday-night shouting was familiar to the whole parish. The children used to come out to listen, and children could listen; for, although noisy, none of today's shocking vulgarisms were part of his drunken eloquence. He had a pair of large brown eyes that blazed in the dark like two little lamps. My father said the devil was standing in him, but it was a good-humoured devil enough.

Not all were boisterous in drink as Jem. There was Tom Healy. He would come home humming to the ditches, 'The Gates opened wide to the poor and the stranger'. He would have sweets for us children, too, though these same sweets often carried from his pocket a coating of tobacco-dust. If he wasn't too far gone he would tell his usual tale of mystery, 'The Big Dog in the Long Garden'. The big dog was a rather fleshless skeleton, but he barked and prowled bravely in the long garden of imagination.

Then there was Dan the Butt, a cranky fellow down whose spine the east wind was always blowing. He hated the east wind. He seldom talked, had the power of silence; we listened as we would listen to the priest. He had been in the English Army, and had seen, he said, the bright roof of Constantinople Minaret and the turban: that was something childhood could listen to.

A fellow, nicknamed 'The Bachraw', a big, round-shouldered man, with a white, woolly beard, used to turn up occasionally. He had the appetite and tongue attributed to Conan Maoil. He had some ugly words and litanies the length of a wet Saturday. He was terrified of lightning. I remember him once during a thunderstorm kneeling at a stool by the dresser praying, with a voice and gesture that would have done credit to a saint: 'God and his blessed Mother, deliver me.' The Bachraw was a good tradesman; he could cut a pair of uppers from a piece of leather where another wouldn't get a pair of toe-caps. He could stitch with machine speed. If one was foolish enough to hamper his bow as he drew the waxed end, that one was likely to get a lively reminder in the form of an alleged accidental punch on the nose or mouth. After administering one of these sore cautions he would turn round puzzled-like: 'The curse of Hell on it, but that's the second time the day I hit the wall with me bare knuckles.'

Garrett Plunket was the most lovable of them all. He was an old man and sensitive. He was intelligent, too, and told no barefaced lies. He could work and talk at the same time – a rather rare accomplishment among that tribe. Some of them in the excitement of the story might forget the boot between their knees altogether, and to clinch an argument might bring down the hammer with disastrous effect on the said boot or perhaps their own knee-cap. When some of us children would take a rasp or other tool off Garrett's bench he never thought of charging us with that heinous crime. He would look under the bench and inside old boots – where missing tools were fond of hiding – and then back to his bench. The missing article would have reappeared, and Garrett wondered at his blindness.

One day in June he gathered up his tools. 'I'm goin',' he said simply, but with a finality we knew too well, and he was gone. He was found dead near Trim a week afterwards.

He must have been death-stupid going, for he left behind him as remembrance – his cobbler's hammer and his spectacles.

(*The Irish Times*, 16 July 1936, p. 4; Kavanagh's first prose publication)

Sentimental Ploughman

Barney the ploughman was sitting between the handles of his plough with his back to the horses. He was smoking his pipe, but nervously not placidly. He was a tall, long-jawed fellow, a man who had dreams that never came true. He was aged between fifty and sixty. Like most adult countrymen, he had grown old, but not adult. His heart was a schoolboy's. The field he ploughed was his own.

The winds of March were bleaching the brown quilt of the seedbed. A few yards away a crow was pecking hard at one of last season's potatoes, which protruded from the edge of the furrow. The field ran down to the railway, the county road ran parallel to the railway, so that Barney's field commanded a fine view of the travelling world. On the railway paling a sparrow was making tentative fluttering advances to his love. Along the road a boy passed singing.

Barney was taking in the scene, and its beauty made him sad and humble.

Just then I arrived, and my intrusion scattered his pensive thoughts. He came back to his normal self.

'Did ye see any nice women, lately?' he asked, after the usual preliminaries.

'Can't say I did,' I replied.

'This part of the country's gone to the dogs as far as the women is concerned; a shockin' bad selection.'

That was the kind of Barney. From morning till night he played his temporal solo on an eternal theme. A casual observer would probably form quite a different opinion of Barney's nature. He might, if he happened to be a town-bred poet, look on this ploughman as a sort of primitive pantheist. If the observer belonged to another sentimental school he might grow lyrical in praise of the glorious ploughman, the backbone of spiritual and material Ireland. But only a man who himself had lived inside the shell of that life could really know the truth.

Barney's romanticism never got beyond the talk stage. At no point did the tremulous line of his thought become earthed in actuality. It was always something far, far away, although the symbols were native.

'It's a holy dread to the world, anyhow,' he said solemnly.

'A holy dread is right,' I said.

'Did ye go to the dance on Sunday night?'

'Oh, I just looked in.'

'Well, what were they like?'

'Oh, just the usual crowd.'

'Isn't that a dread?'

He furtively kicked the brown clay with the toe of his boot. His pipe had gone out, and he stuck it in his pocket.

'That's a good chance for oats,' I said, referring to the field, and also for the purpose of turning the discussion towards less vaporous subjects.

'Arrah, land be damned,' he growled. 'What's in land anyhow? – A bite to ate, and a bad bite at that. The man that would stay on land is a compound eejut.'

'I wouldn't say that,' I said.

'No, because ye don't want to tell the truth. Don't ye know in yer heart that the farmer is an unfortunate animal?'

'I know nothing of the kind.'

'I say,' he began in a lower voice, 'ye didn't happen to eye Betty Brennan when ye were comin'?'

'I didn't.'

'So ye tell me there was a rubbishy selection at the dance. I don't know what happened all the nice women that used to be on the go. There's only the riddlings left – only the riddlings.'

It may be necessary to explain that the rough, ill-shaped grain and choppings of straw left on the sieve is called the riddlings.

'Nothin' only the riddlings.'

After a short silence he began again, this time in a much less pessimistic tone.

'There's a damn fine piece of stuff,' he said, referring to a noted heart-breaker.

'You might swear that,' I said.

'I had a mind to send her word.'

'You had?'

'I had,' he repeated. 'I know I can go there if I put meself about.'

'You're a lucky chap,' I said somewhat cynically, and also a little enviously, even though I believed Barney's hopes to be founded on middle-aged vanity. He shook his head and emitted a sniff to give an impression of contemptuous indifference to such an easy task.

'Huh,' he grunted, 'there's nothin' in it when ye go the right way about the business. A man with a dacent farm and in a fair way of workin' can get the best of them.'

'I wonder.'

I thought for a moment that our conversation would break off on a disagreeable note. He shifted as though to recommence ploughing, but again took up his old pose.

'Would you believe me if I toul' ye that Mrs Murphy put it on strong to me about her Katie?'

'I never said I didn't believe,' I answered.

'Well, she did,' he said with emphasis.

'That's a terror,' I said. 'I thought a Civic Guard was doing duty there.'

'Civic Guards bedamned,' he said. 'What's a Civic Guard? – a cop dependin' on his week's wages. If he lost his job what would he be but a barefooted gossoon? Begod if I hadn't the measure of a policeman I'd go and drown meself. Do ye mane to say that a twenty-acre farmer can't best a Civic Guard? God help Ireland if that was the case.'

'I'm sure you could best a Civic Guard,' I said; 'but at the same time you'd have to admit that a Guard's wife has an easy life, and most women like the easy life.'

'Yer right in what ye say, but still ...'

'Hello, me hearty fellas.' A third person arrived like a blast of furious truth to ruffle the bored, drooping flowers of our talk.

'What are yez condolin' about?' he asked

'Oh, the usual,' I replied.

The newcomer laughed.

'It's a holy terror to see fellas like yous on the wit of the childer. God, it would be enough for young fellas to be blatherin' about nonsense.'

'With all yer bummin' yer not married yerself,' Barney challenged.

'I admit that I let the time slip by,' the newcomer said, 'but if I'm a lone pilgrim itself, at least I'm willin' to admit my mistake. An oul' man talkin' about young girls is the worst of the worst. What kind of oats are ye goin' to sow here?'

'Newline,' Barney said, 'I'm gettin' a barrel of it; and yer right about the women, I'm only an oul' cod,' he added.

'Indeed, yer not,' the newcomer said, 'sure yer not passin' sixty?'

'Only fifty-six comin',' Barney said, with some satisfaction.

'Only fifty-six!' the newcomer said, with affected surprise. 'That's young for Ireland.' And with that the dynamic stranger left us to resume our suspended codology. Barney was cheered up when he considered his comparative youth.

'Any man ought to be married at fifty-six or -seven at the outside,' he said.

'A man's young till sixty in Ireland,' I said.

'I disagree with that,' he said. 'Sixty is a trifle on the oul' side.'

'It may be just the littlest tripe,' I agreed, 'though at the same time not dog-ould.' The ploughman was prancing in the furrow like a two-year-old colt.

'I'll do it when I get things squared up. In the manetime I'd better be gettin' a move on, for, as the fella said, whatever stands the work should go on.'

He spoke to the horses, which, lifting slowly, rhythmically, a forepaw, together moved up the hill.

The sparrow on the railway paling was still and more audaciously pursuing his chosen one.

It was a spring day, and yet … Spring only awakes diffuse thoughts in the Irish countryman.

Dreams, dreams, dreams. Guns, guns, guns.

'You are not such a practical man yourself.' Who said that? It doesn't matter. I have an answer ready:

'I'll do it out here when I get things squared up.'

(*The Irish Times*, 30 May 1939, p. 3)

Europe Is at War – Remembering Its Pastoral Peace

Midnight in Dublin. A wild, but not cold October wind is driving rain against my window. The last buses are swishing by on the glassy-bright streets. The radio in the flat above me has stopped forwarding to this address the mixture of blather and jazz which is called propaganda and which is supposed to influence the masses.

Such of it as has filtered through the ceiling has had another effect on me.

Being an Irishman I should be abnormal if I didn't dream, think and write of far-past peace and quiet in pastoral fields when everybody else is thinking in terms of war.

And just now I remember. Oh, no, I see. In the mirror of this mood I see. What?

An October evening in a country place. A small farmhouse among leaf-lamenting poplars. In a garden before the house men are pitting pota-toes. A cart is heeled up. Two men are working at the back of the cart unloading the potatoes with their muddy hands, while a boy with a sta-ble lamp stands by the horse's head.

The horse snaps at the top of a tall, withered thistle.

'Howl on there, Charlie,' the boy says, and gives a tug to the rein. 'Have yez them near emptied?' – he addresses the men.

'Half a minute, Tom.'

'Then I may pull down the shafts?'

'Aw, yes, ye may.'

'Listen chaps,' one of the men says as he gropes about him in the darkness, 'did any of yez see the tail-board?'

Now they are tackling the horse.

'How many links do I drop?'

'Aw, it doesn't matter a damn: we're only goin' to run the cart into the shed.'

'Right ye be.'

The blowing wind rattles a loose sheet of corrugated iron on the cart-house. An old bucket takes a fitful run in the wind. A woman standing in the doorway of the house calls: 'Will yez be long?'

'Half a minute, Ma,' one of the men, who is her son, replies.

'Then I may wet the tay?'

The three shadowy figures go into committee to discuss this important question. After a while the son of the house replies: 'Wet away, Ma.'

There is the rumble of heavy-laden carts passing along the little road.

In the mirror those rugged men sitting high on their loads of potatoes and potato stalks become figures of romantic allure, sculptures pedestaled in the mud-walled temples of rural Ireland. And I can hear them – Tom, Mick and Paddy – as they pass the time of day to the men in the garden.

'Good evenin', chaps.'

'Good evenin', Mick. Soft-lookin'.'

'It'll not be so aisy gettin' them out now.'

'Ye may have bags of weather.'

And the carts rumble on while the poplars continue to lament. Poplars, the banshees of the forest.

Would that be the nostalgic cry of a cow outside the yard gate? We will soon know. 'Will some of yez come and open this gate?' That's Mary with the cows.

'Run Tom and open the gate.'

'I had an awful job with them cows,' says Mary. 'They were broke out in Healy's clover, and only for Maggie Quinlan I'd be after them all night.'

'Holy fiddlesticks,' Tom says.

Across the 'street' the cows dash towards their byre, the boy preceding them with his lamp. The son of the house leads the horse to a tub of water, at the same time calling out: 'Tom, run out and pull a wisp of hay for the horse.'

The second man, cleaning his muddy hands on the legs of his trousers, follows Mary into the cow-byre to … help her to tie the heads, of course.

'Quit that oul' codology,' Mary's suppressed voice can be heard.

The wind rattles the door of the byre. Flying chaff from the haggard is silver in the spotlight from the kitchen window.

The horse is still at the tub. The woman comes to the door.

'I have the tay wet this quarter of an hour,' she says. 'If yez don't come in soon it won't be worth drinkin'.'

'What do ye want us to do anyhow?' her son replies. 'Tell a mad dog to run madder.'

Two yellow lights appear round the bend of the road, and the tinkle of bells is heard.

Tinkle, tinkle, cleaver's bells
In my heart your music dwells.

The cleaver was the fowl-dealer. Most of the cleavers hailed from Crossmagalen and its environs.

Outside the house he pulled up and spoke to the woman.

'Good evenin', mam. Have ye any …?'

'Good evenin', Joe, what are ye givin for good oul' hens?'

'Two bob for good ones.'

'Troth and sowl, Joe, yer not too dangerous. They may let ye out.' The woman goes to the gate, and, leaning on it, falls into pleasant, non-professional conversation with Joe.

I never knew a cleaver save one who wasn't a romantic. And the tales they carry from house to house have in them still something of the old folk-magic that made news newsy in the happy days before journalism was invented.

And says she to me, 'I'd see ye in hell's blazes before I'd let Molly go with ye.'

'Be the … be the …'

'That fared very well. I can get me pick of them,' says he. 'I could thatch a house with me women if I wanted.'

'Isn't he the consatey pup.'

'I was talkin' to him the other day and the crack came round and do ye know what he said?'

A loud gust of wind blows a hole in the ballad.

'Ha, ha, ha.'

The laugh without the joke that gave rise to it is as bad as marriage by proxy or a kiss over the telephone.

'Wasn't that a good one?'

'I never heard better.'

Ah blow, blow thou winter wind as loud and ungrateful as Shakespeare wished, but why could you not suppress that destroying roar? The golden coin of good talk is falling in the pit of silence, beyond the power of poet to redeem.

'Well, good evenin' Joe. If yer round here on Tuesday or so I'll have a few good hens catched for ye.'

'Tuesday! Right. Good evenin', ma'am.'

The woman returns to her house mumbling to herself and fiddling with her marriage ring. She always does this when she recalls some good yarn.

'That hay is a terror with thistles,' says Tom, as he stands with an armful outside the horse's stable. 'I don't know how any baste can eat it.'

'Put it there,' the horseman replies; 'he'll eat it before he eats the manger.'

Well, the horse is stalled. Even the cows get tied up at last, and Mary and her partner in the cattle trade emerge from the cow-house. And, like four angels of romance, those children of my dream shuffle across the cobbled street and enter the lighted kitchen.

Only now is the woman wetting the tea. She understands the delays associated with the day's work on a little farm.

And where did those four angels go that evening? To Duffy's for a game of 'nap' or to the village to see the last train come in. The last train of pre-blackout brightness that was their cinema. Then the loafers outside the pub studying the evening paper.

Maybe there will be a row. Some drunken fellow may want to express himself in fistic action. I can see two old farmers sipping their pints and talking shop.

'I have them all out and pitted.'

'I'd be finished only for the bleddy rain.'

For a moment I avert my gaze from the mirror of memory, and am again aware of Dublin and the last blue-lit ghostbus passing. I remember some wild talk of a war in Europe. Who is this referred to it? Oh yes, the radio commentator. But I know that beyond the headlines, beneath the contemporary froth and flurry, the tide of humanity flows calm.

And was I once part of this simple, deep life? Did I once experience the joy of being one of those people, part of that experience? The joy of it. Stark and lonely it might seem at times, grey and forlorn as the night poplars of late autumn, but it was real life among real folk, without the fake conventions that put gilt on tin-pot souls. No highfalutin culture.

Cruel and vulgar those folk might be at times or vexingly peasant-deceitful, but there was in them in a greater or lesser degree something of the sensitivity which is part of the poet's misery – an unprotected heart.

It is midnight in Dublin and Europe is at war.

(*The Irish Times*, 25 October 1939, p. 8)

To the Corn Goddess

These handfuls of corn from the furrows of a tiny field, Demeter, lover of wheat, Sosicles, the tiller of the soil, dedicates to thee, having reaped now an abundant harvest; again likewise may he carry back his sickle blunted from shearing of the straw.

Phillipus *

Chug, chug, chug. What do you imagine that these queer symbols stand for? Neither Greek, Latin, Civil Service Irish, nor James Joyce, they represent the echo in my memory of a steam-thresher pulling out from some evening haggard.

An evening in late September. The period is around five years ago, when I first decided to abandon this kind of threshing and to join with Blake in threshing the stars of bright truth from their husks of material words.

Threshing the stars is a bitter task, as Blake discovered. And when one is weary of the flashing firmament of the intellect it is, indeed, soothing to wander back the long aisles of memory to taste the human symbols of the starry harvest.

Threshing time. The romantic smell of steam-engines. I never see a steam-engine with fun-fair or circus but I want to run over and smell it

---

* The epigraph is from the translation of a poem by Philip (Philippos) of Thessalonika, who lived in Rome and wrote *Garland* c. 40 AD.

like a flower. Once on an English common the owner of a fair saw me sniffing one of his engines and came to inquire if I had asthma. But it was my own childhood and youth I had been tasting. Threshing time in my own country. The trailing machinery by narrow roads and disputed right-o-ways. Would any small or large farmer give as much as one inch of his land to make room for the thresher? Not likely. And there were thus some unfortunate fellows who lived far in off the main roads to whom the old flail descended from druidic times. I heard the sound of a flail. As a matter of fact, I used one about seven years ago. The flailer opposite me gave me a blow on the head. He said I wasn't handling my threshing gear correctly, and, there being no standards of flailing, I had to accept a bump on the skull as a funeral offering to Tradition.

But when the petrol tractors came everyone was modern. Yet there was no thresher like the steam-thresher.

And the women and children standing by their yard gates as the machinery passed. The engine-driver nods his head to the women, but in a grand heroic way. At the tail of the machinery three weary men with dirty faces trail. Two of them are 'feeders' of the thresher, and the third man is the farmer to whom the machine is now going.

But the best time of all was the evening after the threshing at some neighbour's. Undiluted joy like a stranger's wake.

We might be tired, those of us who had assisted at the threshing during the day; but, with wheels stopped and pitchforks dropped, we could survey the scene with detachment, as though we were looking at a picture. The rick of straw might be 'going a bit to the hollow' and the yield of oats poor, but that wasn't our worry.

There was only the laughter of lovers in the chaff and the talk of old farmers by the gables. Listen to that evening talk.

'That's a well-built rick. Great straw, too. I often saw worse hay.'

'Good pratie-oats straw.'

A young girl speaking: 'Aw, do, Larry; ask me father to let us have a dance.'

The young man addressed is leaning against the wheel of a cart smoking a cigarette.

'I wouldn't think a damn of putting it up to him,' he says.

I myself, as usual, even then, am standing apart from the light-of-heart-and-foot. I am engaged in a very high-brow argument with an old man who 'nearly knows as much as a schoolmaster'.

Some way like this the argument ran:

'Are ye trying to throw it down me guts that there's better poets than Tom Moore?'

'Ever hear of Milton?'

'Blatherskite. I wouldn't give a second-hand chew of tobacco for any poet but Tommy.'

'A fella would imagine he was a relation of yours.' And then that old fellow gets into a rage; you daren't cross him. Now his language becomes very unliterary, violent. He wouldn't think a ha'p'orth of striking me.

'You young fellas know the devil and all, I forgot more than the half of yez ever knew.'

And that haggard debate breaks up in disorder.

'I say Barney is there anybody out there that wasn't in for tay.'

Barney is the proper-rioter of the place, and that's his good wife, Mary Ann.

'Barney, would ye be willin' to let us have a dance?' a young man says.

Barney, who up till then had been enjoying the flattery of the young man who had been telling him how excellent his corn was and so on, suddenly changes the tune. Flattering is all very well even when nobody is deceived by it, but this is another matter. He is like a hail-fellow-well-met, from whom the other hail-fellow has tried to borrow ten bob. A request like that takes the good out of friendship.

Anyhow, he'll ask his wife, Mary Ann.

So exit Barney into the open jaws of his wife.

'Julia, Julia,' the young man calls to the girl who had requested the dance. He turns to me, 'Did ye see Julia?'

I reply honestly and accurately, as the eternal observer in novels: 'The last I saw of Julia she was juking around the rick of straw with Black Mick.'

'Good God! Are ye coddin' us?'

Very foreign politics is being discussed in all its deepest implications by a man who had once been a candidate (unsuccessful) for the old Poor Law Guardians. He never got over the importance of his public life.

But it doesn't really matter. We are all being educated in the school of experience whether we are unwilling or not.

Barney trying to convince his hard-hearted wife has his hands as full as a Central European diplomat. 'Now that'll do ye. Bringin' a rowdy crowd about the place.'

Ah, there are other considerations which eventually turn the scale in favour of the dancers. There are the pair of daughters: Julia, already referred to, and Bridgie, who up till now has been sacrificed to the devil of my literary limitations.

Bridgie, no more than her sister, is inside helping mother to wash up. Youth must have its fling. A great pile of chaff in the moonlight is golden. Only chaff! The stars are threshed from their husks, and did they have a good dance? They did. Tea was served in the room back of the kitchen fire. The music was supplied by a melodion and fiddle – the civilized half of a newly-formed jazz-band. But an account of the dance must wait.

There is now other work to be done. Stray corn sacks to be gathered up and smoothing an occasional hole in the yard where the engine stuck his toes.

The moon over Slieve Gullion shines as poetry-coaxing as the moon over a cruising steamer when the celluloid lovers of Hollywood are waltzing on the deck. Barney, to get the annoyance of Mary Ann's tongue out of his mind, goes out to the loft to look at his pile of corn.

'There is a good sixty barrels in it,' he says to himself aloud. 'The victory the second done powerful, but that pratie-oats isn't worth wasting ground with.' He lifts a handful of the grain and squeezes it hard. 'Not a bad sample, not bad at all.'

(*The Irish Times*, 8 November 1939, p. 4)

A Winter's Tale

It was a wet day in December. A cold, north-easterly rain was spitting on the bare grey hills of south Monaghan. On such a day little useful work could be done about a farmer's place.

But Pat McCabe, the old slave-driver for whom I was extra man (he employed two regular servant boys), had a wonderful knack of getting work out of abnormally lazy men under abnormally bad weather conditions. He was well aware of his talent, yet there were times when, as he expressed it, he'd need to have an eye in the back of his head to keep us at it.

The two regular hands – Barney Duffy and Johnnie Daly – were experts in the art of 'batin' Mick' – killing time. I, myself, was always so fond of work that I'd lie beside it. Still, the work got done. For, although McCabe was a small, dirty, and stupid scrap of a man, he was as authoritative as Mussolini, or Captain Ahab in *Moby-Dick*.

He had a farm of about fifty Irish acres – all hills – one half of which lay north and half south. He had a wife, too, Rosie, but she remained in an obscurity as deep as the obscurity that enfolds the wives of famous men.

'I wonder now,' said Barney Duffy as we sat at the breakfast table wiping the bacon grease off our chins, 'I wonder now what dirty job Oul' McCabe has for us the day?'

'Ye may bet yer sweet life', Johnnie Daly replied, 'that he'll not have us idle.'

Regretfully I concurred with this metaphysical punter. McCabe knew how to preserve his authority; he never let us in on him; we never knew the night before what particular tasks were to be ours the next day. He did all the planning, and an excellent planner he was. If, for instance, we happened to be picking a pit of potatoes he would know to the minute when we would have accomplished the job. We'd have finished by a quarter to six unless the devil entirely was on us, and so he would have a job to run into the moment we had finished the potatoes. His policy was this – and it was sound policy – no matter how lazy a workman might be, provided he was kept going, he'd get over the work. McCabe had no use for fellows who made a bit of a rush and then took a rest.

The man of whom I speak so harshly was out in the street, in the rain and in his shirt-sleeves. As soon as we had the last tint of tea drained from our mugs he was in on top of us.

'Now, me lads,' he cried in a high-pitched voice. 'Out to the loft with yez. Bottom all the barley bags.' He turned to me: 'You'll do the sewin'. The packing-needle is there on top of the dresser.'

I got the packing-needle and a ball of twine, and the three of us went out and up to the loft in great good humour.

The loft was a large one – seventy feet long; it was the envy of the district. I heard more talk about McCabe's big loft than would give any piece of architecture a decent start on the road to immortality.

One half of its length was taken up with spilled oats; the other half contained the twenty sacks of barley, and the usual trumpery and implements that lie on farmers' lofts during the winter. You know the sort of things – tables of reaping-machines, scythes, etc.

Very interesting place on a wet day. There was a musty romantic touch about it.

The bottoms of filled sacks decay if left standing for any length of time, hence the necessity for re-bottoming them. There is a bit of trade in putting bottoms in filled bags, and I was something of an expert at this trade then. We turned up half a dozen of the sacks at a time and sewed new sacking on.

In this instance we turned up half a dozen sacks and left them there. We lay down on our bellies on the spilled oats and talked.

Funny thing! but it's the only subject that never becomes boring even in the mouths of the most stupid.

What's that you said?

I said there's one conversation theme which springs eternal.

Is it the theme of God?

Not at all, you oul' cod, you. Women is the theme. Did you never spend a day or an evening with farm-labourers? If you had you would have realized the durable quality of sentimental subject matter.

'Damn it,' Barney began, 'but that one we were talkin' about last night is a dandy piece of stuff. You didn't happen to see her this mornin'?'

'I did not,' Johnnie replied. He spat out a grain of the corn that he had been chewing. 'She's all right, mind ye,' he said. 'There's plenty worse than her.'

I was not privy to the focus-point of this tale. 'Who is she, anyhow?' I asked.

Barney advised me to query a certain part of his anatomy. 'We'll do the talkin' and you can do the watchin',' he said.

I was lying nearest the window. 'There's some one after goin' in,' I said.

'Who the hell would it be?' Johnnie wondered.

'Aw, God only knows!' Barney sighed. 'I don't give a tuppenny damn what any bleddy get says,' he continued, 'but I think she's the best in the parish.'

We stopped talking for a few moments. The rain dancing on the slates provided us with a musical programme. Looking through the window I could see the apple trees in the orchard bluely shivering in the sleet.

A leaf fluttered towards the sticky, dark earth of the cabbage garden. A crowd of hens were standing on one leg in the doorway of the horse stable.

'Women', Johnnie started suddenly, 'is all a cod. Any man that follys them is an eejut.'

'She's the best in this parish, anyhow,' said Barney, 'and I wouldn't think a hate of doin' a bit of trade there.'

We laughed. I was observing Johnnie Daly's laugh, and I thought I detected a touch of jealousy in it. 'Who slights me horse would buy me horse' is good psychology.

For once in my life, at least, I was somewhat detached from the emotional centre of disturbance.

'There's Julia Brady,' Johnnie said, 'I'd put her up against any girl ye mention.'

Barney made a Joycean comment – one word which in our country was perfectly expressive of contempt.

'She's none of yer big oul' mopes,' Johnnie went on, 'all of her that's in it is good stuff. The half of these big women, do ye know what it is, they'd put a man out of house and home keeping them in grub.'

'Well yer a funny man,' Barney said. 'The one yer after mentioning is neither big ugly nor little nice. She's more like a thing ye'd see goin' about with Duffy's circus.'

'I wonder,' said I, putting in my cutty, 'what do women talk about when they're be themselves.'

My wonder query was ignored.

And the two servant boys continued their discussion as we reclined on the oats.

I got up and lit a cigarette.

'Hey, damn yer sowl,' Barney shouted, 'put round the fags; don't be so bleddy mane.'

A mouse ran up the wall; I flung a handful of oats at it, but without effect.

My two companions were laughing loudly.

'So ye tell me that?'

'God, she must be an imp of hell's blazes.'

'When it comes to that, women's all the same; the Ten Commandments don't matter ten grains of oats in the wind up.'

'You're right,' I butted in.

The conversation stopped suddenly. Was that a step coming up to the loft door?

We all jumped to our posts. Barney, with great presence of mind, gave a kick to the three human moulds in the oats.

'Here, hurry up with another sack. Wonderful barley that.'

I was plying the packing needle with energy. McCabe came softly in. He came down on us like a soot drop, but we were prepared.

'What's the weather like outside?' I inquired in an offhand way.

McCabe made no reply. He was looking all round the loft. He walked over to the oats where we had lain and studied it as a finger-print expert would the impression of human fingers on a bank-manager's roll of butter.

'Chaps,' he said at last, 'if yez didn't earn yer breakfasts will yez try to earn yer dinners. The day is clearing up nicely, so I think I'll get yez to drive dung.'

Day clearing up, indeed! It was raining cats, dogs, and a considerable quantity of plain water.

'You take the bay horse, Barney, and you the kickin' mare.'

Then he turned to me. 'You can go home. I'm paying ye twelve and a tanner a week all found, and I'd be in pocket if I paid ye to stay at home. Ye ought to have been a preacher.'

As I turned to go home, I looked back once and there were the two servant boys backing their carts into the face of the dunghill.

I looked and listened and thought about it more than somewhat. Tomorrow I'll revisit that scene after five years; I expect that nothing has changed.

(*The Irish Times*, 7 December 1939, p. 4)

Christmas in the Country

'You'd never think it was Christmastime,' said my friend to me as we wandered along the country road on the Saturday.

'It's probably the weather,' I said, 'more like spring weather than anything else.'

'No, it's not the weather,' he said; 'it's our imaginations that have become atrophied.'

He gazed wistfully ahead, and then went on: 'We have no faith. Faith feeds on imagination, and during the past number of years our imaginations have been dying slowly. Take Santa Claus, for instance. Children are no longer asked to believe in a metaphysical Father Christmas. In every shop and store, from Woolworths to the street stalls, you have Father Christmases, complete with red gowns and white whiskers. Nowadays seeing is believing, and that attitude is destroying our imaginative faith in the eternal unseeable things.'

'Good mornin' to ye, men.'

'Good mornin', John.'

That was a neighbour going by in his cart to plough. He stands up in the cart beside the blue-painted plough and trails a lazy horse behind the cart.

Christmas or no Christmas, the farmer must keep on the move.

'So you think there have been such affairs as old-fashioned Christmases?'

'I do,' he replied.

'You live in the past,' I said. 'Do you not realize that this lovely December day is as intense with spirituality as any day from medieval Christendom, or Ireland's Golden Age for that matter. Ever read Whitman? There will never be any more perfection than there is now, nor any more of heaven or hell than there is now … Why should I wish to see God better than this day?'

My companion did not reply. He had vanished; for he really was part of myself. I was alone with my thoughts.

And somehow it seemed to me that a good deal of the joy had vanished from Christmas. We have carol singers on the radio; holly and lighted candles in our homes, mummers and the wren boys, but still.

No; Whitman was right. There never was a better time than the present, and there will never be a better. Here is an old man coming, after drawing his old-age pension. He might have stepped out of William Carleton's stories. He is an old man and his coat pockets are bulging. Bulging with sweets for his grandchildren, but also bulging with dreams. 'Bulging' is a funny word, slightly ridiculous, it destroys the poetic world I wish to evoke. Reminds a person of a flaw in the tyre of a bicycle.

How-an-ever!

'Me sound man, Paddy,' he cries. 'How is the world usin' ye?'

'Can't complain. Dammit you're getting younger since I saw you last.'

'Keepin' the best side out; keepin' the best side out. What do you think of the German now?'

We talked under our breath, because of the Censorship laws.

On that Saturday evening I called at a neighbour's house. Over the kitchen fire hung a twenty-gallon pot, and the woman of the house was sitting beside it driving logs of wood into the fire.

'A happy Christmas to you, ma'am,' I said, on entering. She returned the compliment with the traditional compound interest of the Gael and then said: 'I'm boilin' the oul' puddin' and I'm blessed to God if it's worth the trouble. But nothin' would do Jemmy but me to make a puddin' of some sort. He said it wouldn't be like Christmas at all without a puddin'.'

I backed up Jemmy's view.

And then Jemmy himself came in. After we had gone through the usual courteous formalities he went to the fire and looked into the pot.

'I hope the water doesn't get in on it, like last year,' he said.

'I hope not,' his sister said. 'Troth, there's some money's worth in that puddin' – a pound of raisins, a pound of currants, mixed spice and candied peel …'

'I hope ye put the two bottles of stout into it,' Jemmy said.

'I put one of them in it,' the woman said, 'and I think it was any god's amount.'

Jemmy returned to his tidying up of the yard and dunghill. I, after a few moments, managed to evict myself from that too urgent kitchen. Curiously enough, Christmas Eve has been the traditional day for making the pudding. Generally speaking, it would be suspended in the pot from the crook, at noon, and would be boiled in approximately six hours. No sooner would it be out of the pot than it would be sampled, and a few years back I remember a queer character who used to make a tour of all the neighbouring houses to sample the puddings. This fellow was a huge, swarthy fellow, with a bottomless stomach. Although in many matters his opinion didn't carry much weight – he was slightly half-witted – in the matter called a Christmas pudding he was a conne.

'What was Mrs So and So's puddin' like?' he would be asked.

'Boys o' boys, it was very plain. No raisins at all in it.'

'What do ye think of ours?'

'It's grand. What's to bate it?'

Some few years ago a neighbour who owned a large boiler used to facilitate his poorer neighbours by allowing them all to boil their puddings in it. This boiler, which was attached to the pigsty, was a hundred yards distant from the dwelling, and one Christmas Eve a crowd of unChristianlike young men made a raid on the boiler and carried into captivity several of the puddings. Of that affair, I can only remember one poor woman's curse: 'Me darlin' puddin'. May the devil pull it up out of their guts.' And in less printable language she prayed that they might get the dry murrain from the eating thereof.

On Christmas morning I noticed that the old country church was lighted with electricity. Three barefaced glaring bulbs took the place of the tiered, 40-candler chandelier that hung from the ceiling. One hundred and twenty candles stood there unlighted. They looked sorrowful as skilled workers whose work has been taken over by machinery. Only kept there for show – a glorified pauperism.

And those candles could be gay, as well as solemn. There was that candle which, on a couple of Christmases, made a business of dropping hot grease on the bald, shining head of the village grocer, until he looked like a man with a large wen on his skull.

Christmas Day itself has been a dull, dreary day since I remember it. Everyone kept to his own house. A family day, and there's nothing so tiresomely smug as a family day. Once, I believe, we visited on Christmas Day, and now we have put on a hypocritical respectability that is killing.

I got up and went for a walk across the hills. I looked down on the sweet little houses in the valley. Everything was restrained. The smoke rising from the chimneys stole into the sky like a visitor entering the room of a sick child.

A great calm rested on the land. It might be Peace on Earth, but looked more like a laboured quiet.

And then I looked in the withered grass at my feet.

Of all the wonders! A buttercup, a yellow buttercup on Christmas Day. Exciting.

As I looked at the golden petals in the grey grass, I felt spring among the hills. Spring in the heart.

(*The Irish Times*, 30 December 1939, p. 8)

Some Evocations of No Importance

'What were the happiest moments in your life?' a man asked me one day. The happiest moments are those that are most vivid in the imagination. The imagination is, I think, incapable of evoking moments of sorrow.

It is a summer's day and I am aged around twenty-two and I am drawing me coal from the station.

There is no work as easy as manual labour. There I was, me face black, sitting on the sate-board, me legs crossed, letting the fields look at me. Ah, the fields looked at me more than I at them, and at this moment they are still staring at me. The humpy hill beyond the railway at the Beeog's lane. The house where the two yellow-faced brothers lived is roofless but, unlike most cabins of its class, the right masons must have built those walls. Best of bleddy walls. Could nearly be roofed again.

I am thinking of what I heard me father say of those brothers. They spoke Irish, as did their two nieces who were alive at this time, and when one of the brothers died the other lamented him loudly: 'Mo graer, mo graer,' he cried.

This is bad phonetics for the sound of 'my brother' in Gaelic but what's the differ? But everyone said that if he had been half as good to him when he was alive he'd have him still.

I can see across to Harry Conlon's on the side of the hill in Drumnanalive.

Somebody is driving a sow up the hill. I don't suppose I was ever up in that field. And it's curious how you get a sense of travel to strange lands in going to some field less than a mile from your home. And you get the feeling of returning from a long exile when you revisit some field that you had walked through as a child.

There are several fields I long to see again. There is the corner under the Rock in our Far Field, down beside the stream, where many's the hot summer day I sat with my feet touching the cold water and watching the violets that grew on the cool, shaded bank.

There is a pad there which leads into Caffrey's field and another into Woods', and I used to go that way when I was in tow with Johnnie McCabe.

Stones were always rolling into the stream at this point, and never a week passed that I hadn't to go up there and pull them out, for this stream drained our meadow, and when it was plugged in winter you couldn't go to Meegan's Well without being up to your arse in gutter, as the fella said.

We were always talking about all the extra land we'd have if a few of the cuttings were sunk a foot or so. Every few years we were able to get a number of local scraidíns (scraping small farmers) together to do a week's work on the drain. (Streams were always called drains.) Generally speaking, the combine tended to thin out as each man got as far with the job as would drain his own low-lying meadows.

And that's the way it was when I was in wo (vogue) in that country.

This is a new cart I have. No danger of the shoeing coming off the wheels. I peep over the dashboard. God! did I speak too soon? There's a shoeing there looks like shifting. Ah, no, it's all right –

'Hardy.'

'Hardy.'

A neighbour on his bicycle has caught up with me and cycles along holding the dashboard.

'There's a bleddy good slack you're drawing, Paddy.'

'It's not slack, it's a class o' nuts. We got a bargain in it. Wigan.'

'What are yez wastin' on it?'

'Thirty-five bob a ton.'

'That's bleddy chape.'

'Good value all right. There's a terrible scabby field of oats – White's.'

'The worm got it. Do you know what? It looks more like a miss that stripe up the middle.'

'I wouldn't think so. Good evening, Joe.'

'Evening, lads.'

'There's a man won't be long in it, Frank. Shocking failed.'

'I hear they sent him back from Dublin without doing a damn thing for him. Opened him up, to make out. Cancer's a shocking disease.'

'Shocking.'

'I must be going. I want to buy a lock of Jeyes Fluid for we have a cow ready to calve, and you never know.'

'So long. Might be seeing you the night.'

'I may be at the Cross.'

'So may I.'

The hard-stemmed wild weeds that grow on that ditch! And yet they have a curious sort of attraction for me. It's not a ditch you'd like to sit down on, but just the same it is part of your life.

Why do you remember this particular part of the road so well? I know. Because this spot, for no special reason, reminds you of yourself going with your mother to the station of a Monday morning carrying the baskets of eggs and butter on the handlebars of the bicycle.

'And remember what I toul' you, to clane out them hen-houses and whitewash the roosts. And don't forget to put the porringer on that wee calf and not have him sucking the other calf's nabel.'

'Don't forget to bring me back *John O'London's*.'

'If I think of it. There's Mary Faley ahead of us. I don't want to catch up with her, for she'd pollute a person with her oul' talk about the wonderful man Cissie got. As far as I hear, the devil the much he has, a few scabby acres in the wilds of Derrafanone, at the back of God's speed where the devil shit the big needle. Might as well be transported. And there's another thing – for God's sake will you cut them nettles at the Meada gate, for they sting the legs of me every time I go out into the Meada. It wouldn't take you ten minutes.'

'I'll do that.'

'And you might, if you have time, tidy up that oul' haggard. But don't kill yourself. Don't try to take it all away in one graipful. Nothing for you only the lazy man's load. Go light and go often. Bad luck to her, she's waiting for us. Good morning, Mary. I think we have loads of time.'

'Well now, I'm not so sure. Father Gillan passed me at Little Bessy's and it can't be that early.'

'We're safe enuff,' say I, the scientific man. 'The signal is not down for the up train yet. Once we get this far before the signal is down we are in bags of time.'

'Patrick, you could nearly put Mary's basket on the carrier.'

'Don't bother, sure it's not that heavy.'

'It's a nuance if you have a light basket, Mary. Give it to him and don't be killing yourself. Good people's scarce and bad people ought to try and mind themselves. Didn't poor Micky Duffy go off very sudden? When I heard he was dead and buried I couldn't believe me ears. I met him in the Carrick fair – was it two months ago or three? I think it was around April. When did we buy the drop calves, Patrick? Was it at the fair or an ordinary Thursday?'

'Ordinary Thursday.'

'The Lord save us and bless us, but it's a sudden world. But sure he has his family reared.'

I leave them at the station, where already a number of women are waiting for the train to take them to the Dundalk market, a great weekly event in that country at that time. A social event. That is one of the mistakes the price-controllers and planners make. We don't live by the guaranteed price alone. The controlled price killed all the fun. But people still manage to have a little.

The village of my native place is built around a disused graveyard. In that graveyard stands a somewhat stunted Round Tower. Liveliest spot in the village is that graveyard. The nettles and weeds are in blossom. Somebody who may be a commercial traveller waiting for a train is going through the graveyard, stumbling over the fallen headstones in the matted grass, reading old inscriptions. The tomb of the McMahons is here. A Protestant church stands in the graveyard beside the Round Tower. It is probably out of commission by now. Is there e'er a Prod in the parish at all?

I drive round by the Civic Guards' barracks and up past the Far House. At the door stands a bundle of twigs and a scabbard full of Tysacks – scythes. The great maker of scythes was Tysack, though some people would swear by the ones Bolger made. The Bolger was on the heavy side.

Would I ever dream of going in to have a bottle of stout? Never such a thought in me head at that time, and look at me now.

Ah, well, times change and we change with them. Do times really change? I am not so sure. We change. Thinking back into my youth, I know I am occupying another body with a soul that is not quite the same. I am not so innocent now. I have learned to desire, and that is unwisdom.

Up the sunny, dusty road to the station. Some bollocks is after shifting the bleddy wagon down towards the stop-lock. I'll have to back in now. I tie the reins round the crossbar and hop over the side-board into the wagon. It's an easy wagon to fill from, for it has a smooth unpatched bottom. And the shovel I borrowed from John Parr is a powerful great shovel.

Nicely, nicely, I fill the cart. I shove the sate-boord along the tail-boord so that it will make the back of the cart higher and the coal will be in no danger of falling off going up Ednamo Hill.

Far away are cities, far away. I am a young man in the depths of the world. But I do not feel young. I feel very old.

Somebody asked me if I was twenty-two and I got red in the face. He said I looked twenty-two. And at a dance at Annavacky deck someone else said I wasn't 'dog ould' and I felt he believed I was and wanted to console me.

Age is the worst complex I have ever had. I remember writing before I went to bed one night:

> *The last year of my teens is passing to-night*
> *And lonely am I for ...*

I could remember the rest if I tried but I am ashamed. The bad verse I wrote was something atrocious. Not the right kind of badness either.

Have I the courage to quote bits of these verses? One of the first was appropriately called 'The Pessimist'. Cannot remember that one. But I do remember the one I wrote in the *Dundalk Democrat* – 'Lines on an Old Wooden Gate':

> *Battered by time and weather, scarcely fit*
> *For firewood: there's not a single bit*
> *Of paint to hide those wrinkles and such scringes*
> *Tear hoarsely down the silence – rusty hinges:*
> *A barbed wire clasp around one withered arm*
> *Replaces the old latch with wanton charm ...*
>
> *This gap ere long must find another sentry,*
> *If the cows are not to roam the open country ...*

A whole column of that. Needless to say I got no payment, though all the neighbours said I must have got a tidy sum for it.

'The Bard used to make hapes of money writing for the *Democrat*,' they said.

As my imagination is levelling the coal on top of the load, trimming round the dashboards, my present intellect is reflecting on the fact that good taste is not a natural development. The so-called simple folk fall into the pits of weary cliché and convention. 'Teenage' and similar words, all sorts of vulgar abbreviations, are the notes of simple folk getting 'educated'.

The keynote of simple folk is bad manners, familiarity. They intrude on one's private soul. The only tolerable simple people are those we have manufactured in our evocative memories. Of course, there were some who had remarkably good natural manners, but on the whole ...

Well, there's a damn good load of coal. Getting even better at this side of the wagon. I can't have less than fifteen hundred on that cart.

I get sitting on the front-boord with my feet on the shaft, pick up the reins and go on my way home.

It is a hot day and the old graveyard is a-hum with bees and flies. Aye, aye, aye! Aye indeed!

(*Envoy*, July 1951, pp. 22–7; also 'The Flying Moment' in *X*, June 1960)

Sunday in the Country

As I left the train I walked on to a country road, a familiar road that now appeared somewhat strange, and that was now on this late September evening as silent as a room in which the clock has stopped. It was in this place – Inniskeen in the County Monaghan – that I was brought up. I knew every field, every stone in the road, every short-cut and gap. Memories crowded me round.

No human being was about to disturb my meditations. I think now that the Spirit of Place has a more powerful attraction for us than friends or relations. A tree, a stone or a field recreates for us the happiest – and the saddest which is the same thing – moments of our lives – in other words, our moments of most intense experience.

One often hears of men who declare that they love the ground some lady walks on; it is no exaggeration, we do love in that way. How well I remember those ash trees as I went to Mass on Sundays. About what year would that be? I remember now. And I was wearing a new brown suit and my hair was very thick and …

All last weekend I argued with my mother and my friends against the quality of living which is possible in this poor tillage country. We attack what we love. Nothing profound about that, for love is an enslavement, an irrational thing against which we hold out as long as we can. But surrender is happiness. Of Saturday night in the country I once wrote in a poem, part of which I quote:

In a meadow
Beside the chapel three boys were playing football.
At the forge door an old man was leaning
Viewing a hunter-hoe. A man could hear
If he listened to the breeze the fall of wings –
How wistfully the sin-birds come home!
It was Confession Saturday, the first
Saturday in May; the May Devotions
Were spread like leaves to quieten
The excited armies of conscience.
The knife of penance fell so like a blade
Of grass that no one was afraid.

To attempt to show the religious life of a people as something apart from the ordinary business of living is a false approach. Some Protestant Sabbatarians criticize the football-playing Sunday and all that. But in fact in the Catholic tradition every day is something of the Sabbath.

I promised myself that I would write of Sunday in the country. Sunday in the country has not changed much since I was a child. Except that in this part of the country, which is I am afraid typical of all parts, there is a great scarcity of young people. On the road on which I used to live there are a score of strong farmers and only one of them is married. What you get usually is two brothers and a sister in a house, or a middle-aged son and daughter and an old mother.

For all that, Sunday morning begins with someone getting up early, making a rushed cup of tea, and off to first Mass.

Then the others get up, one to milk the cows, the other to let out the hens and feed them. When these little things are done they begin to get ready for second Mass. The person who has been to first Mass gets ready the dinner. Regarding this item a change has taken place in the national diet. Due to the scarcity of bacon, bacon-and-cabbage has become a thing of the past. To fill this lack a butcher has set up in the village and the Sunday joint is as common among the small farmers of south Monaghan as it is in Stillorgan.

Another change has been caused by the scarcity of farm labour. Farmers who used to employ two or three men have none now. The casual harvest men – known locally as 'gawthins' – who used to come up from Crossmaglen and south Armagh for the harvest, are today all in the millionaire class. When I was a boy these amusing fellows congregated outside the church on Sundays waiting on farmers to employ them. Little they then realized the fortunes that were to be theirs when in the Klondyke of a little store of tea or rivets or of God knows what they would stake their claims.

Walking in fields is my favourite occupation when I return to the country. Last Sunday I caught in these fields the same old magic that they had for me before. So quiet, so easy on the heart.

Threshing mills are set up in haggards. The potato stalks are withered. I do not know anything I love so much as a potato-field at this time. A friend I once knew used to say that I wrote too much about potatoes and cabbages and not – I suppose – enough about roses. But I might pause to ask a question. What is the quality of beauty in art or in nature? It is what happens to you when you look at something. And looking at a cabbage can be a more thrilling experience than looking at a rose. Beauty is an energy.

On Sunday evening a few people walk along the roads and lanes. Some go to Benediction in the chapel. Some are to be found at the crossroads […]

Monday morning came.

> The air was drugged with Egypt. Could I go
> Out the gate to the City of the Kings
> Where art, music, letters are the real things?
> The stones of the street, the sheds, hedges, cried no.
> And I saw one turn her head as she went down
> The blackberry laneway, but I knew
> In my heart that only what we love is true,
> And not what loves us. We should make our own.

(*The Standard*, 5 October 1945, p. 8)

Ash Wednesday in Inniskeen

From Carrickmacross to Crossmaglen
You'll meet more rogues than honest men.

Ah, God be with oul' times and God be good to them all! Only the other day I was thinking and musing on my country career, and visualizing myself coming home in the cart that once notorious road and letting the nag in to take a drink at the stream that spread out at the corner just at the bottom of Magoney Hill. And then up past Magoney school where we used to be at the Irish class.

Oh the evocative poetry of place names! Fegevla, Shancobane and Oghil Cross. Then up Baragroom – the gloomy road well named.

But the moment that my imagination most brilliantly lights up is a moment on Ash Wednesday (it is Ash Wednesday as I write this) and I am over on the Pass filling in ruts. The Pass, which was a cart-track to a few fields which ran on the edge of a cut-away bog, became such a persistent thing in our lives that it graduated to the importance of a capital initial.

There was a wire paling on one side and the paling too took up a lot of time. As usual I have gone off the fags though so far I have never succeeded in getting beyond the Sunday. Five fags a day was my consumption in those days but just the same I liked them. I have a weak will. I have often felt that if I could ever manage to get off the cigarettes I would achieve something valuable. But every time I went off them they became my inspiration, and I shame-facedly went back to them.

On the hill beyant across the angle of the bog my neighbour Jack is ploughing his pratie-track. He too has gone off the fags, and he has a strong will and he will give a disheartening leer when he catches me smoking.

I shout across to him as he turns on the bottom headland.

'How are you doing 'ithout the fags?'

'No bother.'

'You're lucky. I'm starved for a smoke.'

He has a poor opinion of me. He always had. Everyone in the country has a high opinion of Jack, because his uncle was a noted footballer.

'Is the ground dry enough for ploughing?'

'Dry as male. There's a day id dry anything.'

'God, there's a goodle of blood in it still,' say I, hoping that my cliché will help to establish me as a man of merit.

As we talk another man comes along.

'Me soun' Owney.'

'How are you, gassan?'

'This is an awful bleddy oul' Pass.'

'It needs to be bottomed with big mollockers of stones,' says Owney as he picks up the crow-bar. 'God, there's a damn handy bar and what you might call the right point pieces on it.' He glances around him. 'Kerley's pratie-track is very dry. Very hard weather on cattle, that.'

Owney straggles off and there down the road comes Jack's father, a stern man. (He is still alive, aged around ninety. He was telling me when last I met him that his father was born in the year 1800 and I wondered if that wasn't a record for two generations.)

What I never can imagine is the age I was at that time. I may have been eighteen or nineteen. To think that at that time I didn't know that there was such a thing as literature or that at that moment people as young as I were parading up and down Grafton Street. There I was, a man in the middle of a bog lost in life. I wonder would I have been happier if I had never broken out of this chrysalis?

There I was – and as my imagination evokes again – looking with passion into the mirror that is the water in a hole out of which I have pulled the rotten stump of a paling-post. And straining the wires on the poplar upon which the gate was hung. And never knew that there were beautiful women in the world. Falling in love with the least offensive trollop at a 'stir'. Remember we used to call small dances 'stirs'.

I had no ambition to escape, for I didn't know there was any place to escape to. What I eventually did was done without apparent impulse. Almost by reason.

'Patrick!'

'What?'

'Come home and give us a hand with the churning, and don't forget to take home that good little bar, for I want you to go to the village for a couple of bags of Inja Buck.'

'Righto.'

'Here, take them cans and bring us in some well water while I scald the churn.'

Over the rushy meadow and along the stream to McArdle's well beside the railway. Off to the village for the bags of male.

I threw the harness on the mare (and that reminds me how recently I was reading a verse quotation in this journal which spoke of the plough chains – the traces – being attached to the straddle. No. The traces in ploughing are attached to the back-band or back-rope as the case may be. The straddle is only used when you put the horse in the cart.) At any rate I gave the mare a few rubs of the curry-comb and put her in the cart, and off with me to the village [...]

'Good evening, young fella.'

'Evening, Hughie. Making the best of weather.'

My evocative memory has revived. I am back in the cart on my way to the village. The sudden transformation is dangerous. There are shallow people who might say that a man who once drove a cart should not give his views on cultural things. They are wrong. Life is life. The March wind blows across the hills of Ednamo.

'Very hard weather on oul' people, Paddy. Aye, very hard weather on oul' people. Ah, sure that's the way with the world, as the man said.'

The man returns to his trimming of the hedge.

'Go, on, Polly.'

(From 'Diary', *Envoy*, March 1951, pp. 67–72)

The Seed of Poetry

The Ruins of Time build Mansions in Eternity – Blake

'The last week of March or the first week of April, that's the right time to plant the spud,' Mat said.

'Any time the ground's in order's the right time,' I said, using, like Mat, the traditional formula.

Mat, the man with whom I had been chatting in this profound manner, was one of those happy unfortunates of the tillage country who never had a spud of his own to plant – except, of course, boiled ones. He was a poor labouring man, yet to hear him talking you'd imagine that the tribulations of twenty acres of bad land were his. He was a thick-witted fellow around forty, with a nose like the sock of an old plough, and – not comparing the brute beast to the Christian – he had a set of yellow teeth like the teeth of an old horse.

We were planting potatoes. It was morning, around nine, and though the sun was shining bright, a hasky wind was blowing from the east. It was coming towards the end of Lent and I had given up the cigarettes, and I was young and I felt so idyllic as I stood on a height and drew in deep breaths of chill. As one grows older, Spring becomes a sad time, for it reminds us that although the earth renews itself we are not renewed – in body at any rate:

The trees were in suspense
Listening with an intense
Anxiety for the Word.

How I loved the dust on the dry headland of a potato field. A cart-load of seed was heeled up on the headland. Four bags of treble X – superphosphate – stood at intervals along the headland. The drills had been opened and the dung spread on the previous day. Three children, with bag aprons filled with seed, were dropping the seed at an average distance of fourteen inches apart. That was the distance Tommy Duffy ordered. Tommy himself had his horses backed into the double-plough ready to yoke up.

Mat, who had put on a bag apron made out of a manure bag and had filled it from one of the bags, plodded over the headland, heavily weighted with the fertilizer. He had on his round face a look of shining pride; for shaking what he called the 'phoster' was an honour. The boss was moping around the headland like a man who had lost something.

'What did you lose?' asked Mat.

'The draw,' Tommy said; 'did you see it?'

'It was on the plough yesterday,' Mat said. 'Somebody must have taken it.'

'Stole, of course,' Tommy said, 'what else?' He toed the clay. 'No mistake about it, but I have good neighbours.'

'And the muzzle's gone, too!' Mat cried.

Tommy stared fiercely at the plough. 'The muzzle gone, too, that's enough for you anyhow. The muzzle and draw whipped off the plough. Oh it's me that has the good neighbours. Take the eye out of your head and tell you you were better without it.'

I pointed to a small piece of iron near the plough. Tommy stopped and picked it up. 'Here's the muzzle-pin,' he said, 'and that just shows you.'

Tommy was another version of his man, Mat. Because he made sure never to say anything original he had got a reputation for soundness of outlook. 'I tell you what you'll do, Mat,' Tommy said. 'Run over to the house and you'll find a bit of a chain over the door of the horses' stable – inside.'

'And how about the muzzle?' Mat asked, when he had hurriedly got rid of the apron.

'Aw, we'll tie it on the rack some way.' Mat went off at a trot, and considering that he was anything but streamlined he managed to cover the ground.

'Isn't this a fine how-are-you of a Monday morning,' Tommy lamented to me. 'And it's that half-chawed eejut of a Mat I have to thank. He'd drive a fella astray in the head. He's all right for a bull-dragging job like filling dung or cleaning a drain, but for a handy job … And he couldn't make a thumb-rope: no, not if his life depended on it. He's dear at jaw-wages.'

'You're lucky to have him,' I said, 'especially in these times.' I agreed, however, that his inability to make a thumb-rope was a drawback. And just then Mat returned.

'Well, did you get it?'

'I got a bit of a chain,' Mat panted and threw down the chain. The boss knelt beside the plough. Suddenly he sank his fingers in the soft clay and fished forth the missing draw, to which was attached the buckle known as the muzzle.

'No use in talking to you, Mat,' he said. 'Where was your eyes?' He turned to the laughing children and shouted: 'What way is that yous are dropping the seed? Pinking them. Stoop your backs and put your hands down with the seed. Have yous rheumatism?'

Mat commenced to shake the manure. I walked alongside him carrying on my shoulder the drilling-bar which would be used instead of a double-tree when the plough was coming back closing the second drill. The wind blew the stuff into our eyes.

'A bad day for shaking the phoster,' Mat remarked.

'Blind your eyes,' I said, and I stepped back a few drills.

'It's not that,' he explained; 'a moist day is the right day for putting the phoster to work. This is a bad hasky day for the job.'

Then I crossed the fence into the grazing field, and as I did so I was also walking back and forward in time.

There were coltsfoot blossoms growing on the green height and the daisies were coming up. And the straw that had been offered to cattle

in winter was being blown through the leafless hedges.
And I did not know that I wanted anything of life.

> *And sometimes I am sorry when the grass*
> *Is growing over the stones in quiet hollows*
> *And the coltsfoot leans across the rutted cart-pass*
> *That I am not the voice of country fellows.*

(*The Standard*, Easter 1948, p. 19)

H.E. King Spud

Talking about happiness and happy days, I always remember the taking out of the potatoes – or lifting them, as they say in some places. There was something beautiful and exhilarating about the smell of the dry brown clay and it was supposed to be very healthy. (In the old days girls with anaemia were put to doing a few days over the good earth.)

Our local method, which I can believe is still in use, was splitting the drills with a swing plough or a double plough if you had one. I hadn't. I never liked the digger; there was too much stooping and not enough repose, and also you needed a number of hands.

But I remember my labours in a field of ours named in Irish Cúl an tSiopa, or the back of the shop. The barn where the implements were stored used to be called the shop.

It was much easier work where you had a good crop and that I must claim I invariably had, for the reason that I was terribly lazy. All my neighbours spent days grubbing and paring and battering at their potatoes and potatoes dislike being disturbed. (I may be contradicted about this but I have my experience.) The potato belongs to a parched, bonehard country and anyone may see the mollockers that are to be found at the heart of a hard lump of soil.

My policy was to shove on the potash and from then on as far as possible leave the potato alone.

Taking them out, as I say, was a great pleasure especially if the Octobers were fine as in my memories they seem to be. And there I was with my sister, one each side of a basket, gathering away. The cart was heeled up in a convenient spot and we filled it till it was about half full and then pulled down the shafts and filled in the front. My cart was a small Monaghan cart and I think it only held sixteen baskets.

There were different kinds of basket – a green one and a withered one – and there was a basket-making business in the vicinity of Carrick-macross which was started by somebody or other.

There was also, while I'm on the subject and before I forget it, a maker of sieves and riddles in that area: his name was Quinn and I used to see him prowling about hedges looking for a nice straight nut-free trunk of ash. Beautiful riddles and sieves he made, so light compared to the wire one. The fine sieve could take hair-grass out of hayseed.

Round about hay harvest time he was to be seen with his ass cart piled high with these lovely articles on his way to the shopkeeper who bought them from him. You could use one of these riddles to eat your dinner off in the old fashion. (Hope I'm not boring anybody.) I was talking about the baskets that were made from the common sally. I have never seen one in a Dublin shop but I suppose they would have no use to a city body. No potatoes to be gathered or stall-feds to be fed.

What pleased me about gathering the praties, as I remember in Cúl an tSiopa, was the rhythm we worked to. Having grubbed me drills first, I 'threw out' a number of drills and then let the mare graze around the headland. Then meself and me sister Josie started to gather. A well 'threw out' drill was handy. The thing was to go deep enough not to leave potatoes under you and yet not too deep to produce too much clay to be teased out.

I, as the dominant male, lift up the basket and carry it to the cart. When the cart is full I put the mare in it and drive it home up the Beeog's Lane, for this was an outlying farm …

The mother calls from the doorway: 'Can I wet the tay?'

'Wet away, Ma,' I answer.

I cover the potatoes with straw, loose out the mare, and in no time I am sitting in an oil-lamp-lit kitchen eating a feed of flour bread (soda bread, they call it now) and tea and eggs with an appetite I wish I had these days. Outside the moon is bright in the sky and over that coun-tryside there lies some mysterious beauty which affects me, though at this time I cannot analyze it. What would I not give to be able to bring back those days! There is no going back. As I wrote before, the real happiness in that life was its unconsciousness. When we are unconscious we are closest to the Eternal. We have to shut our eyes to find our way to Heaven.

Of course I also uprooted potatoes by the spade method. I don't think I was what you'd call a top-grade spadesman. In certain cases the spade was essential. For digging an 'early pot', for instance, into which afterwards you might put a ridge of cabbage seed. Digging those early pots remains in my imagination. Going off with the bag, the spade and the bucket. You were supposed, if you were anything like a decent spadesman, to weed the ground as you went. Some haverils would leave a seam of scutchgrass and faraban between each dug drill that was a shame.

Incidentally, does anyone use the name faraban for a certain weed? I can't remember its botanic name but I do remember about a man who on his deathbed was asked by the priest if he forgave everyone and he answered that he forgave everyone and everything but the scutchgrass and the faraban. The word faraban is in Dinneen.*

Not all my potato memories are pleasant, though the unpleasant one is not really vivid in my mind. It was towards the end of World War I and my father had bought an acre of stubble for green crop on the conacre system at something like twenty nicker. Anyhow I know that he nearly went out of his mind over losing his head so badly at the letting, but the result paid off. I remember I cried in the wet frosty clay as I helped to gather some of these potatoes. If the Lord spares me I intend during the next few days to return to that potato country and maybe spend a day in a potato field. [...]

(*Irish Farmers' Journal*, 1 November 1958, p. 16)

* Rev. Patrick Stephen Dinneen, *Irish–English dictionary; being a thesaurus of the words, phrases and idioms of the modern Irish language*, revised and enlarged edn (Dublin 1927).

The Turkey Market

[...] I remember, too, going to the market in later years with a load of turkeys. Lost years – I pick them up memory by memory.

Pulling a bag of hay for the mare and leaving it carefully in the body of the cart. Taking in the seat-board in case it should rain during the night. Everything is ready. I am as near contentment as any man could desire. Contented except for the worry that it might freeze during the night and that the road would be slippery.

'Do you think it will freeze, Frank?' My neighbour and myself both look up at the starry December sky, and the verdict eases my mind. 'You'll have no frost while the wind's from the south.'

Up in the morning early. Lamp lit on the table. A bright fire under a swinging kettle.

From the excitement of the bright kitchen I go outside to let the mare to the water at the boghole. Halfway down the path she wheels round – the rogue – and sneaks back to get her oats first. 'Go on now and take your drink.'

We speak to animals as if they were Christians. She sees there is no way out of it, but my opinion is that she only took a few sips of water. I gave her her oats, curried her, and put on the straddle and breeching.

Then as I am giving a glance over the cart for no particular reason, my mother comes to the door and, looking up the valley towards the east where Orion is in the sky, she says, 'Isn't it a lovely morning, thanks be to God.'

'A good job it didn't freeze and the mare not sharpened.'

'Is that Cassidy's cart I hear?'

We could hear the somewhat petulant rattle of a cart, that short jolt of impatience which told us that the vehicle was being loaded in some neighbour's 'street', and we were so filled with the sense of community, of being poised for a great adventure.

It was still dark as I climbed over the wheel into the cart loaded with turkeys and got sitting high on the seat-board with the winnowing sheet under me and the bag of hay at my feet. 'Run in for the bottle of holy water,' my mother called to one of our household.

Out of her cupped hand she sprinkled the cart and its contents with the holy water. The gate was opened and down the dark lane I went, a young man bogged in unconscious happiness.

I remember that market well. It was during the Economic War, as it was called – and a bad market it was. The day turned out wet to make things worse and there we were, helpless country folk, staring at each other in the shadow of St Patrick's Cathedral, with those rueful looks which are impossible to describe, but which are funny in a perverse way.

I was there for an hour before anyone asked me what took me out. Geese, oddly enough, were a better price than turkeys. Frank Cassidy, a neighbour, was selling his geese to the townspeople at sevenpence a pound. When my mother arrived by train I had not yet sold a turkey.

The only buyers in the market that day were smugglers – the cleavers from Crossmaglen. And though nobody has a higher opinion of the cleavers of Cross from a romantic viewpoint than I have, at the same time I could never recommend them as wholesale buyers of turkeys. Two of these amusing buyers were now examining my load of turkeys. One of them held a bird by the legs while he felt its breast. 'That's an oul' warrior,' he remarked to anybody who might be listening. 'He is not,' I answered back hotly. 'There's not an oul' turkey in that load.'

'What are you looking for them?'

'Eightpence a pound,' I said, very off-hand, and looked away to conceal the awfulness of my asking.

The cleaver shoved the turkey back into the cart and pulled the sheet over it carefully with an air of finality. He was walking off with his companion in roguery when I called him back. 'What will you give me for them?'

'I'm full up,' said he. He consulted with his partner. 'Could we take any more?'

'They'd want to come right,' said the other.

A second examination of my turkeys began. 'A crooked-breasted one, that ... I say, Joe, looka the legs of that. That's an oul' one in earnest ...'

The sheet was once more drawn down. The two buyers stood by the tail-board. 'I'll buy the hens off you at three and six apiece; the cocks are no use to me.'

'A fella would think I stole them,' I said, as I fixed the sheet and made unnecessary adjustments to the lynch-pins at the tail-board.

'You didn't come out to sell, young fella,' said the cleaver, 'but I'm telling you before the day's out you mightn't be so stiff.'

He was right in his prophecy.

I doubt if all we got for that load of turkeys would leave a man drunk, yet for all that, as my mother and I, having eventually disposed of the birds, made our way through the crowded streets, we felt free and elated. The Christmas Spirit was around us. The countrywomen, with their egg-baskets and their dark clothes and blue felt hats, could not be depressed by the badness of a market.

For without running to piety, it can be said that these women – in spite of what they might say – were not primarily interested in the money. They were taking part in a way of life, a life rich and complete, that in its flood carried down to the great sea of their destiny boats loaded with the merchandise of the soul.

(From 'A Conversation with Memory', *The Standard*, 7 December 1945, p. 1)

I Went to the Fair

'I say – give me your hand, give me your hand, give me that hand?'

No response from owner of hand.

I have just been thinking that I have never seen in print a proper description of a traditional deal in cattle in a country fair. To remedy this defect I have gone to the typewriter on more than one occasion, and on each occasion I failed. A deal in cattle or other animals went by a strict formula: the lines the actors said never varied but the emotions put into them swept all the strings. I must confess that I was never much good at a deal. I used to imagine that I was doing everybody a good turn by cutting out the divides and the hand claps not realizing that I was betraying Shakespeare's instructions to the players. I was looked upon as an iconoclast, a spoilsport.

'Here give me that hand?'

The hand of the potential buyer is given reluctantly. The seller stares at the buyer's palm in a meditative way. As he holds the buyer's hand by the tips of the fingers the other hand goes up and down in a wavy motion. 'Here, I tell you what I will do, I tell you what I will do, I tell you what I will do – twenty-seven all up and you'll have luck in my baste.'

'And you'll have luck in my money.'

The seller reminisces: 'I know your people and I know yous are dacent people and … sure I knew your mother and like that I'd like yous to get her.'

'And sure wouldn't I like to buy of you. Don't I know all ablongin' to you and they were a credit to the country.'

'And they were nothing to the people ablongin' to you.' Traditional courtesy obliges a man to repeat the mispronunciations of his neighbour. 'As dacent a people as stood 'ithin the parish of Donaghmoyne.'

'Twenty-five if you like now, if you like now.'

At this the seller becomes very dramatic. He is no longer holding the other person's hand in a slack casual manner. He is no longer whispering: he is shouting and we feel that some fantastically generous offer is going to be made.

'Here, here, I'll be as good a sport as you, I'll be good a sport as you.' Down comes the palm with a mighty slap. 'I'll be as good a sport as you – twenty-seven with a crown luck.'

The buyer takes his cue: he grabs his opponent's hand and shouts, 'And I'll be as good a sport as you.' Voice dies to a whisper. 'Twenty-five all up.'

It might well happen that neither of these was a genuine buyer or seller, that they were merely putting on a show for some slow-witted mother's son: this was quite a common occurrence. At this point a third party turns up. Sometimes that third party is the actual owner who is there to carry the play further. The three-card lads are only trotting after these men.

Generally, however, the deal was on the level and the middleman, the 'tangler', was authentic too.

Enter the tangler. 'What's atween yous?'

'There's nothing atween us,' both say.

The tangler delivers his speech:

'I know yous both and yous are both dacent people and yous'll both do as I say – divide what's atween yous.' Both principals remain mute, standing stiffly to attention. 'It's you that has the right pair of good-looking daughters that id keep a fella out of the gutter, and begod you might be buying more than a cow.' Sudden excitement again. Tangler grabs both parties' hands and with a great struggle brings them into contact by the skin of the tips of the fingers. The deal is made.

Aw 'deed aye, them was the days. How well I remember the Sparrow Madden. He was a dealer in gorries (local name for bonhams). He was a thin little fellow, couldn't write his name, but is a rich man now, thanks to the Border. In gorry markets, where it was usual to find the husband and wife on opposite sides of their little cart of bonhams, the Sparrow would go up to an old man who had a young wife and in his pretended drunken voice – pretending he didn't know them too – he would say:

'How much for them chaps?'

The man answered humbly. The Sparrow replaced the sheet on the cart, and then had a short confab with the wife. At that he would turn again to the husband and shout: 'You'll do as your daughter says, you'll not break your daughter's word.'

This would embarrass any normal man, but it was seldom it embarrassed any of the hungry scraidíns of farmers who were to be found guarding donkey carts full of bonhams in that part of the country. Oh hell, to the embarrass or embarrass.

And then there was the horse dealer from Crossmaglen who once paid a tribute to my innocency of expression. This man dealt in crooked horses – and he, too, is in the money today, thanks to the same Border – but as he was so well known very few people would dream of approaching a horse that had Mr X or one of his well-known friends at its head. So he employed young, innocent-looking chaps to stand by his vicious horses and sell them for him. I occupied this post on one occasion and proved that I was never meant to be rich. A poor woman and her gowdy of a son came up to me. Mr X was in the vicinity but for all that I gave her the wink as secretly as I could.

The son didn't take the wink as quickly as his mother and the result was that I was never asked to sell a horse for this horse dealer again.

Just after the war I happened to be travelling north – travelling first class on that occasion – when I fell into conversation with a very gay fella on the opposite seat.

It was my old friend the horse dealer and I had told him all about my experiences with him before I remembered him. He enjoyed the joke immensely. Indeed he was a very cultured fellow in the generous traditional way that is to be found in rural Ireland. He had heard a lot about me; he had read everything I had written. He himself had made a stack since those distant days of the early 'thirties.

'How did you do?'
'Aw, sure there's no money in the job I'm in.'
'Aw, just the same.'

(*Kavanagh's Weekly*, 21 June 1952, p. 3; also 'The Cattle Fair' in *X*, no. 7, pp. 255–7)

The Dundalk Market Train

The Monday train that carries the small farm folk to and from the Dundalk butter and egg market was returning with its load of open-mouthed but shrewd passengers. The compartment in which I sat was crowded with five people and about a dozen large baskets. On the seats and under them were plough parts and hampers holding potatoes, and in one corner were three pullets tied together by the legs. A woman was explaining that she had exchanged four cocks for the pullets and was pleased with the bargain.

Opposite me, beside the woman, sat a Louth farmer, a fellow of about seventy – small and tight, and in that condition of fake drunkenness which farm men put on to their hail-fellows with whom they are transacting business. This man was also pretending to be deaf when it suited his purpose. On the seat beside me was a drawling, dawdling – but as cute as they're made – small Monaghan farmer. His little girl of eight or nine sat beside him, or jumped about and played with a ball and lead pencil. The small farmer, Larry, had his heart set on buying a load of wheaten straw of the Louth man, whose name was Joe. The fat woman, with a bosom like a bolster of feathers tied in the middle and a series of red chins in multiples of three that disappeared into her black blouse, had her eyes fixed lovingly on her three pullets, but was assisting the straw deal forward.

'I say Joe, would you sell me a lock of that wheaten straw?'

The prospective buyer leaned over with his palms on his knees and a look of weak, watery supplication on his knowing face.

Joe stuck his pipe still deeper into his mouth and stared vacantly at the child. He grunted in an absent-minded way and then spoke through his nose: 'Man alive, that's a shocking nice wee child.' He glanced out the window where the little fields were being dipped in the gold of late autumn. 'I'm damn but the turnips could be doing with a sup of rain.'

'He wants to buy a load of wheaten straw of you, Joe,' the woman shouted in his ear.

Joe spat out nervously and his head trembled a little. 'A shocking nice wee girl.'

'Would you take a fellow's word for a half ton on the cart? I only want a lock to thatch the cart-house. I wouldn't have to weigh it. You'd take me word?'

'Why wouldn't I?' Joe stared straight in front; and he spoke in that indifferent, noncommittal tone which suggested that he didn't want to sell and was trying not to make a 'bad fellow' of himself. He changed the subject. 'There's a man and I saw him at Kilkerley chapel last Sunday and he got shocking stout of himself – Paddy Brady. Do you know what I'm going to tell you, it was there with me to recognize him. "I'm damn but," says I, "you're not Paddy Brady?"

'"And do you not know me?" says he.

'"As much as," says I; "man alive you mended a terror." I tell you that was the man done well for himself and his family!'

'He had an extra family, Joe. Why the likes of them girls to do a day's work at anything you wouldn't meet from Hell to Ballyshannon. I remarked one of them at the altar in Kilkerley the other Sunday, and I never saw such a smashing girl. Do you know them, Larry?'

Larry was bored; he was only interested in the straw. 'I say Joe, what would you charge me for a half a ton of that straw?' he drawled humbly.

Joe cocked his head like a dog listening at a closed door. 'Would you take the whole rick?'

'Now what in the wide world would I be doing with the whole rick? Sure there must be the guts of ten ton in that rick.'

'They're making paper of it now, I hear,' Joe said half to himself. 'If you broke on it you'd have to take a cut down to the ground and not have it in the rot heap.'

'I'll do that alright, don't fear.'

'You might and you mightn't.'

The woman was bowing and talking pettishly to the child. 'You'll have to go to school the morrow. And you have your nice new pencil.'

'Aren't you going to come home with me?' Joe addressed the child. 'Making paper of it now, I hear. I tell you this war is no bloody good to the farmer. There was some rise in the last two wars I remember, but this one isn't worth a damn.' He sucked his pipe meditatively, with his eyes on the handle of a butter basket.

'What about that straw?' No answer.

'He says what about the straw? Are you going to make a deal with him?'

The child offered Joe her ball. 'Keep it yourself like a good girl.'

'What age is she, Larry?' said the woman with a large smile that showed a mouthful of yellow teeth from which the gums had receded, leaving her molars like a row of icy axes hanging from a beam by the handles.

'She was eight last May.'

'Lord! O! You won't find till she'll be able to do little turns for you. Larry you ought to put her on for something. Being an oul' pratie-washer is the last of the last. Nothing like the schooling no matter what they say. The dry foot under you from one end of the year to the other. Working about a little farmer's place is nothing but pure-bred slavery.'

'Nothing but the God's honest truth you're saying, but as the fellow said she has plenty of time before her yet. I say what about that straw? Are you going to sell me half a ton?'

'Joe, are you not going to tell the decent man about the straw? Don't sing dumb.'

'Aye, too,' was all Joe said.

'Well, that's the way,' the woman sighed. 'Larry you're just as well off not to have a son. I have three boys, and I can tell you it's no joke keeping them in style these days. The boys are worse now for the style than the girls. Off every Sunday to the hall and not able to get up on Monday morning till the sun ...' The train was roaring through a cutting. 'Some of the men that's on the go these days, they'd pollute a person,' I could hear the woman saying. 'Sunday-men – that's all they are.'

'The halls have the country mad,' said Joe.

'What about that straw, Joe?'

The train was pulling up at a halt and Joe was staggering to his feet. The woman gathered her baskets and worked her way to the door after him. There was only Larry, his child and myself left. 'The right oul' haveril that fellow,' Larry mumbled to himself, 'drive a rat to hell and back for a ha'penny. I tell you it's no wonder that fellow has them on their edges.' Larry was speaking partly for my benefit. 'Skin a flea for his hide.' We got out at the next stop.

(*The Irish Times*, 20 December 1941, p. 6)

The Stir

'Why aren't you coming down to the stir?' the son of the house said to me in a grumbling voice. I was sitting in the kitchen listening to an old man telling old stories. I wasn't pulling my weight. After all, the stir had been organized for the young people, and for me to stay sitting in the kitchen listening to the old people wasn't very courteous. The stir was being held in the Big Room behind the fireplace. In the Little Room on the other side of the kitchen (it was a one-storey three-roomed house) the tea, or supper if you like, was being served. It was from the Big Room and those taking part in the stir that people were being called in rotation to supper, so I reluctantly left my old story-telling friend and, stooping my head (I was always big for my age) to avoid striking it on the low lintel of the Big Room door, I joined the merrymakers at the stir.

The stir was what they called a private dance.

The dancers were seated round the walls on the side-boards of carts which rested on bags of meal, the girls mostly on men's knees.

A noted entertainer from the town of Louth was present and had just concluded a song. The jazz age was beginning and it was a jazzy type of song; I thought it marvellous. He was about to begin another song but the son of the house who was M.C. was about fed up with him. It took him the best part of an hour's forcing to get the singer started and now it was nearly as hard to get him to stop once he had got warmed up.

'Take your partners for a one-shtep.'

But the man from the town of Louth was off again, to my great delight. The majority of those present were out of sympathy with his new type of song though through force of habit the end of each verse received the traditional encouragement of 'Rise it, ye boy ye!' and 'Good on ye'.

It was a summer's night. The harsh call of the corncrake kept up a continuous rhythmic beat. From the horse's stable came an unusual noise. Was the horse caught in the manger? The son of the house glared at the man from Louth as much as saying, you have frightened the horse, then he rushed out. He returned shortly: nothing wrong.

The eight people who had been having supper in the Little Room filed back into the Big Room. The daughter of the house tapped eight other people on the shoulder with the words 'Go on down now'. She passed me by and I felt wounded; this was a real test of how well you were thought of. I was almost a next-door neighbour but it showed you how little was thought of you when it came to the whipping of crutches. And there wasn't more than two more lots to be served. I would probably be left to the last, and so it happened. But I was grateful for all that; after all, I had been invited.

The Little Room was very little. A table had been placed lengthwise along two beds. Four of us sat on the edge of the bed and the other four jammed against the wall on the other side.

There was bags of bread and jam; it was a great feast and we all felt inclined to gaiety.

I was a bit uneasy; I seemed to be under suspicion. A second daughter of the house who was in charge of this department had what I was later to discover were all the attributes of the owner of a lounge bar. She had a stern and nasty attitude that would stand no unconventional nonsense. That terrible fear of the unconventional is a queer thing. Most people have something to conceal and the unconventional is always likely to bare the secret. I had merely stretched myself for a moment back on the bed.

Shortly afterwards the M.C. looked in the low door and stared at me. I never ate a male's mate that did me less good. Gingerly I stabbed with my knife for the slices of bread. I put on the jam with trembling hands. I did everything gently.

Next thing was, didn't the leg of the bed on my side give and we were all on the ground with the cup of tea held – if we were lucky –

poised above our foreheads. We managed to get to our feet. It transpired that the leg of the bed was a sack of oats that had slipped sideways. I eventually extricated myself from the awkward situation and the rest of the supper passed pleasantly.

I remember that Little Room well. On the damp walls hung all the usual holy pictures that were to be found in a small country house. On the mantelboard over a rusty fireplace stood a faded photograph of a wedding with the bridegroom wearing side-whiskers. Grandfather of the M.C., I suppose.

'It's a bleddy good stir,' I said.

'Make a dousing wake,' said the fellow opposite me when the daughter of the house had gone for more tea.

We were not conscious of any element of pathos though the material was there. Pleasure is comparative.

When everybody had supper the stir got going in earnest. The fiddler played and left as few gaps as possible through which the man from the town of Louth could enter with another of his jazzy songs. I protested loudly that I thought the man from Louth damn good. Then the M.C. said: 'How about yourself giving us a stave?'

'I would, only I can't think of the words of any song,' I said.

There was silence. I tried to think but no song came to my memory. Just as the silence was being broken by jeering banter I recalled the words of 'McKenna's Dream':

> *One night of late I chanced to stray*
> *It being in the pleasant month of May*
> *While all the green in slumber lay*
> *The moon sank in the deep.*

Sang it right through in spite of interruptions. And as God is me judge when I was finished I tossed my head from side to side and said what a million singers had said before, without knowing that anyone had ever said it before – 'A good song but a very hard song to sing.'

(Unpublished, c. 1957)

The Marriage Market

Seeing a film which purported to deal with the marriage customs of the Irish* awakened my imagination to what I knew of this subject. Was there ever anything peculiar about the way we had of getting married in this country? Very little, unless one wishes to descend to the forced-humour level of the folklore collector who, like the average newspaper-man, has to find wonders in the commonplace or bust. There is always supposed to be a symbolic meaning in all this lore.

There was nothing different worth writing about in match-making in rural Ireland from what takes place in every country, on every level of society.

There has been a lot of talk about the 'made match', and the suggestion is that it was a very commercial proposition. Marriage is, in a general sense, a commercial proposition which concerns more than the two principals.

There seems to be some sort of idea that in America people get married for love and love alone. If this were true, it would be giving so-called love a position it does not deserve. In America it is supposed to be all romance; it has to do with necking, and not with collaring money. In the film we saw the romantic American bridegroom shove the bride's fortune into a furnace, and it was the only time I have ever seen an American being contemptuous of cash. Of course, it was only

---

* *The Quiet Man*, directed by John Ford.

meant to be fiction, and meant to be an escape from the reality.

Romantic love is a pleasant affair, but something far more satisfying is the practical proposition. Shaw pointed out that the real test of equality is in the intermarriageability of the classes. You can have that romantic stuff, and go through with it, only if the economic level of the parties is the same. There is no trouble in a man marrying his economic equal, but then few men want to do that.

Love may be a reality but –

The first thing that any man should get into his head is that women are brutally practical. There are the exceptions but, generally speaking, when a man gets his heart broken on the rocks of romance it is due much less to his emotional or intellectual defects than to the fact that the woman realizes that, as a husband, he will not do. The position here [in rural Ireland], where so few get married at all, is not to be taken as a true guide; a woman here has to be impractical.

Economics is the key to the marriage business, and in no place more so than in romantic America.

It takes as much business acumen to land a rich heiress as it does to make the same amount of money in ordinary commerce. Now and again, you find a rich woman marrying a poor man who happens to take her fancy, but it is a rare occurrence. For one thing, it is nearly impossible to meet anyone on a different economic level than oneself. You may meet them in a sort of way, but there is no teeth in the grip. Subconsciously, all those encounters begin with 'No'.

People with approximately the same amount of hard currency meet at dances and other social meeting places and, though they may not be wildly attracted to each other, the money in their respective pockets knows that they are meant for each other. It is a hard world and the romantic films cannot give us escape from it.

One thing that can be said in favour of the Irish traditional method of getting married is that it worked, and it worked because it was the same practical method that is used everywhere.

It was based on sound psychology. Silly feminists, who are never feminine, have created the notion that women like equality (as it is called), that they must not revert to the bad old days when they were mere chattels. As far as the parents are concerned the daughters are chattels and the daughters are never more pleased than to know that they are being bargained for as mere chattels. Not much pleasure in having your dignity and being eligible for Parliament if no one wants you. On a deeper level, there is even pleasure for a woman in the thought of being a slave. In fact, it is in the male, too, born of sloth; we all want someone to lean on, someone to do our thinking for us. If I myself got half a chance I would buy a ready-made suit of thought.

The women were clever when they wanted to be slaves; it is a great luxury. The rural Irish system of going about the marriage business was as follows. The man set his eye on a girl whose father, he knew, was able to give her a decent fortune. The amount of the fortune would be well known, for neither the girl nor her parents any more than in other reaches of society were anxious to conceal the bait.

'She may be small,' said a father of his tiny daughter, 'but I'll put as much money on her head as will make her tall enough.'

Having picked out the girl, the man went through the usual introduction ritual. He 'sent word' by a well-wisher that he would like to call to discuss the matter, and would he be welcome.

There was nothing outlandish about this; in fact, it was strict formality, a very necessary thing in all our dealings with people. I saw where one of those agony-column advisers in a Sunday newspaper advised a questioner that, if he fancied a girl whom he saw in the street, he should speak to her, that the days of formal introductions were over. That was bad advice, for such acquaintanceships start off on the wrong foot; one or other of the parties feels that his or her dignity has been injured – I made myself cheap, sort of. There is a tremendous temptation to cut out the formalities, but it is a mistake as far as my experience goes.

When the formal introduction was gone through the man was generally advised that he would be welcome, and so on an evening arranged, accompanied by a friend and armed with a bottle of whiskey, he called at the girl's house.

The companion opened up in the following manner. (On one occasion in the late 'thirties I happened to fill this office.)

'I suppose you know what we came for, so there's no use in batin' about the bush.'

'How is your mother this long time?' says the woman of the house to me. 'I didn't see her this long time, and she's the right good woman and reared the right good children.'

After this, my man took over his own bargaining.

The bargaining went on in such cases often in the presence of the girl who, as I suggested earlier, had no intention of being insulted.

She was seeing not the mere man who wanted to marry her but her future and the future of the race, for that more than the man is what women marry.

She dreamt into that future, saw herself as the woman of a house, accompanying her husband to fairs and markets, and that is the real pride. There was nothing used to attract me more than seeing a newly-wedded wife up on the seat-board of the cart beside her husband, who usually was nothing to look at, looking at the world with confident eyes.

The romantic method is amusing enough, if one doesn't believe too much in it. The cinema has encouraged somewhat simple folk to take it seriously and to ignore the hard reality that lies behind the marriage business.

But sanity is bound to return, for women are always sane, and they have very little use for romance that leads nowhere. Women suffer love-making mainly to please the man, but the real romance they believe in is the knowledge that he has a salary that will support a wife and family, or is otherwise in a position to marry her. The thrill of the possible is the only thrill. This is true for both male and female. The thrill of the hard earth when we come down out of our daydream and look the reality in the face is something that cannot be simulated.

Incidentally, why do we dream and live in clouds? Because we realize that there is no earth to come down to.

There was romance in Irish love-making – the romance of the 'made match' resided in the word 'made'. It was life going on. From the point of view of complexity it had less of the twists that go with commerce higher up. One could be folklorish about it, if one did not take it seriously.

I am back in a country town as I write this; it is a Fair Day, late in the evening. There is a rumour going through the crowds that a match is being made in Donnelly's pub. It has been going on for hours and negotiations are in danger of breaking down. We wait tensely. Then a fat woman comes out of the pub with a smile on her face. There is a shaking of hands all round.

Someone rushes up to the fat woman:

'Did you agree?'

'It's all settled.'

Everyone is excited. We are in the midst of continuing life. The fair is alive with tomorrows.

(*Kavanagh's Weekly*, 14 June 1952, pp. 2–3)

Old Wives' Tales of Ireland

When I was growing up in the North of Ireland thirty years ago, the dispensary doctor was – or he ought to have been – a frustrated character. There were few diseases, according to us, at which a doctor would be any good.

We had Murray, the bone-setter, and Jackie, who had the 'secret' for the cure of the whitlow. His powerful plaster was believed to be useful also in cases of cancer. My own father had the cure of the jaundice. He got the prescription out of an old medicine book, but his patients didn't know this. They thought it had been something remarkable passed on from father to son.

The business of midwifery was under the control of two old women, but over and above all these, who might be called quacks and for whom there was something to be said, were the witch-doctors. And, as often happens in the case of other religions, the people who believed least in the superstition were the priests of it.

In the second house from ours in the lane lived Harry McElroy. It was believed over a very large part of that country that Harry's touch would cure erysipelas, or the rose as we called it. Of an evening I often saw as many as seven or eight suffering from something they thought was the rose asking the way to Harry's.

He had two cures, the long cure and the short cure. If you were poor, he touched the sore spot once with his hand as he mumbled a Christian prayer. But if you were rich, he had to visit you in your home for nine consecutive days.

You may ask: Did these people get better? In every case they did. But nobody knows what they got better from – the question is one of diagnosis.

I remember my younger brother got a swollen foot one time. The old people of the neighbourhood gathered in and said it was the rose. So send for Harry. There was a long discussion. My father, perhaps knowing the fraud of his own cure, after a long think decided against it.

It was a good job he did, for the swollen foot turned out to be a bad case of septicaemia. He was lucky to get over it, for there was no penicillin or anything of that sort in those days.

When a child got mumps, an ass's winkers was put round his neck and he was led in and out of a pigsty three times by one of the opposite sex, who kept saying in Gaelic:

'Hugadh a lecna, mucna, mucna.'

'Take the mumps, pigs, pigs.'

It happened to myself.

Nearly all children's diseases were looked after by witch-doctoring. I had the whooping cough. My godmother came and put a red tape round my neck. In the case of girls, the godfather did the job. Another sure cure for whooping cough was bread made by a woman who was married to a man of her own name.

A stye on the eye was cured by one of the opposite sex pointing gooseberry thorns at it nine times for nine days. If you failed to get at the stye in the moon it came in with, that same stye would keep on coming back till that moon came in again.

Another cure, and a horrible one, was for scarlet fever. There was in the old village graveyard the ancient vault of The McMahon, a noted clan, and this vault was full of the skulls that gravediggers threw up. A member of the family of the sufferer had to go to this 'skull-house' at midnight and bring home a skullful of water from a stream that ran before someone's door, and give it to the child to drink. It wasn't every man would go to this graveyard. We believed in ghosts, as well as cures.

These beliefs are far from dead yet. I was back in my native place a couple of years ago, and knew of a man who had a sick child. What it was I didn't find out. But the cure which he was performing was bringing the child to the blacksmith's forge every morning for nine days. The blacksmith carried the child three times round the anvil, and eventually dipped it in the trough. If a customer had arrived before the man with the child, the cure didn't work and he would have to come back the next morning.

It was all a mixture of downright madness and ignorance, and how so many of us managed to survive is a tribute to the Life Force. A good many did die, or were left with complaints that stayed with them all their lives.

There was one woman who had the cure, as we put it, of sciatica. A young fellow who lived beside me got a bad hip which he thought was sciatica. On his own old side-car – his jaunting-car – he drove of a winter's night ten miles to see this woman. The cure was to dip his leg in a stream that ran beside the woman's house. It had to be done at midnight. This poor chap got the best of cures: he died from pneumonia and had no more trouble with his bad hip.

The basis of all this belief is the desire to believe in miracles which is in all men. Life itself is a miracle. It is easier to get people to believe in a miracle than in factual evidence, because the miracle is evidence of something beyond the prison walls of mortality.

(*Family Doctor*, vol. 2, no. 7, July 1952, p. 364)

Gut Yer Man

'Go on, our Micky –'
    'Gut yer man –'
    'Bog him –'
A football match is in progress in my imagination, and I must admit that I am not a spectator but in there, ploughing all around me, making myself famous in the parish as a man that never 'cowed', even at the risk of a broken neck.

'Aw, Kavanagh, the dhirty eejut.'

'How could he be an eejut and him a poet?' one of our supporters replied, and my traducer had no comeback.

The battle raged up and down the stony field. The team we were playing was a disgusting class of a team who used every form of psychological warfare. For instance, when one of them was knocked down he rolled on the ground and bawled like a bull a-gelding.

Then there was the time when I put the ball over the goal-line and a most useful non-playing member of the opposing team kicked it back into play. We argued and there was the normal row.

The referee came up and interviewed the non-playing member of the opposition, and that man replied: 'I never even saw the ball. Do you think I'd tell a lie and me at Holy Communion this morning?'

What could we say to that?

Of course we had our own methods. We never finished a game if towards the end we were a-batin'. We always found an excuse to rise a row and get the field invaded.

Ah, them was the times.

For one year I was virtual dictator of that team, being captain of the team and secretary and treasurer of the club. There was no means of checking up on my cash, which gave rise to a lot of ill-founded suspicion. I remember I kept the money in an attaché-case under my bed. It is possible that every so often I visited it for the price of a packet of cigarettes, but nothing serious.

I once went as the club's representative to the County Board. We had to defend ourselves from a protest against us being awarded a certain game on the grounds that the list of players wasn't on watermarked Irish paper. I pointed out that the list was written on the inside of a large Player packet and that Player packets were made in Ireland. This did not impress. Nothing I said impressed, as I hadn't the clichés off. It took a good deal of conspiring to depose me from my dictatorial post. Members of the team met in secret groups to know what could be done, but as soon as I got wind of the conspiracy I fired every man of them.

In the end they got rid of me, but it was a job.

The man responsible for my deposition was a huge fellow, a blacksmith, a sort of Hindenburg whose word carried weight. He was a great master of the cliché, but sometimes he broke into originality as when the time we were going for the county final he wouldn't let us touch a ball for a week previous as he wanted us to be 'ball hungry'.

Ball hungry as we may have been, we lost the match, and I was blamed, for I was 'in the sticks', and let a ball roll through my legs.

The crowd roared in anguish: 'Go home and put an apron on you.' And various other unfriendly remarks were made such as 'Me oul' mother would make a better goalier.'

Somebody has said that no man can adequately describe Irish life who ignores the Gaelic Athletic Association, which is true in a way, for football runs women a hard race as a topic for conversation.

The popular newspaper has driven out the football ballad, which at one time gave fairly literal accounts of famous matches –

At half-past two the whistle blew

And the ball it was thrown in,
The haro Murphy sazed it and
He kicked it with the win'.

Then there was a ballad singer who used to sing –

The catching and the kickin' was mar-veel-e-us for to see.

After the ballad came the local paper, where we were all Trojans in defence and wizards in attack. I once got a lot of kudos from a report which described me as 'incisive around goal'. No one knew the meaning of the word incisive but it sounded good.

These reminiscences have been inspired by a Dublin barman – a native of my own district – who said to me: 'I often wonder you never wrote about the time you were playing football for the Grattans. Do you mind the Sunday we played yous below in Jackie's meada beside the river? And big Hughie on the side-line with an ashplant ready to cut the head of e'er a man that kem 'ithin a mile of him?'

'Vaguely,' I said.

'Aw, you must remember. Weren't you playing that day?'

Then it came back.

She was a brave mother who willingly allowed her son to play football. Most mothers would 'be out of their minds' worried over their sons on the playing fields, never knowing when he'd come back to her a 'limither for life'.*

'Many's the good man the same football put an end to. How I remember the poor Poochy Maguire that got the boot in the bottom of the belly and never overed it. If you'd take a fool's advice that you never took you'd lave the football alone.'

'Things have changed since them days.'

'That'll do you, now. What about young Kiernan of Cross that was killed in Cavan?'

As soon as the player came home he was scrutinized by his mother.

* A 'limither' was a man fit only for begging. According to Kavanagh, 'Limiter' was a phrase used in the Middle Ages by mendicant friars who were licensed to beg within prescribed limits (*RTV Guide*, 24 February 1962).

She had sharp eyes as a rule and was able to see the deep cut over his eye which he had been trying to conceal with a lock of hair.

'You got a kick?'

'That's only a little thing.'

'Little thing! Aw, God knows but it's me that's the unfortunate woman. I heard the roaring down there in that stony meada of Jackie's, and I didn't know at what minute you'd be brought home to me half dead. Did yous win atself?'

'A draw.'

'Yous were never able for Donaghmoyne – with all your bummin'. Get the black porringer from under the stairs and put them pair of eggs in it ... No, never during soot were yous fit to bate Donaghmoyne.'

'Only for the referee –'

'Only for something the sky id fall. Yes, only for something the sky id fall.'

For all this my imagination finds difficulty in focusing on this period – and one should always trust the imagination to light up vital things. All sporting subjects are superficial. The emotion is a momentary puff of gas, not an experience, and I know now why I have been unable to write about it at length.

I have noted that in *Ulysses*, that compendium of commonplace emotions and goings on, only the punter speculating on the result of the Ascot Gold Cup comes into the theme. So sport can't have been very vital, for Joyce had a mind like a sponge. But all these opinions of mine are barren. It is none of my business, and one should always try to extract the comedy from life and not see it moralizingly.

'Hello.'

'Hello.'

'How are you after the game last Sunday?'

'A stiff leg.'

'I know what that means.'

'You're right. Can't sit down without the leg straight out in front. Shocking bleddy nuisance. We were in very bad luck. Sure, Paddy Keegan had an open goal in front of him and he shot forty yards wide. The man that id miss that id miss the parish if he fired at the chapel.'

'Bad all right.'

'Desperate. Pity Trainer wasn't playing. Mother won't let him.'

So the two men on opposite sides of a stone fence talk on.

My brother was telling me how one lovely Sunday morning he was taking a stroll outside San Francisco on the edge of the Pacific when he saw, hurrying with little bundles under their oxters, men of a rural Irish complex.

Sometime later he came upon a Gaelic football match in progress. Everything was as at home: There were the men running up and down the unpaled sideline slicing at the toes which encroached with hurleys and crying: 'Keep back there now, keep back there now.' And all around the pitch the familiar battle cries of the Dalcassians were to be heard:

'Gut yer man ...'

'Bog into him.'

Not a man of them had ever left home and the mysterious Pacific was just a bog-hole, gurgling with eels and frogs. Yet, there was something queer and wonderful about the sight, or the thought.

Then Inniskeen came on the field and they were stuffed with pride,
They fell before the Fontenoys like grass before a scythe.

Yes, says he, they fell before the Fontenoys like grass before a scythe.

('Diary', *Envoy*, August 1950, pp. 79–83)

Return in Harvest

During the harvest time I visited my native fields and former neighbours for the purpose of recording some of the people I used to know so well.*

For certain reasons I now think we approached this matter from the angle of a common fallacy. Men are often accused of having two differing views on a subject and are called two-faced. What we say when we are involved in ordinary intercourse with people may be different from what we think when we sit down with ourselves to reflect. There is a notion current that there is some special virtue in what in radio is called the 'unscripted discussion' and that you will get the truth out of people when you catch them off guard. I don't believe this. When a man speaks impromptu he speaks on the surface. You have to dig for truth and when you have found your truth in all its humility you have to have the courage to utter it.

It would be wrong for me to say that I was disappointed in my former neighbours; on the contrary they seemed to me to have almost the serenity and order of a work of art, a quiet humorous attitude to life, a source of delight in a Ballybunioned society. Amid the loud leppin', roaring balladry and boring professional Irishism of Kerry and Galway which is totally without humour – I could realize that something had

* This article is based on the script of a programme broadcast on Radio Éireann in September 1953.

103

continuous life out of history. Notwithstanding the arrival of the tractor and the combine harvester the spirit I found here had not changed
in a hundred and fifty years. This was the society to which Carleton
gave a voice. Indeed, the tractor and combine harvester have helped to
keep the tradition alive by taking over the burdens which tend to bru-
talize men and women. Anyone who has ever done a day's tying of
heavy lodged corn with thistles in it will know that he would be in no
mood at the day's end for amusement or relaxation. The trouble about
this modest humorous authentic living is that it requires a very subtle
technique to get it across on radio, or in writing for that matter. The
advantages are all with the loud, roaring obvious melodrama. Because
the loud and melodramatic is unreal nobody is involved. You are dealing with an artificial thing, a convention.

Mediocrities, which is another name for a kind of person incapable
of love, worship the conventional, because it can be learned. It is with a
convention, the veneer, that what passes for Irish literature in the past
fifty years has mostly been concerned. The basic emotion behind this
was hate. Hate or evil is not what people always think – it is negation. It
is not deliberate. It is the absence of love and love is the essence of genius.

Beware of anyone who sees you as picturesque, as a character. When
someone dislikes you he refuses to see beneath your mannerisms, your
peculiarities. Love, which as Chesterton shrewdly pointed out is anything but blind, sees into the unique wonders of the loved one's heart.
Most of those from Synge onwards who wrote the externals of Irish life
– which weren't even true – weren't deliberately bad; they just weren't
good enough, and humble enough. They lacked the courage and humility to admit to themselves that they had no real love perception.

Since then nearly all writing about Ireland has proceeded from this
point of view. You have plays in which barbarous characters are set up
so that audiences can feel superior. The audiences which only yesterday
were humble folk from the small fields have taken over the function of
the idiotic Ascendancy, and authors have turned up to invent a lower
order that one can be superior about.

Great liberality is permitted towards these mythical characters in
the use of murder, infanticide, drunkenness and outrageous bawling.
The new middle-class audience of theatre and books is falling back-

wards in its efforts to prove itself broad-minded. Liberalism in language and behaviour is the real sign of art and if murder, rape and bigamy are not present how are they to know whether the thing is art or not?

Now, I am quite willing to allow that the sentimental side deserves to be punished. This sentimental side which cries out that Miss Mary Murphy's book on God is the greatest thing since St Augustine. Between these two closely related horrors the sincere and authentic artist has a lean time. The artist is a moralist and yet he is not a conformist; he has no friends for he is not bawling in a pub on the one hand and he is not screaming hysterical piety on the other.

I realize that at this moment many people may be wondering when we are going to get to south Monaghan, but actually we are only now passing through Mullacrew and have still a few miles to go.

So that gives me time to put down a few more points.

In going on this journey I was subscribing to another fallacy and I hope I'll be allowed to blame nobody but myself ...

There are certain people in Ireland who will be heard saying that so and so has done for Ballina what so and so has done for Cork. Once upon a time a reviewer of a poem of mine said that he hoped that somebody would now do for other regions of Ireland what I have done for south Monaghan. He was attributing virtue to the place. Of course if anything I had written had the slightest value it would be as true for a Chinese as it would be for a man from Drumnagrella. It would be in fact truer for the man from China, for the man from China would not have his judgment confused by local colour. The test of authenticity in a work of creative thinking is this. If you say of a character in a novel by a Chinese, an Italian or a Frenchman – 'How Chinese, Italian or French' – you are dealing with a bogus article. But if you can say at once of such a character: how Irish! then you have the real thing. For the exciting thing about people is not that they are different, but that they are alike – and it is only when they are alike that they can be unique.

We are now passing Channonrock Cross. On my left is the road to Carrickmacross, on my right to Dundalk. Many's the time I rode my bicycle this way.

There is a thing which is often said that is the thing about the simplicity of the countryman and his language minted direct from experience. It is true indeed that a good deal of poetry is dispersed throughout rural parts. I remember an old woman, a centenarian, being interviewed in these parts a few years ago and she spoke of the bad old days when the labourer would have to work from the stars to the stars. And a returned American emigrant whom I often heard my father quoting who said that when he came back he thought that the bushes ought to know him. There are as I say quite a lot of these freshly minted images but on the whole when the Irish country person or ordinary person whether of town or country utters himself he is anything but simple.

Of the ordinary rough-and-ready balladry of the country this is not so true, but when a country body begins to progress into the world of print he does not write out of his rural innocence – he writes out of Palgrave's *Golden Treasury*. The Assyrian has come down like a wolf on the fold of much Irish balladry. In another way Francis Ledwidge, whom some people call the poet of Meath, did not write out of his Meathness; he wrote out of John Clare. The first stop out of total rurality is complexity – imitation. The plain countryman and of course the plain townsman when he comes to a city loves concrete buildings and chromium plate. I remember, when I came to Dublin for the first time, being disappointed with the façade of Trinity and wondering why they didn't get a good plasterer to float and pebbledash it.

And now here we are in my native village of Inniskeen within two miles of the Armagh border and one mile of Louth.

The Fane river flows lightly over the pebbles, the old round tower is still there. The only thing I notice is a very large number of new houses all built in the usual suburban style.

We entered Dan McNello's shop and, as I did, I remembered myself as a small gowdy of a gassan standing in the grocery part of this shop beside my mother who was ordering the Christmas goods. During my rural days I don't think I ever frequented the pub sector and I don't suppose we would be blempt if we made up for it on this occasion.

Among those in the pub when we arrived were Tommy Crawley, Owney Hanratty and Peter McArdle.

'How are you, Tommy?' says I.

'The best, Paddy,' says Tommy. 'God, Paddy, I was only the other day talking about your mother, the Lord be good to her, and it's herself was the right dacent woman, and the time I was doing the ploughing for her. Do you mind the oul' swing plough? That was the best swing plough ever was in your country. Petey McArdle here often put a point piece on the sock.'

'Is that a fact?' say I with all the usual fatuity of the interviewer.

'Damn good plough alright,' said Petey.

'Yez were joined with Dinny Brennan that year. The oul' kickin' mare ...'

'She belonged to a road contractor and would only work quiet in a cart,' I said.

'I was the only man ever could make her plough, Paddy. She ploughed away the whole season till we were closing the drills for spuds in Dinny's field. We were damn near finished and yourself and Dinny were lying on the gravel beside the oul' boiler at the gate when begod she let go. "Loose her out to hell," cries Dinny.'

'I remember it well,' I said and drove my forced laugh in among sincere company. At this point my neighbour Owney Hanratty, a light-hearted fellow of eight-five, joined in.

I led off at my most inane. 'Did you ever know me to do any work?'

'You carried bags for me at the mill and I found you all right. Of course you never killed yourself and sure weren't you right.'

'I was fairly intelligent?'

'Sure you were intelligent: only you were intelligent wouldn't you have to work the same as the rest of us.' Owney's memory was working. 'Do you mind the day you jumped off the cart and I thought you were killed?'

'Oh, yes.'

'Down at Candlefort Lane. I was going up to McCoy's to draw oats and you were going to sarve Mass. You jumped off the cart and everyone in Paris Row thought you were killed.'

Owney went on to tell a mysterious story about a woman who died in childbirth. It all happened in that most remote and mysterious of all periods, the period immediately preceding one's birth.

I often heard my father talking about this woman's death, how for the three nights preceding her death he used to stand outside his door listening to the banshee crying for her. My father believed in the banshee, and in this he wasn't far wrong for the banshee is surely the Irish muse – a weird intangible thing.

'Owney remembered the funeral. There was a tradition in that country that wherever a funeral had gone a right-o'-way subsisted thereafter. Apparently the owners of this right-o'-way stopped the funeral with the words, conveyed with great power by Owney: 'Lave her down, damn your souls. Lave her down.'

Tommy Crawley left down his glass of stout and re-joined the debate. 'Do you mind the day when you were drawing home the oats when you nearly tore the leg off Josie?'

'Tore the leg off Josie?'

'Yes, I was on the rick and could do nothing. The mare pulled on, with the traces caught in Josie's leg. And the mother roared and cried: "Are you going to kill the girsha?"'

Curious how I should have forgotten and these people should have remembered. There was imagination here.

At that we left the pub and made our way in the general direction of my native townland of Mucker. Indeed, as a fact I might say that in that village only one Irish mile from my birthplace I was not quite at home. A man's range of geographical interest is very limited. A few fields, a few landmarks, are all that our imagination needs or can contain.

On our way towards Mucker I remembered the Beeog's Lane and I concentrated my memory on the wiry grass that grew on the banks of the road, remembering how I had often sat there. And I saw a hump of hill and on the top of that hump I was a young man of twenty and it was a day in early April and we were sowing oats. And I felt the sharp wind of April that was blowing hope and sadness. And I could be again myself as I was looking over the hedge at the long white road that stretched far away.

And beyond the railway level-crossing was the house I was born in. Once it was home, now it meant almost nothing. Deserted and the spirit departed. We drove past the gate over the top of which I had so often leaned happy, unconscious, warm and comfortable at the heart of the myth. The worry of my fields was around me then. And that is how we perceive the beauty that vitalizes us – when we are doing something else. We must be involved in love.

We passed many important landmarks of my childhood – the Gullet and the Big Bush and Woods' Gate and Cassidy's Whaal – what does 'Whaal' mean, by the way? It is a real Gaelic sound. And then we pulled up at John Lennon's house. Many's the day, as the fella said, meself and John wrought together and listened to his father telling stories of the great fist-fighters. Jim Corbett and Jack, the Nonpareil, Dempsey that he had seen in action in America.

The leading question was 'Do you remember …?'

I wanted to remember my way and I was helped to remember my way back into the warm myth of my rural days.

'Do you remember the time we were cutting the corn in the Well Field,' said John, 'and you grabbed all the Champion spuds out of the basket when the dinner came out? You'd eat nothing but the Champion, they were very floury.'

None of this may sound very exciting but in the atmosphere this conversation lived. It was the story of private lives, the only story that is of any importance, the story with which the poet is always concerned.

(*The Bell*, April 1954, pp. 29–35)

Part II

from 'City Commentary'

As I entered by the City Gate on my way to Áras an Uachtaráin on Saturday, I was the only pedestrian on the sun-flooded landscape. This was the special entrance for those who were to be received by the President. On either side of me the lawns showed acres of good wheat. The hazy air was vibrant with the wings of bees. Walking along that avenue, that is as healthy a mile as ever I footed, I could imagine myself rambling up to a palace of the Ming dynasty.

But it was better as it was. I was going to meet for the first time a literary man who had become President of his country. Nothing more romantic than that in Chinese literature.

After the presentation of the trophy, at which the President spoke lovely Irish, we broke up into groups on the lawn. There was a great run on autographs. The only autograph in which I would have been interested would have been that of the man who helped to secure me several cups of tea, Mr J.J. McElligott. Incidentally, to find how he spells his name I have just searched in my pocket for a ten-shilling note.

I next found myself in argument with Mr Boland, Minister for Justice, an intense man of sincerity. In this discussion I was supported by one of the most delightful persons, Mrs Dr Ryan, who is perhaps better known as Máirín Cregan. The ceremonial lowering of the flag to music that is somewhat plaintive was impressive. That was the end of the Garden Party.

*

I record with pleasure the news that my friend Mr J.P. O'Reilly has been appointed a temporary District Justice. Mr O'Reilly is well known in literary circles and I think I have on a few occasions alluded to him as the 'literary lawyer'. Some time ago I mentioned a law case in which he was engaged and in which the Book of Kells was invoked as an authority. He is an Oxford graduate and was a contributor to the *Irish Statesman*, the paper in which I first began. This always gives a man a special place in my affections.

Sunday was Croagh Patrick Sunday and I wish I could see the dawn from that sacred mountain on such a morning. Clew Bay and all the little islands. It happened that I could not sleep and I went out to the streets sometime before six. Dublin does not encourage early rising. On Sunday morning even the gas comes on late and the town itself is as sleepy as a town in Pickwickian imagination. I commented on this to a man who was selling papers and he rather agreed with Dublin's attitude. 'It's not that we're lazier than London,' he said, 'but we show a bit of discretion.'

A Toast to a Man of Letters
G.B.S., 87

O, G.B.S.
I a XX –
R2 –
2 U!
4 I B
OTT.

(*The Irish Press*, 27 July 1943)

The Tailor and Ansty

When I read *The Tailor and Ansty** my first wish was to meet this engaging couple. A short time ago my wish was granted.

In Eric Cross's book there was no mention of the fact that the Tailor lives in the middle of Goughane Barra, one of the most enchanting beauty places in all Ireland.I got the idea that he lived in some wild, remote place, out of the reach of everyone. It is wild, but not remote. There is a daily bus from Cork, whose terminus, Ballingeary, about forty miles from the city, is only three uphill miles from the Tailor's home.

Wheeling my bicycle up that mountain road, I kept my eyes wide open, watching out for the image of the Tailor or his house as they were formed in my imagination. It was a late August evening and the sun had gone down. Looking once to the left on the crown of the hill, I found myself looking in the open door of a house whose gable was to the road. Sitting at his hearth, and gazing out at me and the world, was an old humorous man, wearing a black hat. Could this be the Tailor?

In reading the book I conceived the Tailor to be a sharp-faced fellow and perhaps a little slim. The word to describe him is genial. His face is broad, and there is an aspect of softness and gentleness about him. There is also in him, I think, just the faintest suggestion of melancholy; but of this I am not sure. It could be that, considering the way

* Eric Cross's book *The Tailor and Antsy* (1942) features Tim Buckley, a tailor and irreverent *seanchaí*, and his wife and sparring partner Anastasia. The Tailor's frank account of Irish folk customs resulted in the banning of the book after publication.

that this grand Irishman has been treated, I may have read what was in my own mind. Those of us who have ever written autobiographies can realize the position of the writer if he has to live afterwards in the auto-biographical place.

But the Tailor is happy, and so is Ansty. Ansty was leaning on a broom near the seven-generations-old dresser when I entered to a flour-ish of welcomes that were blazing with sincerity. In the book I got the impression that Ansty was rather a spitfire and something of a nag. Of the pair, I think that Ansty is the more delightful character. She does not say much, but there is a pungency about her comment that tickles deeply.

Although the Tailor's copy of his own book fell a victim to that book-hatred which throughout the ages has not failed to pose as a Christian virtue, it lives in his memory. He is not worried because the book was burned. 'I have it all by rote,' he said, laughingly.

'Eight and sixpence,' said the practical Ansty. 'I had a mind to grab it out of the fire.'

When I had introduced myself and found that many of our friends were mutual, the conversation turned – as conversations usually do – to gossip about our friends and their work. Being a great story-teller himself, the Tailor is a critic of other story-tellers.

'What do you think of the stories of Frank O'Connor?' I asked.

The Tailor was striving to light his pipe at the time. '... Frank ... Frank's stories haven't enough wonders in them.' The Tailor doesn't believe in naturalism.

'And you know Pat O'Connor, too,' I said, referring to the bearded son of Andrew, the sculptor, who was so well known in Dublin a few years ago.

'He's a particular friend of mine,' he said with dancing eyes. 'Be the mockstick of war he came over here from France about ten years ago and ...'

'France ... France,' Ansty, who was sitting opposite her husband with her palms on her knees, kept saying in an undertone.

Very modernistic people are, often without knowing it, heavily in-fluenced by puritanism and these are liable to read into the Tailor's rich medieval view of life their own narrow views. Sometimes people like these gurgle with delight to think that the good old pagan survives in the Irish peasant. The Tailor and Ansty are great Christians.

Ansty got standing on a chair and unhooked a piece of bacon from the rafters. It was getting near dinnertime. The Tailor is an expert in slicing bacon against his chest. He also peeled and chopped some home-grown onions. He is inclined, when visitors of the open-mouthed variety call – and they call plenty – to give them what they came to get. But with me I am glad to say he kept to hard experience. 'Of all the blindisht men that ever was he was the blindisht,' he said about a certain man we knew. His pronunciation of blindest was the emphasis of sincerity. He leaned over to me and spoke with the wooden pipe deep in his mouth.

There is nothing the Tailor and his wife love so much as company. Their instinct for hospitality is akin to paternal and maternal instincts. Almost everyone who comes to Goughane Barra calls on the Tailor. I was afraid that when this crowd of sightseers came that they would shatter the spirit of the place. But no danger at all. He and his wife are equal to the world.

Finally, when leaving, I got both himself and his wife to give me their autographs. They have applications for these from all parts of the world. They signed in good handwriting that had only the hint of a tremor in it. Timothy Buckley, The Tailor. Ansty Buckley.

(*The Irish Times*, 18 September 1943, p. 2)

When You Go to Lough Derg

In the Basilica on Lough Derg the young priest was speaking to a congregation of about two hundred pilgrims. He was speaking about St Paul and what Paul had said about Christ. Listening to him and observing the congregation, the thing that struck me most forcibly was the freshness, the recency of Christianity. Lough Derg is no museum piece. The old stalk of Christianity ends in influences that have both colour and scent – and thorns too. The absence of thorns, I might remark, is one of the signs of senile decay in a bush. It might have been AD 100 or thereabouts and all the excitement of the New Truth was stirring the imaginations of men and women. Perhaps there were people present who had seen Christ. From the way they prayed a man could think so.

That was my first and strongest impression of Lough Derg when I went there for the opening of the pilgrimage last week. I arrived in the little town of Pettigo in the evening at three o'clock. I had only time to take a bare look at the village that is half in Northern and half in Southern Ireland. The village has no bookshop that I could find, though going on pilgrimage with a book might lessen the tedium of the place – and reading is not prohibited by the rules. The only book on sale in Pettigo was a new version of the prophecies of St Columcille, but I didn't come across that piece of fiction until the return journey. The bus took us up the hill that got barer and bleaker as we climbed. On one side I caught a glimpse of a pretty stream that must have some trout in it as there's an anglers' hotel in Pettigo.

At the end of about a four miles climb we came to the ledge over the lake. At the pier the boatmen were getting ready the boats. The sun was shining on the scene as it always seems to do when I go on pilgrimage. Down below us in the hollow of waters is the holy island. It looked so completely unnatural. Around stood the bleak depressing hills like walls shutting out the green sensual world. The Basilica in the sunlight looked like some fairy castle that had been transported there. The white-washed cottages might have awakened my poetic imagination. But the place is too real, too valid, to encourage the romantic attitude.

As soon as we arrived on the island we had to take off our boots and our pride and commence the Stations. And of course we were fasting from the night before. A most interesting character whom I met on the bus took a deep interest in my spiritual welfare. He explained the Stations to me as well as giving me a leaflet. This man who made the pilgrimage twenty-seven times in twenty years was a mirror reflecting a Christian optimism and fortitude that is unusual in the modern world.

'If I started telling you of my good luck I wouldn't be done talking till tomorrow morning.' And he went on to tell me how he had been sick, on the point of death, and had recovered. A few years later he split his skull 'from there to there'. He pointed to his ears. 'And I'm as fit today as any man here.' Those were only a few of the disasters that had befallen him and the fact that he recovered was due to the mercy of God. The majority of the pilgrims appeared to be of the business class. The reason may be because farmers are busy at this time. I did meet one large farmer, the father of ten children, from whom and his wife and farm he goes every year to Lough Derg, full of confidence that on his return everything will have prospered. I met a well-known ballet-dancer, on the night of the vigil during one of the intervals. I saw her on the concrete pavement at the back of the church having a Scotch dance explained to her by a girl in a tartan skirt.

Although, on paper, St Patrick's Purgatory is not such a terrible punishment, in actuality it almost reaches the limits of human endurance. Most people find the vigil the worst part. For me the worst was the austerity, the prostration of both mind and body that is seldom relieved by any flamboyant life. The coat of heavy protective piety is hard to pierce down to the bare heart.

On the second day we had no Stations to make and so were free to lounge about on the rocky height in the middle of the island. I sat there a while and listened to the conversations. 'Is it down be the lighthouse in Fanad that you live?' That was an old woman speaking to an ascetic-looking young man who had cycled eighty miles ... 'A bloater's kipper ... What was the name of the young fair-haired priest that said Mass this morning? ... Were you "sitting" last night? ... Why can't you see something good in it? If one soul is made more virtuous, more pure, don't you think that is good?'

It is to be regretted that sinners don't come to Lough Derg any more. As one of the priests on the island said to me, when a modern man sins now he doesn't believe in sin. He rejects the fundamental fact of sin. The ethic has been torn up by the roots. And yet even then there is something in men which compels them to dredge the harbours of the soul in self-denial. Lough Derg is above everything else a challenge to modern paganism. If a man brings his pride with him there's sure to be a fierce battle. The only thing that disturbed me on Lough Derg was the absence of obvious mental or spiritual struggle. I like dramatic conflict, the inner convulsions that erupt the burning lava of the soul through the crust of piety. That is the way of the Catholic Church which has nothing whatever to do with Victorian smugness.

'Why are you here?' I asked an old man.

'I'm practising for the next world,' was his answer.

I remember Lough Derg with pleasure. I remember the old white-washed cottages with their open hearths and cranes and crooks and a healthy smell of lime. The Basilica has the virtue of usefulness and simplicity. The Stations of the Cross in stained glass are pretty in the way of minor effeminate art, but are too small.

I remember the sunlight on the buildings and the sound of the bell that called us to prayer. I remember the deep seriousness of every official from the Prior down to the humblest maid-servant – their anxiety for the pilgrimage and the pilgrims. And there is one other thing I should like to mention. It is often said that girls go to Lough Derg to pray for husbands and men for wives; if this is true it is a Christian desire. Is there anything more holy than the deep longings of the human heart? Ultimately it means the desire for Reality – for the Holy Grail of God's Truth.

(*The Standard*, 12 June 1942, p. 3)

Down the Shannon to
Clonmacnoise – Pilgrim at the Oar

Everybody we met on Sunday last at Clonmacnoise said that by boat was the proper way to approach this noted place. It was the way St Ciarán and his monks went fourteen centuries ago. For all that, hardly more than a few did; they came by car, trap and bicycle, while the Shannon, noble, most smooth-running steed, was scarcely stirred by an oar.

And it struck me that this was typical of the attitude of our age. Most of us want the quintessence of things, not seeming to realize that the labour and pain with which all happiness is surrounded is often the best part of the joy – afterwards. That is why the remembered joys of childhood are so sweet.

But let me not moralize too much, forgetting that myself and my companion, Patrick O'Connell, of Listowel, are rowing the eleven long miles down the Shannon from Athlone. My companion turned out to be a well-known oarsman. I provided the enthusiasm. The sun is shining on the calm waters. Around the bend of the river are hazy blue distances over Hy-Brasil.

Six swans take off with a great splutter and flutter. A cormorant is perched on top of one of the navigation sign-posts. We see donkeys by the edge of the river. There is a little field of oats in hand-ricks. Poor enough country this in south Westmeath; it is what is called in unpoetical language a Congested District. Cottages with yellow roofs of newly threshed oaten straw.

As we slowly glide down the broad river we watch before us and behind us, wondering if we will see other pilgrims coming in boats. But no sign of any. With the exception of the navigation signs, there is nothing that would appear strange to St Ciarán here today – except perhaps the fewness of travellers on the great waterway.

As we go down we have now Roscommon on our right and Offaly on our left. What do we know of Clonmacnoise? We try to remember and Rolleston's famous translation is nearly all we have to fall back on.

> *In a quiet watered land, a land of roses*
> *Stands Saint Ciarán's city fair,*
> *And the warriors of Erin in their famous generations*
> *Slumber there.*
>
> *There beneath the dewy hillside sleep the noblest*
> *Of the clann of Conn ...*

We were on the lookout for hills. We owe a lot to those old poets, so truthfully have they been the recorders of history. There were hills in the distance. And then once, as we rounded a bend, we saw the two towers of the great monastery standing out from the side of a hill.

As we swept round a wide meadow the outline of the old buildings became clearer. We could see 'Ciarán's plain of crosses' and for a moment I was amazed at their number till I began to see that this was the congregation – among the crosses all right – attending High Mass.

The chant of the choir came down to us in our boat and echoed somewhere among the hills. It was beautiful to hear and I tried to dream into the bare bones of this reality the warm breath of a transcendent emotion! To sit like a child and let the wonder that is the history book of old graveyards, old hallowed shrines, do what it would with me.

We pulled our boat on to the land and hurried up the slope from the river, across the wall into the graveyard where High Mass was being celebrated. Listening there I realized that I might well be standing over the bones of Roderick O'Connor or one of Conn the Hundred Fights' sons; or of any of those whose very names bring the past alive [...]

A group of men were standing by Clonmacnoise's famous Celtic cross trying to span it with their arms. I was told that anyone who can clasp his hands around it gets a gift. If that be the case, I have a gift, though I do not know what it is.

The great enthusiast for Clonmacnoise today is Mr Patrick Molloy, the local schoolteacher. He it is who takes the leading part in the Long Station – as it is called. The Long Station is, in some ways, similar to the holy exercises practised at Lough Derg. We had not time to complete this, for it takes the best part of two hours and a half.

About half a mile down the narrow road towards Shannonbridge is St Ciarán's Well. It is an ordinary little spring, well shaded by a couple of stunted hawthorn bushes. Everyone there – including myself and my companion – took a sip of the water from a glass jam-jar that was handed round. Kneeling on that soft meadow, something of the breath of imagination started within me.

I kissed the ancient stone which represents St Ciarán's head – which is worn smooth by the lips of pious people – and kissing it, I, too, felt that I had not come here in vain. The repose that arises in the heart of Christian humility charmed my worries away.

At least four thousand people did this Station. There was a procession half a mile long which filled the whole width of the narrow road.

On the whole, Clonmacnoise today is a poor place. But, standing among those old dignified ruins, one could realize that, as some writer has said: 'Clonmacnoise was once a queen.' Here is Dervorgilla's chapel. Talk about sermons in stones! Dervorgilla the romantic, the impulsive, who ran away with one of my ancestors and afterwards repented of her folly!

Curious how little is really known about Clonmacnoise in the common traditions of the people! Except for Rolleston's poem, this university of Ireland's golden age appeared but a name to most people I met.

We watched it from our boat as we departed. We knew, too, that St Ciarán had not forgotten us, for as we pulled upstream, the wind blew behind us, blew strong, and to us it was the Saint who had set it blowing.

(*The Standard*, 14 September 1945, p. 1)

from 'Round the Cinemas'

On my first appearance as a film critic I should, perhaps, make a generalized statement on what my attitude is likely to be. A critic should have an attitude, a bias, for as some writer has said, 'scales which are evenly held may contain nothing'.

There is no writer more liable to deceive – and perhaps none more biased – than the one who gives the impression of being impartial.

Letting the facts speak for themselves is an immoral principle when we all know that facts and figures can be selected to prove anything.

I am fully aware of how embarrassing self-revelation can be. In my head there is the woefullest anthology of bad poetry, and for years I have been terrified lest this mangy cat of my youth's bad taste might escape from the bag. So when I announce that my taste in films runs to comic stuff – Pop Eye, Laurel and Hardy, Abbot and Costello, the Marx Brothers, etc., the prospect is terrible to contemplate.

I used to like gangster pictures, but since nowadays the gangsters are always enemies of democracy they have become a bit of a bore.

I cannot abide 'musicals' or films in which large numbers of airplanes continuously roar, and above all I am allergic to 'hospital' pictures in which crowds of young handsome doctors and nurses with masks on are rushing through long corridors to the operating theatre.

The handsome young surgeon is in love with the beautiful nurse, but, in spite of this defect in his reason, he will save the life of the rival on the table.

Finally I remember with real pleasure, and could return again to see them, only three films: *Pygmalion*, *The Petrified Forest* and *The Cheat*. Perhaps it is significant that two of these were originally plays, and in them appears the incomparable Leslie Howard, whose loss must forever be lamented.

Thus to the Irish cinema world, which has a higher percentage-to-the-population of filmgoers and no film factory – or studio of its own – I make my bow.

Some film critics handle this industry as a very precious 'Art Medium' but from what I have seen this week the medium is empty of any kind of intelligence [...]

(*The Standard*, 22 February 1946, p. 3)

The Story of an Editor
who was Corrupted by Love

The first thing we must emphasize is that we* are not closing down primarily for lack of money or because our circulation was too small. Our circulation was remarkably large and was rising; last week we sold out. As for money we did, it is true, put a notice in the paper last week saying that we would carry on if we got a thousand pounds. We intended that thousand pounds to be a token of the intensity and enthusiasm of our readers; if among them there wasn't one or a group who would be willing to support us to that extent then we would take it that we had no real public.

Money was important but it definitely was not our main problem. Our main problem was two-headed. First, there is the absence of writers and, secondly, the absence of an audience. Like the chicken and the egg, it is hard to say which of these comes first. Perhaps the audience is the more important. An audience makes a writer as much as a writer makes an audience. As Keats, or it may have been Shelley, pointed out, a creative writer is like a musical instrument slung from a tree branch upon which the winds play, and the winds are the audience. It is the need of the audience which produces the voice.

Oddly enough, although there is no ultimate audience there is just

*Kavanagh's Weekly.

enough coquetry to draw out writers who are then left with a hunger that cannot be satisfied within that society. This attitude runs throughout all parts of Irish society, the cowardice which withdraws from sudden and dramatic decisions, a particularly Irish form of immorality.

This has been true of Ireland since the beginning of history and the result is that Ireland had no literature till it turned to the English language and found an audience outside the country. There is a constant complaint that such writers as Frank O'Connor sell their country, but the gutter journalists who make these complaints don't see that we have only ourselves to blame.

Why there is no audience in Ireland for serious thinking is an interesting question. Once again it springs from the cowardice which will not go to the logical dramatic conclusion of its original tease.

It might be said that history is to blame. Ireland has been for nearly a thousand years in a state of disorder. At the same time there were periods, when the native Irish Chiefs were in sole control, when the country was at least as placid (or as excited) as Elizabethan England. Yet that society produced nothing that wasn't trivial. The so-called Gaelic poets weren't worthy of the name; they were nothing but drunken, clowning entertainers, and this was because there was no audience which would understand or encourage the serious and dignified and ultimately gay.

Such Gaelic literature as there is has no gaiety or love of life in it, and that is the purpose of the poet – to give people an enthusiasm for life, to draw their attention to the wonder of the fields, of the weeds.

We might explain our failure away by attributing it to the smallness of the country, the thinness of the population. Again, this will hardly work as an excuse. Very deep down in our historical roots there is some sort of cynical disbelief in life. Nothing matters but the momentary sensation, whether that sensation be wine, women or song. So it is that we are one of the most drunken nations on the earth. The Americans and the Swedes drink a lot, too, and these countries have practically no literature, nor today any spiritual basis for literature.

We would go so far as to say that not only has Irish society never believed in the value of literature but it has never believed in Christianity. There is no dramatic abandon in Irish society, no wild enthusiasm for any special idea as in England. We, therefore, have neither saints nor poets. The Island of Saints and Scholars! It is a remarkable thing how in the face of the facts Ireland should have established to its own satisfaction its poetic and saintly nature while at the same time attributing to the English, who have produced what is probably the greatest literature of mankind, the qualities of stolidity, unimaginativeness, lack of poetic life.

This is a very curious affair and it may have something to do with 'compensations' of a Freudian kind.

At all events there is no audience and no desire on the part of that section of the public with the most influence to create such an audience.

As we said in another publication, the keynote to Irish thinking is summed up in the phrase 'And where will that get him?' when someone refers to the achievements of a great poet or thinker.

Undoubtedly it will get him nowhere if you don't believe in the God of Life, the God of the grass, of the sun.

What kind of a world would it be if there was no hope, if we all felt and said with the average Gael: 'Where will that get him?'

There would be no Shakespeare, no Homer, nor a Saint Thomas Aquinas. There would only be, as here, men swilling themselves into forgetfulness.

In our time the Welfare State is doing all it can to produce some sort of synthetic substance which will take the place of a divine purpose in the lives of people. Organized holiday camps, organized drama groups, schools of acting! Bring in the masses of the people, give them an interest! What a futile effort this is! It is the way the world is going, trying to find a remedy for the logical despair that must follow on materialism.

There is a great deal of talk about the materialism of the Soviet. It may well be as materialist as they say, but it is so logical in its materialism and so passionate about it that it must eventually come out the other side and give rise to a great spiritual flowering. The Western democracies, particularly America – and Ireland which draws some of its poisons from America – are quite as materialistic as the communists but cannot see that they are.

There is nothing evil in communism that isn't rampant throughout Ireland today. Despair is on its way and although Despair may seem an immaterial thing and not nearly as important as a Pact made of silly words between Highmania and Lowmania, it is the one monster to be feared. Despair is the monster which fills the pubs, which eventually drives people into war. Anything to forget the futility of life. In Ireland we still have a strong Catholic religion, at least on the surface, but how deeply that religion influences men's minds is another question. Out of our experience we cannot say that we found it influenced men on any fundamental issue. When we listened to men being themselves it was not religion that spoke but money and materialism in general.

We would hate to live in a solemn world where people took Art seriously. There is despair in the heart of that enthusiasm too; it is only another attempt to get out of the way of the monster.

One must beware of being too logical about anything.

If we go on in a logical way we come to cage bars. But Hope soars gaily above these logic bars. There is wonderful freedom for the spirit in the world but we must beware of demanding the ultimate answer.

'Why?' is God.

We sensed this terrible need and we felt that we had in our small way a remedy for it. We believed and we still believe that something is still possible in this country.

For instance, the national radio station is financially independent and is not forced to be subservient to the opinions of illiterate journalists; it doesn't have to compete with Radio Luxembourg. Yet it never puts out an idea nor to our knowledge has ever given a forum for the discussion of any idea of the slightest seriousness. (Seriousness in our language is another name for gaiety.) It has tossed back at the people of the rural parts a lot of 'kitchen comedy' stuff that never was true, not to say funny.

It puts on every so often a number of names of well-known Dublin citizens in what it calls a 'free debate' and the people of the rural parts have no means – or will have no means now that we are gone – of knowing that these well-known people are silly, superficial fools whom no one outside the conspiracy of mediocrity would dream of taking seriously.

Then it has its 'Art' section.

Hours of dull music, because music is free from ideas, are inflicted on the listeners.

Music is also Art.

Then there are the Poetry Programmes. It may well be that throughout the country there would be many people willing to believe that poetry was not the greatest bore in the world, that it was not a punishment. But to kill any such belief Radio Éireann has a 'Verse Speaking' choir which pumps out the most atrocious and boring drivel.

Never an idea from one end of the year to the other.

All this Art stuff is part of the world of commerce. It is phoney and meant to deceive the public; it is the fiddler playing while his companion picks your pocket. The only thing that matters is people – thinking, dreaming, hoping, loving. Life is the great good. But these people being mediocrities and cowards don't want life or ideas; they want to establish the lie that the futile world they inhabit is the best of all possible worlds.

We are sorry to have to record that Éamon de Valera has been the great patron saint of this mediocracy. Though nobody more so than de Valera has preached the Spirit of Ireland, few men who have ever become leaders of this nation have been less in touch with whatever is vital in that spirit. And that takes some doing, for the leaders whom Ireland has put on pedestals have in general been an unworthy lot – O'Connell, Parnell, de Valera – empty, vainglorious, featherers of their own little emotional nests. England has been much luckier, but then England has hardly ever put a leader on a pedestal. Churchill, the hero of the Hitler war, was thrown out of office at the conclusion of that war. There is an adult tradition in England, and it extends to literature in a big way – even in these days of the Welfare State. They have a traditional sense of values.

The questions we never ask ourselves in Ireland are: Do we believe in anything? do we care for anything? If the answer is 'Yes' we must then ask why therefore is a man who is eager to discuss and reflect upon serious subjects considered bad news and box-office poison. One doesn't expect the masses of the people to be philosophers but one expects to find a minority who think, whose influence is felt throughout all society.

Subsidiary to the question of the absence of an audience is the absence of any writers of real sincerity. Among the older school you have clever fellows, but when you read their work you realize how thin their

experience is. Writers like that fit in among the second-rate English literary journalists who cling as bitterly to their cliché, to their set literary
conventions, as do the true-bred Gaels to the worship of another kind
of mediocrity. In fact the literary journalist of this kind is even more bitter in his possession of such beliefs (as that Elizabeth Bowen is a genius)
than the Gaelic worshipper of the bucklep and trivia.

It is usually taken for granted that there was a great literary renaissance in Ireland within the past fifty years. How little of all that writing was of the slightest merit! Yet poor as most of it was, it was an
attempt at imaginative activity along the right lines. Without a doubt
it was a movement of mediocrities and has arrived at its logical conclusion, but while Yeats was at the head of it the mediocracy squirmed.

Yeats as a poet conformed to a convention and in a great deal of his
verse was insincere, but as a man and a thinker he had a wonderful
sense of morality. He was not a Christian yet he can be included among
those who would agree with Chesterton that 'To the pagan the small
things are as sweet as the small brooks running out of the mountain but
the broad things are as bitter as the sea.'

Being a cunning apologist Chesterton attributed solely to Christians this passionate desire for the broad bitter sea of reality.

According to Chesterton's definition – and we agree with him –
there are few Christians in Ireland.

Now and again a real Voice of the People is heard. Sean O'Casey, for
all the Protestant kink in him, is a voice of the people. O'Casey's instinct
for life sent him to England at the earliest opportunity. Here he would
have been trampled in the Dublin gutter; in England he was drawn out
though he is by no means a remarkable thinker or very creative.

It can be a pity that a writer has to depend on a strange audience.
Although an English audience is awake and aware and alive to the
nuances of the imaginative world, it is defective in some ways. Writing
for an English audience a man has to abandon those intimate details
which mean everything to his integrity, for with the best will in the
world only a few rare spirits will get these delicate touches. Joyce was
wiser when he went to Paris. He found as an audience that unsettled,
generous, Paris-American society which is ready to appreciate anything
– even Ireland. In England an Irish writer to some extent is drawn into

giving the English what they have been told is the real authentic Irish thing. At the moment, due partly to the Hitler war, the English audience has abandoned its comic view of the Irish writer's angle, and about the only place now where phoney Ould Oireland is tolerated is in Ireland itself. See the film of *The Quiet Man,* which has been gobbled up by an enthusiastic Dublin audience. You wouldn't get away with that trash in London. However, there is still a strong touch of the old tradition and it is not good for the sincere portrayer of life.

As will be observed, the writer of this still believes in the people; he knows that there is no virtue in race; he believes that there should be a virtue in religion and that men who purport to hold a transcendent belief in the Communion of Saints, the Resurrection of the Dead, etc., should be wild with a spirit of imaginative adventure and love of life. There is something of that in the country but it is either blotted out by the tradition of society or grows out of its faith and hope into what makes our political and business leaders. Judged in that light it cannot be too deeply founded.

Although there is no obvious audience in this country, writers of merit could be encouraged into existence if there was any sort of interest in imaginative things among those who manage to climb into authority.

For instance a Cultural Relations Committee was founded by the Government. This kind of semi-political body would not be satisfied with the simple sort of merit that would be the offering of such genuine writers as we might have. It has a large Government grant of over £10,000 a year and it has to be pretentious. The result is worse than useless, it is vile. With one thousand of those pounds per year all the creative writers that Ireland would ever be likely to produce at a given time would be sumptuously provided for. As with the £1,000 which we sought from a reader, that £1,000, too, would be a token of the attitude towards the sincere writer.

Now and again we have discerned some faint flickering of the light of genius but there is nobody to encourage it into full life, as we would have done had we been able to continue.

Did this Cultural Relations Committee give us any support? They were one of our nastiest opponents. Their object is the encouragement of the non-thinking, of the low mediocre, of all those things which make their loutish world seem better than it is. Then there is the Arts Council, worse if such were possible than the Cultural Relations Committee.

The members of these two bodies wear the cultural smile which withers all life within range of its venom. The members of these two bodies sat in pubs and roared with hysterical laughter as they read our weekly paper. As we shovelled shovel after shovel out of the Augean Stable that they inhabited, their anger and hysteria increased. They cried that we were destroying all they had so patiently excreted. If in the future this piece of writing here is read it will be a guide to whatever man of talent happens to come across it.

It might almost appear that in our condemnation of the Cultural Relations Committee, the Arts Council and allied bodies, we are being angry because they didn't support us. We couldn't have accepted support from such vile bodies. Once again, as with that £1,000 which we didn't receive, the desire would prove the validity of the enthusiasm. If they wanted to give it we wouldn't need to receive it.

So far from Ireland being too poor to support sincere writers, there is far too much money available for 'culture'. There is an immense amount of money available for the use of the drunken clowns of Commerce, for those who are willing to put on an act to salve the conscience of low types. With the money available from taxpayers' pockets for bad art, dull music and dilettante film-makers, all the writers which the country would produce would, if they got a share of it, be utterly demoralized. No, it must be clearly pointed out that Ireland is not too poor to support writers of merit. Let us not labour the point too much.

It is because we know that we could have eventually, after our hearts were broken, swept these enemies of promise out of existence that we are sorry we shall be heard no more from this platform in this country.

As part of the encouragement of talent, small publishers could be helped – which would, of course, include ourselves.

There is no reason why we should have to defer to London. Standards were made here in the eighteenth century and to some extent in the early part of the present century. The Cultural Relations Committee brought out a number of pamphlets, all of which were pernicious gestures to Commerce. Now to come down to more personal matters:

In producing this paper we produced a curious effect on our readers.

They were split in two. We had friends of a vague kind and enemies of a fairly precise kind. What makes people hate a sincere statement is a question that the Editor of this paper cannot answer; it has something to do with morality, with that part of morality which puts, as it were, willy-nilly its author on a pedestal. Gods do not put themselves on pedestals; on the contrary, they dislike pedestals. The public puts them on pedestals that it may have the pleasure of knocking them down.

Our readers were many and at a pinch we might call them friends. But as a serious reading public they were not worth considering. Week after week they bought our publication, enjoyed it, but in no way co-operated, never wrote in or showed their interest. Their great defect was their inability to discriminate.

The Editor would like to believe that they read the paper for the ideas; he knows that many did, but hardly enough.

He still believes firmly that beneath all the public noise there is in this country a warm, kindly and tremendously generous instinct which may some day be implemented. The Editor refuses to disbelieve that he has friends who are nearer to being disciples than friends and of which many are women. It would be wrong not to record this belief here, and he does so in defiance of the fact that the response to the paper's appeal for support was anything but generous.

One reader wrote in to wonder why we ever started the paper if we couldn't make it pay; this shallow and immoral view came from a man who has a big reputation among pub-crawlers as a man of integrity and intelligence. It is ridiculous to ask a paper of ideas to pay its way. What might pay its way or would be readily supported is the 'literary' magazine which an undiscriminating public recognizes as a literary magazine. In other words, a magazine that conforms to a well-established pattern; this kind of publication will get the support of the Sweep and the various business monopolies.

The idea that every activity of mankind can be measured in terms of money is a rather insane one. In fact, with the arrival of the Machine Age and the Atom Age the old relation of money to labour is breaking down. A new system for distributing the goods of this world is needed, and if that system could be established without bringing with it the despair of materialism a really wonderful world would be created. We could have imaginative ideas, all the gay things of the world freed from the tyranny of money.

But this man who wrote in represents something in Ireland. He is intelligent, but he – though this may be a reaction to personal failure – is committed to the Dublin notion of a respectable honest worker. What is a respectable honest worker who doesn't try to 'bum' for his living?

He is often a man in one of the better-paid professions, of little talent and particularly with no talent for filling that part of time which is called 'leisure'. Once you get 'leisure' in the world you are in touch with society's sickness; there is no leisure time in a healthy society or individual. If something appears to be at rest it is in decay.

The Irish or at least the Dublin idea of spending leisure time and of becoming a man who pulls his weight in society is to sit in pubs for three or four hours each evening. Then off to an expensive restaurant for a meal. That is being a non-bum, that is being a healthy member of commercial society.

Those were our friends. We had enemies, too.

The Editor learned a very useful lesson from his experiences with this weekly paper.

For more than ten years he had suffered from the delusion that he had in Dublin a large body of friends of a special kind. These friends were friends of his genius. They felt that he deserved to be supported.

They were all 'cultural'; they were all engaged in various liberal works – good Samaritans, defenders of liberty, helpers of the poor, some successful commercial writers. The keynote to all their characters was kindliness. These gave the Editor to understand that they were working for his canonization as eagerly as the supporters of the cause of Matt Talbot are working, and that they were only waiting the opportunity to do something to advance the ideas in which he believed. True it is, he caught whiffs of a humanitarian stench on many occasions; he got an inkling that these people loved the poor and defeated so that they might steep their stinking hearts in the precious ointment of poverty. They wanted something over which they could exercise power. It was for this reason that these people were pleased to do all in their ability for the Editor so long as he would guarantee always to remain poor and ineffectual, never to enter into competition with the world on any serious level. How right Oscar Wilde was when he remarked that anybody can sympathize with failure, but that only a great saint can sympathize with success.

They kept telling him to stick to ballads, to what he knew of country life, but not to start talking about such abstruse matters as money and politics.

Then the Editor, who for so long provided these people with a potential subject for the exercise of filthy power, began to take a hand in the game, and the venom that was openly exuded by his cultural friends would be impossible to describe. It is no mere melodramatic persecution – maniacal delusion; it is very real, so real that as that same Editor sits at his typewriter on this hot summer's day in 1952 he is finding it hard not to splutter with ironic laughter over his machine. He will always remember with gratitude the ultimate goodness of these friends of his for at last fully exposing their hands. He called their bluff and is a wiser man today than he was three months ago. The only power that is worth while is knowledge, knowledge of oneself and of other people in relation to that self.

Individuals never seem of much importance in the hurry of contemporary events, but it is by individuals that history is made, and the individual who has been editing this paper has moments when he is not overwhelmed by the roar of the present day, and he knows that what has happened to him will be of very great importance in time to come.

This writer has no paranoiac notions of messianic importance; he is more amused than anything else that he should have been in a small way the instrument that could record the people's need for a purpose and a passion.

> Yet having said all this he feels
> That he should go down on his knees and pray
> For forgiveness for his pride, for having
> Dared to view his soul from the outside.
> Lie at the heart of the emotion, time
> Has its own work to do. We must not anticipate
> Or awaken for a moment. God cannot catch us
> Unless we stay in the unconscious room
> Of our hearts. We must be nothing,

Nothing that God may make us something.
We must not touch the immortal material
We must not daydream tomorrow's judgment –
God must be allowed to surprise us.
We have sinned, sinned like Lucifer
By this anticipation. Let us lie down again
Deep in anonymous humility and God
May find us worthy material for His hand.

(*Kavanagh's Weekly*, 5 July 1952, pp. 1–4; this essay constituted the entirety of the last issue of the paper.)

The Old Road

Here's to the dust of the old-fashioned road,
Here's to the old Mud-Bound Macadam
For the gravel that lifted, the marks that would hold
This tribute! we hope it will glad 'im.

Out on a quiet road beyond Finglas we came upon a group of men playing skittles. Most people know the game – five short wooden pegs standing within a circle to be knocked out of it with short sticks.

'It's your peg,' said one of the men; and it suddenly dawned on us that the word 'peg' to describe a throw or dart was a bit unusual. Can it be that the word is 'peck', which means to dart or throw?

At any rate there they were, teenage boys and sixtyaged men having their evening game. And watching them our minds went back to country days and the various road games that were popular before the full arrival of the motor age. Even the most remote by-roads have cars on them now.

There was a game called peggy or piggy, which was a form of cricket. The peggy itself was a short stick about three inches long and an inch in diameter with pointed ends. When you tapped the end of the point with your striking stick it hopped off the road, and then you, if you could, hit it in mid-air and sent it as far as you could. You had three strikes – except in certain circumstances.

A circle about a foot in diameter was traced in the dust of the road

(God be with the dusty roads) and you first pitched the peggy towards the circle. If you succeeded in putting the peggy clearly within the circle your opponent got no innings.

Our name for putting the peggy in the circle was, of all things, 'fat'.

If, on the other hand, your peggy was half in and half out of the circle, your opponent got either one or two blows at it according to whether more of the peggy was in or out.

Having sent the peggy as far as you could down the road, you judged how many spangs – strides – it would take your opponent to reach it in and you gave him a few less.

Then he came lepping along the road with his longest strides while you counted. Seventy you gave him and he did it in sixty-nine, and so instead of you getting the score your opponent got it.

Another road game that had quite a vogue in our schooldays was called 'duck'.

A large flagstone – the table – was placed on the middle of the road and we all looked for suitable 'ducks'. The duck was a nice round mollocker of a stone. 'Pitch till we see who's going on table.' We all pitched our ducks, and the man farthest from the table was 'duck on table'.

The object of this game was to fling your duck at the duck on the table, at the same time crying 'duck', and then to recover it and get back to the butt without being tigged by the man on the table.

Sometimes the whole crowd of players would be on the wrong side of the table. But if one of their number succeeded in getting back to base and could then knock the duck off the table, all his companions would be able to get back: for the man 'on table' was powerless when his duck was off the table.

Duck-down, as we sometimes called this game, was inclined to be dangerous on the shins and ankles. Like peggy, it had an element of cricket in it.

It is interesting to note that these road games were as popular in Dublin as in the country: in fact, they were widespread.

The game of rolling the iron ball was once fairly widespread, too, but now has survived only in Cork and a few other places.

There was – and no doubt still is – the game of quoits, which was sometimes played with pennies, but more usually with large washers.

The good thing about these games – and about all games – is that they kept us looking outward. Introspection is a constant danger.

(*The Irish Press*, 24 September 1954, p. 10)

Bachelorhood Is Tragedy

Nobody has observed that all the writers on *The Vanishing Irish* have unwittingly or subconsciously made a fierce attack on marriage.* They have in effect said that married life is a damnable ordeal, that they, the married ones, are enduring it with their teeth clenched in agony while thousands of cowardly, mean, unmanly men are having the time of their lives living without wives or children.

Now the curious, or maybe not curious, fact is that very often it is those with the greatest potential and capacity for married happiness who fail to achieve it at an early age or maybe at all. One can see the reason for this: to them marriage is such a thing of joy that this kind of idealistic man does not want to fritter away the cash of that potential except at the Moment of Truth.

Nothing to man is so dear as a good woman. So wrote Langland in *Piers Plowman*: six centuries ago. Seeing a good woman and beautiful makes me believe in the absolute abandon with which God loves men. To have such a creature for a wife is a thing of ecstatic holiness as well as of overflowing sensual pleasure.

The least sensitive, least imaginative, the uneducated and unaware go into marriage as they would go to a football game. Slum dwellers and tinkers are all married before twenty. Similarly in countries which

* *The Vanishing Irish*, edited by John Anthony O'Brien (London, 1954): a collection of essays on social conditions, marriage and population in Ireland.

have divorce, which is contempt for marriage, people get married freely and early. They can get out of it. It is just a cheap thing, a thing of democracy and the Welfare State. Young people have to go before a bench of ignorant magistrates to get permission in England. It is something cheap for cheap people. As most people are cheap it works out.

The foregoing part of this article was written last. What follows was written in a hurry and what I have above written is I hope a lucid statement of the scattered views hereunder.

Now read on:

I have been asked to comment on, or reply to, Mrs Sheridan's article in last month's issue on behalf of Irish bachelors.* God forbid.

Mrs Sheridan's article about the selfish Irish male is a species of writing which can be readily recognized as the journalist's lie. I have been a collector of this kind of lie for some years. This kind of lie deceives nobody, is meant to be entertaining, and, of course, is not to be taken seriously. The bachelors with the L.P. records, interest in theatre and ballet, etc., do not belong to Ireland but to Fairyland (modern meaning). Where Mrs Sheridan came across such a large bunch of queerdom I do not know, for I thought Ireland too poor to support many. However –

Here to restate some truths that are already known.

Lifelong bachelorhood is a tragedy for any normal man as it is for any normal woman. Every normal man desires a wife and children. I always feel sad for half men like Bernard Shaw with their self-deceiving lies. Actually to be a bit personal the poet is the most domesticated of animals. Those dilettantes who live on the fringe of their futile culture have it all wrong. Poor things. There is something wrong with the woman who talks, as the newspaper lie puts it, of a 'career' in preference to marriage. It is not less so with the normal man. I know it sounds awful of me to be repeating these commonplaces. But what with that silly book *The Vanishing Irish* and other things it appears necessary.

Why some men and women fail to achieve the highest human destiny is a complex subject not to be answered glibly. It is seldom a con-

---

* Monica Sheridan's article 'Our Tame Ganders' presented Irish bachelors as stay-at-home types as opposed to 'wild geese'. The typical Irish bachelor was depicted as a self-indulgent, fortyish male with a taste for the arts. He lives with his mother, 'a boy forever'.

scious plan or defect of courage as the writers of *The Vanishing Irish* suggest; it is mainly due to the vicissitudes of living.

One cause is being cursed with an ideal. A man who knows what he wants never gets it. Hard pleased and easy fitted was how I used to hear such men described.

Marriage to continue banality is a compromise –

> *... no two ever wed*
> *But that one had a sorrow that never was shed.*

Mrs Sheridan runs on lines similar to the *Vanishing Irish* crowd. She accepts the journalistic myth that in the realms of ethics there is such a thing as an Irish person. In the realms of human beings seeking salvation here on earth passports do not matter. It's good boring fun.

'What do you think of American women?' I was asked many times on my return. The right decent person will take up the idiotic question and play the game. After all, the person asking such a question is a brainless creature parroting the convention. I sometimes got fed up and simply and brutally answered that American women were very like women.

Marriage is a deal with society. The old Irish phrase was that a married man 'joined the world'.

Having got this far I found myself at a loss so I took another look at Mrs Sheridan's piece. I found that she was almost managing to be offensive. She accepts all the shibboleths of the illiterate – *My Fair Lady* publicity-handout stuff.

And 'A man of forty-five drooling over his first born.'

Think of Goethe. At the age of eighty, seeing a beautiful girl walking along the street, he exclaimed: 'My God! if I was only ten years younger.' And Picasso who at seventy has a young family.

No, all that categorizing of people into groups is part of the false values which more than anything else are a cause for whatever marriage-rate troubles there may be. It is the anti-aristocratic flattery of the lower orders. Any idiot can boast of being young at some time.

The papers are full of it in England these days, that is the newspapers which cater for the mass of forty-five million serfs who have the vote, the pools and just enough literacy to read the racing page of the *Daily Express*.

What matters in marriage are the children. There is nothing wrong with the Irish except that class of chap and girlie whose only talent is being Irish who writes about them.

Finally, I have seen and I see every day more beautiful women in Dublin than I ever saw in America.

(*Creation*, October 1954, p. 61)

Roger Casement

I have always been puzzled why Roger Casement should be such a hero, above criticism with certain kinds of people. It is definitely 'politics' to take this view. One may, with safety, be critical of Michael Collins, Cathal Brugha, etc., but not about Casement. It is true that he died nobly, but so did the others.

Then there are the diaries.

For as long as I remember Irish patriots have been *grigging* the British to produce the alleged diaries so that they could be examined by scholars – *if* they had them. That was the big *if*. The typescript was forever being sneered at as a worthless document. Now that the British have at last done what we demanded they do, I notice that Dr Roger McHugh and Dr Herbert O. Mackey have been complaining in the press about having got what they wanted.

I think the time has arrived when it is impossible to claim that the diaries are forgeries. Indeed, the book by Dr Maloney, *The Forged Casement Diaries*, was correctly described by the late Sergeant Sullivan as 'twaddle'. And, of course, Yeats's ballad in which the poet exceeded himself in codology! I am afraid that now the diaries will be available to scholars it will be left to others than those 'Casement committees' to enfold Casement's memory in understanding and compassion.

I am not alone in the belief that Casement's addiction to perverse erotic fantasies was expressed in a verbal way only, and that he was not a practising paederast as in the diaries he boasts himself to have been.

These delusions of sexual grandeur are not rare. His diaries might, therefore, be in a way described as fiction and, at a pinch, little less valid than Molly Bloom's tiresome drivel at the end of *Ulysses*.

As well as all this it must not be forgotten that we are all whited sepulchres. Beneath the businessman's or the politician's formal exterior may be a corrupt mind. I often think that God must sometimes smile when He sees the impeccable businessman advancing on his office.

The mind of the best of us is seldom fit to be seen as God sees it.

Casement's putting the fantasy on paper is an extension of the erotic fantasy. One doesn't have to be a Kraft-Ebbing or a Freud to know this. I remember when I was in America a man I knew used to get highly comic and witty letters from a friend. These he read to his wife. Then one day the wife came across one of these letters and she was what newspapers would call horrified. (Of course, no one is horrified about anything except family misfortunes, loss of large income, etc.) Anyhow, the letters were interlarded with the most complex sexual fantasies which are always so thunderingly dull except one's own eroticism is awakened. This is precisely the form of the Casement diaries.

Now what your average politician appears not to understand, and what your average Irishman did not understand at the time, is that Casement belonged to a profoundly sophisticated society. Casement was a child of Experience dealing for the most part with the children of Innocence. Such a man would be dissembling all the time so as not to shock his friends. He had to live a double life.

The ordinary man brought up on newspaper morality and filled with newspaper pieties which cut out everything of reality is a soft, hysterical and dangerous plasma who should be kept in a certain kind of subjection. These people have no critical basis and are dangerous if given authority. Criticism, even when friendly, they look upon as attack. Casement would be completely outside the comprehension of such simpletons. These should have things explained to them. The explanation should run thus: Don't be prying into what you couldn't understand. Dig your ditch.

Does our acceptance of these facts preclude Casement from his high place in our esteem? I don't think so. The interior of the sepulchre discomfits the hysterical, but sane and virtuous people will take it in their stride. Casement for me as an Irish patriot is another matter.

As I see it, Casement was an English public servant and an English humanitarian which the ruthless machinery of English public service often throws up. To call him an Irishman, as the word is commonly used, is silly. His attachment to the cause of Irish independence strikes this writer as somewhat dilettantish. Trying to organize Irish prisoners of war in Germany showed that he knew nothing of the Irish mentality, and was also perverse. The British executed him because he betrayed his own side. And it must be remembered that in time of war in the small island of Britain the savage and not the sophisticate is in charge. It was a dreadful piece of meanness and hypocrisy for the British to use the diaries to discredit him, as it is said. But it wouldn't have made the smallest difference; they'd have hanged him if the President of the United States, the King of England and the Archbishop of Canterbury wanted him reprieved. During the last war they hanged young Amery whose father and uncle were both in the Government.

The diaries should now be accepted for what they are and forgotten. Nothing can be worse than a constant untruth in our minds. The lie that the diaries are forgeries or that they are non-existent (an Army officer declared them non-existent) is akin to the lie about the National Language, its widespread use and exciting literature. I have often thought that a country should have a group of men well paid and protected as judges are from the ignorant mob whose job it would be to tell the truth. There are such people in England.

Telling the truth is good for society but a hazardous occupation for the truth-teller.

(*National Observer*, September 1959, p. 7)

In Praise of Wells

Meegan's Well, Cassidy's Well, Feehan's Well – these were famous wells in my youth. They still survive in my imagination as well as in reality, though the well as we knew it is giving way to the laid-on supply of water. It is a pity, of course. It is not merely the clear spring water with a possible trout in it for decoration or the thorn bush overhanging it, but something more. Perhaps the thing I most recall is the gossiping women at the well.

I never liked the chore of walking a crooked path of five hundred yards to Meegan's Well, which gave us our regular supply, and I often dreamed that it would be wonderful if there was a spring under our house and we could have a pump put in there. Actually there was a powerful spring under the house and in front of it too, but Nicholas Kearney, the water-diviner, was unable to find water anywhere about our house but on the insanitary site of the dunghill (nowadays known, in deference to niceness but not to vividness, as the compost heap). Not so long ago the present occupiers of that house got another diviner who found the spring mentioned, from which the water is now piped in.

Looking at this spring I thought of all the times I had carried two tin cans of water from the distant well and I was reminded of a rhyme that was in an old school book:

There was a man who had a clock, his name was Mathew Mears,
He wound it regularly every day for four and twenty years;

At length his precious timepiece proved an eight-day clock to be
And a madder man than Mathew Mears you wouldn't wish to see.

And so by me and the well. I felt that I had been put to so much unnecessary work. But it was worth it.

Beautiful things such as wells have ways of surviving. There is first the idea of the holy well, of which there are many in Ireland. There has been up to this present day the belief that it is unlucky to close a well even when it is in the middle of a field and a hindrance to tillage. A well so placed has or had the privileges of 'lone bush'.

One of the most beautiful of holy wells is Father Moore's Well beside Kildare town. One day in the summer of 1954 a friend who was driving me to Limerick suggested that we visit this well, of which I had not heard before. And whatever may be the orthodox holiness of it, its natural beauty flashed into my mind.

The man who told us about the well and the priest after whom it is named did not know much about Father Moore, whose biretta and other vestments are to be seen beside the well. But he did tell us that you couldn't boil the water, a quality attributed to most dedicated wells, and which keeps them from being disturbed. The idea of a well having a dedicated purpose makes it more beautiful than normally; we see it as all beauty must be seen, obliquely: it enters our mind sideways, shyly.

In my native area the most famous holy well was (and is) Lady Well near Dundalk. On the eve of the Feast of the Assumption the people from the neighbouring counties visit it at midnight to bring home bottles of the water. This water was in my time used to sprinkle on sick animals as well as humans.

In the days of my youth, which was still the days of the horse-drawn vehicle, the eve of the Fifteenth of August was an exciting time. In my memory are two visions of that hour. In one we are finishing the cutting of our acre of conacre oats in the top end of Woods's field. Red Rooney is finishing the cutting – with a scythe. I remember the length and texture of that oats because it was an important evening. I can hear and sometimes see Terry Lennon getting ready the horse-cart to drive his family to the Well. The rain looks like holding off, though it was a tradition for rain to fall on that evening.

In a short while the cart rattles down the lane loaded with about six women on two seat-boards, the three back passengers facing backwards. It took a horse about three hours to make the journey one way, and that was a long time to live in the contemplation of nature. That slow movement taught us something that in after-life we are apt to run short of, the patience to be alone, the patience to realize that we live long, not through speed, but through still contemplation. The proceedings at Lady Well in those days were rather rough, but they exuded sincerity and a vital tradition. It was a cultural entity that was around us there. We all spoke with the same accent and had the same patterns of living. Lady Well itself is covered over with a little house and this prevents its well qualities displaying themselves fully. But it is a true spring well all the same, and it evokes in my mind a whole countryside with all its life.

Archbishop Healy published a pamphlet on the holy wells of Ireland which is a rare publication. We owe a good deal to Philip Dixon Hardy for his little book *The Holy Wells of Ireland*, which is easy enough to come by.

Hardy was a stupid fellow, not given to analyzing his real motives, who said that his object in writing was to 'hold up to the eye of the public the superstitions and degrading practices associated with them'. In the course of being angry and self-righteous he gives us a good deal of information. 'It is indeed impossible for any traveller to pass over any considerable part of the country, more especially in the South and West, without meeting with numerous Holy Wells.'

He tells us of the pagan origin of well worship and mentions the Pattern of St Michael's Well, Ballinskelligs, on the 29th September, the feast of St Michael the Archangel, 'which concurs with the Autumnal Equinox and consequently with the Baal Times of the Druids'. But I do not claim to be a scholar. I only say a well is a thing of beauty and a joy forever. And I am aware of the high justice of the fact that the most sacred place of pilgrimage in Christendom is Lourdes, centred round a well.

But such considerations are too vague for me. I think of the common wells again; Tommy Connor's Well was beside the railway, and Rooney's Well was in a hollow among blackthorns. As I remember it Mary Rooney (who spoke Irish) is standing beside the well with a red handkerchief around her head and she is telling me of the prophecy that a coach without horses would go along the road and that it would pass through Owney McGahon's very house. That was the railway from Inniskeen to Carrickmacross, not then built and now closed.

At this point I must remind myself not to be too generally enthusiastic for all wells. For therein lies Essayist's Whimsy. Beauty is personal, and sometimes of no interest to others.

> *However I am glad I brought the waters to life*
> *Of wells that were known to me once by taste and by sight*
> *The hawthorn on the flagged roof*
> *Saying here is the place of Love*
> *And you will never get over it quite.*

(*Ireland of the Welcomes*, September–October 1959, pp. 8–10)

Preface to Trench's
Realities of Irish Life

William Steuart Trench's *Realities of Irish Life* has been for many years a favourite book of mine. And not merely because I was born and reared amid the principal scenes he describes. Or that I went to one of the National Schools he built on the Marquis of Bath's estate in south Monaghan. Or that my grandfather was the first master in that school. He built many of these schools over the Bath Estate, all of the same design, with a belfry in front which made them look somewhat like Stephenson's locomotive, The Rocket. He also built many farmhouses on the estate, and all, like the schools, had carved over the doorway:

B
1859

I never found out whether the B stood for Bath or built.

He is buried in Donaghmoyne Churchyard within two miles of my birthplace and his name is execrated in popular tradition. It was said that so evil was he that the rats invaded his grave and devoured his body.

But for none of these things do I admire his book. I admire it for its courage; the courage to write about the apparently insignificant. This courage was also shared by Philip Evelyn Shirley (related to the poet), who divided south Monaghan with Bath, who was a cousin of Trench's and for whom Trench also acted as agent. Shirley, equally hated, wrote one of the greatest local histories. Shirley's *Monaghan* is the history of small fields, forths and feuds, and is a rare book.

Trench is also the only literate recorder of the Great Famine of Black '47, never known as The Great Hunger, as Mrs Woodham-Smith's meretricious account would have it. His is the only contemporary report of the potato failure and is not listed in Woodham-Smith's book.

Trench is a sharp observer of the social scene – and though through his mid-nineteenth-century eyes he was unable to see the rights of the common man, he had some good ideas. He saw that the subdivision of already small holdings was disastrous. A five-acre farmer left his patch in equal divisions between his sons. Each built a cabin and produced a family. The so-called population explosion had started in early-nineteenth-century Ireland and the Famine was inevitable. He also had the excellent idea of paying tenants their fares to America.

The terrible expedient of the assembled tenantry going on their bended knees and begging Trench in God's name to reduce their rents is very moving, and has been in my own time a well-known form of blackmail. During the Hitler war, when an IRA man was that morning executed in Belfast, a crowd of us (myself included) ordered all the shops in O'Connell Street, Dublin, to close for an hour. One large shop refused until we all (myself included) went on our knees and started saying the Rosary in front of his open door. To assist our devotions a brick was thrown through the window of the shop and then the proprietor came to the door and quickly pulled it shut.

It may be interesting to note that the Office of the Bath Estate in Carrickmacross, Co. Monaghan, now a convent, was once the Irish residence of the Earl of Essex, the unfortunate friend of Queen Elizabeth I. He parleyed with The O'Neill at near-by Essexford, for which parley Elizabeth gave him the hammer.

It is, however, the evocations of locality that move me most in this book. Mullacrew, a village famous for its annual fair.

The Castleblaney besoms the best that ever grew.
Sold for two a penny on the Hill of Mullacrew.

Ireland was an important place in the mid nineteenth century. The people – even the landlords and their agents – believed that their little spot of earth was the centre of the world.

(MacGibbon & Kee, London, 1966, pp. 11–12)

Part III

Old Moore's Poets

'Were you ever around Yeats's birthplace?' I once asked a Civic Guard who hailed from County Sligo.

'Which Yeats do ye mane?' he replied.

'Why, Yeats the poet, of course.'

He never heard of such a poet.

'Ah,' said the Guard after a pause, 'there's no poets now like th' oul' poets.'

'What poets are you referring to?'

'Poets like Henry Frain and Amelia Porter; they used to write some powerful poems in Oul' Moore's Almanac.'

Would you credit this? It is as true a piece of dialogue as ever was written. It took place about five years ago. So what!

The bards of Old Moore's Almanac* are known to the initiated as the Bards of Lady Di – Di being short for diary. Their poetic output finds a market on the back pages of the Almanac under the headings of Charades, Elegies, Rebuses, Enigmas, and Miscellaneous. It is a sort of correspondence. A man in America, for example, writes a charade addressed to some old schoolfellow in Ireland; and the one addressed replies the following year.

* *Old Moore's Almanac,* first published in 1764 by Theophilus Moore of Milltown, Dublin. It included a monthly calendar and weather guide, times of sunrise and sunset, tide tables, dates of fairs, markets and race meetings, as well as a section devoted to verse. The almanac was popular among farmers during the first half of the twentieth century.

*Dear classmate of my pristine days
I hail thee with delight.*

And the reply:

*Dear, gallant songster of the West
Whom I appreciate.
And your eulogic words addressed to me
I do reciprocate.*

The end of the epistle is usually a riddle, for the solution of which prizes are offered. This school of verse has received scant consideration from the commentators. This is an oversight which should not be allowed to drift into eternal forgetfulness. The sentimental bathos which is their natural expression must interpret something in the Irish character. Old Moore was the poet as well as the prophet of the small-farmer community, among whom I grew up. It was probably the same all over Ireland, which explains my contretemps with the Civic Guard. Here is an authentic folk-song. Yeats and Synge might attempt to get down to the people, but the people had no use for them. Before newspaper-reading during the last Great War became a habit in the deeps of rural Ireland, what small farmer ever heard of Synge? Down among the people in those days were the Bards of Lady Di, who could express everything except criticism of Ireland.

Reading these verses one sometimes gets the impression that the bards must be joking, so successfully does their seriousness run to the ridiculous. But such an impression would be all wrong: they take themselves as seriously as ... Readers of a recent controversy in the *Irish Times* can fill in this space according to their literary affiliations.

And talk about that *Stuffed Owl* business!* Why did nobody inform the compilers of that anthology of bad verse that there were still the bards of Old Moore – a rich field for side-splitting research. I know that AE, in reviewing *The Stuffed Owl*, said that only genuine poets were

* *The Stuffed Owl: An Anthology of Bad Verse*, selected and arranged by D.B. Wyndham Lewis and C. Lee (London and Toronto, 1930).

entitled to be quoted when they slipped. With this critical principle no lover of laughter can agree. Anybody who makes us laugh is a benefactor of humanity.

A man in America receives tidings that a friend's baby has died, and he writes:

> *Across the raging seas was heard*
> *The feeble infant's dying roar.*

This gem was discovered by Sean O'Sullivan, R.H.A., and I, with the tears of laughter in my eyes, gratefully acknowledge.

But that is no chance jewel dropped from the moon. Almost any page of Old Moore can show the equal. Opening at random the current issue (note – this is a real random, and not the carefully selected random of book reviewers) I find the following elegy, which ends:

> *He'll sleep, he'll keep his long, lone sleep in the nucleus of life's goal,*
> *That final trend that all must wend and none can e'er control,*
> *Until the Judgment sound shall reverberate around this unstable sphere*
> > *concave,*
> *And the thunder's burst will rend the crust that wraps Pat Henry's grave.*

It is rather a pity that the last line fails to maintain the tragic ridiculosity of the remainder. The poets of Old Moore may die unwept but they will not be unsung.

When the already mentioned Henry Frain died about fourteen years ago there were gallons of ink tears shed for him. Henry was the 'Leader of Poet's Hall', as their laureate is called. Since his death up to the current issue of Old Moore, his name and fame are 'reverberating around this unstable sphere concave'. Then there was the Queen of Lady Di – Miss Amelia Porter, whom my friend the Civic Guard remembered. After her death it transpired that Miss Amelia was a man by the name of Paddy Sweeney. This knowledge had no effect on the elegies for her. As a queen she wrote and as a queen she was mourned.

> *Miss Mary Waldron is in dree,*

Likewise Marcella Wyme;
With Miss Carson and Bee Doherty,
From the City of Brooklyn.
Miss Maggie Doyle, star of renown,
Miss Donegan likewise,
And Sarah Kerr from Omagh town,
Weeps for her demise.

That is no more than a drop in the ocean of tears that were dropped on Paddy Sweeney's grave. Another bard long and deeply lamented is P.J. McCall. It seems that is the P.J. McCall who wrote 'Kelly the Boy from Killann' and other popular songs.

It is among the elegies that the picking is richest. A man laments the death of a rich neighbour's four-year-old daughter:

She's with her uncle, Mr Willie
And they are sleeping side by side.

Reading these lines I get a perfect picture of Mr Willie. I would say that he was one of the old, hard-drinking, hard-riding school. And the author, he, too, reveals a good deal of his peasant humility.

Another bard sings the praises of his wife, who has been his faithful companion for forty years:

My darling is now an invalid, but still her charms remain.

The death of a father is recorded with precision:

At break of day life ebbed away as the clock was striking seven.
That was the time the clock did chime when God called him to Heaven.

But, to get away from the songs of death, let us turn the pages of the Charades. The first to catch my eye begins:

Dear Sol has cast his radiant glance
O'er moorland, lake and hill,

When a riparian stroll I did advance
Along a rippling rill.

Where is the artist of the ridiculous who could substitute a word for riparian to get the funny effect so well? And there are love songs which are a continuous skid off the track:

Her eyes were shyly glancing
And she said with meek cajole
As I had lit the fire of love
She'd kindly add the coal.

Bards who stop writing are urged to return to the fold of Lady Di:

The bards will greet your risen pen
With chaplets round it wreathe.

The only thing Irish which comes in for criticism is the government:

Our Irish legislators
If the truth to them be told,
Have left our people hungry
And standing in the cold.

I wonder did anybody observe John Bull wince a few years back. He must have, for when a new leader named Joe Fogarty had taken up residence in 'Poet's Hall', one of the subject bards wrote:

Bards agree on every hand
At home and in each distant land
That Fogarty should lead them.
Ah, well may England wince to know
We've chosen dauntless Fenian Joe …

When I was a boy there lived in our district one of these bards. He styled himself the Bard of Callenberg, after the townland where he lived. He never spoke except in ryhme. He was in great demand at wakes and in pubs. He was a cripple, and the neighbours subscribed to purchase for him a donkey and cart.

'Ah, that was the right poet,' people said. 'If he had conduct, it's himself that could make the tidy livin' from his poems.'

He summoned a neighbour once, and gave all his evidence in rhyme:

> *Alas! to tell how I was done*
> *By Pat, the Miser, and his son.*
> *I was in Scotland far away*
> *When they drew home my cock of hay.*
> *They promised to thatch my mother's cot,*
> *But no, they left it there to rot.*
> *The rain came percolating through*
> *And smashed a couple, sad to view.*

At the height of his fame he was attacked by a rival bard from County Meath, who accused him of plagiarism. That was the end of the Bard of Callenberg: he never wrote for Old Moore again, and he fell a dozen rungs to the bottom of Fame's ladder. The people were shocked to learn that their poet was copying.

'Ye'd never even it to him,' they said.

However that might be, nobody could lay a charge of plagiarism to the pen of the genius who wrote 'The Feeble Infant's Dying Roar'.

(*The Irish Times*, 9 May 1939, p. 2)

William Carleton

If ever there was a writer of the people as well as a writer for the people, William Carleton was such a one. In a great many small farmers' houses when I was growing up in the north you would be liable to find one of Duffy's prayer-book-like editions of this novelist sharing library honours in the back window with Old Moore's Almanac.

There were traditions about the man, too. But I would not give much heed to these traditions, founded on sentiment mostly. At the same time I think it can be said that among the older generation of rural dwellers there was a warmer interest in writing than there is today.

At one time I thought more of Carleton than I do now. I am beginning to find in him a creative weakness which seems to be common to most Irish writers. While his background lasted he had a rich subject. When he tried to leave it there was just an ineffectual flapping of splayed feet.

It occurs to me to speculate on how true this is of so many of our writers. You find brilliant young geniuses making one fine lyric move, but never the second. You find Colum writing his lovely lyrics and then drying up, Stephens, Campbell, the same. You get Joyce and O'Casey, great while they are dealing with their background, but incapable of taking off for other worlds. America is blamed for Colum's failure, London for the failure of O'Casey and Stephens. In the case of Joyce there is no blame being handed out, because most writers think that *Ulysses* and *Finnegans Wake,* finally, were not the despairing crash into emptiness of a man who had eaten up all his background.

The one Irish writer who projected himself forward from his background was Yeats. His early lyrics are superficial statements of a mood, but in the later work you find him reading the symbol.

> *I meditate upon a swallow's flight,*
> *Upon an aged woman and her house ...*

He has found the second jaw of his pincers and he grips.

The other writers whom I have mentioned would have succeeded no better had they stayed in Ireland. It was just that they lacked that energy of will that makes a Dostoevsky or a Wordsworth. They died of weariness. Carleton had lived his whole youth so intimately with his people that he had more material than most writers of this kind. But in the end he does repeat himself many times.

Another thing I miss in him, and it is related to the other weakness, is much in the shape of a moral purpose. He moralizes plenty though, a different matter. His evangelizing propaganda is pathetic and the only thing to be said in its favour is that it may have helped him to get a civil-list pension. It is said that his writing helped to ventilate the grievances of the peasantry. But Carleton complacently accepts landlordism, and is only anxious to make the landlords more reasonable. In fact, whenever Carlton starts to moralize, philosophize or dogmatize, he is what we would call 'an oul' cod'.

The best of Carleton's work is contained in his *Traits and Stories of the Irish Peasantry* and his autobiography. His longer novels, of which he perpetrated several, are melodramatic and sentimental in the worst possible manner of the period. But in a story like 'Ned McKeown', which is the first of the *Traits*, we get the most vivid, and, in the true poetic sense, romantic pictures of landscape and character. He evokes a scene out of a deep loving memory. Ned, who has not been minding his business, has been getting the ironic lash of his wife's tongue. Here is the end of the row:

> On Ned seating himself to the bacon and potatoes, Nancy
> would light another pipe, and plant herself on the opposite hob,

putting some interrogatory to him in the way of business –
always concerning a third person, and still in a tone of dry ironical indifference –

'Did you see Jemmy Connolly on your travels?'

'No.'

'Humph! Can you tell if Andy Morrow sould his coult?'

'He did.'

'Maybe you have gumption enough to know what he got for
him?'

'Fifteen guineas.'

'In troth, and it's more than a poor body would get; but anyway Andy Morrow deserves to get a good price: he's a man that
takes care of his own business, and minds nothing else ...'

Anybody who has lived intimately with the small farming people will
see how authentic this little tiff is. And it is as true today as it was one
hundred and fifty years ago. Carleton's women characters are idealized,
but not sentimentalized, and through them he has almost reached the
purpose of great art.

There is a subsidiary purpose – a sort of plot – in Carleton's work,
and it might almost be described as the Popish Plot. He holds the
Protestants up as examples of frugality and thrift – and, perhaps, he was
not far wrong. When I was growing up I often heard a ploughman,
going out determined to do a neat job of work, say: 'We'll do this good
and Protestant.'

Carleton claimed to have turned Protestant, but, notwithstanding
these forced overtones, he was never anything – was incapable of being
anything – but a Catholic. All his best work is true to that medieval texture of Irish Catholic life, where the same breath that utters a Hail
Mary suffices to shoo the chickens off the floor or the cat from the jug
of cream. His autobiography, which he did not live to complete, is a
grand book, free from all those anti-Romish asides which are such a
nuisance in their interruption of the narrative.

It is full of self-pity, for small reason. It begins: 'Alas! It is a melancholy task which I propose to execute – the narrative of such a continued and unbroken series of struggle, difficulty, suffering and sorrow as

has seldom fallen to the lot of a literary man ...' Considering that for the last twenty years of his seventy he had a civil-list pension of £200, he seems over-pathetic. Had he lived today, he might have reason to complain.

Carleton also wrote some verse. One poem of his, 'Sir Turlough, or The Churchyard Bride', has a most weird and wonderful incantation, and in some respects it surpasses the excellence of Gray's masterpiece.

It tells the legend of Sir Turlough, who met in the graveyard, on the day upon which his would-be bride had been buried, a beautiful lady whom he kissed. It was the kiss of a wraith, a fatal kiss, and there seems to me to be something of fearful symbolism in the legend.

> *The bride she bound her golden hair –*
> *Killeavy, O Killeavy!*
> *And her step was light as the breezy air*
> *When it bends the morning flowers so fair,*
> *By the bonnie green woods of Killeavy ...*
>
> *He pressed her lips as the words were spoken,*
> *Killeavy, O Killeavy!*
> *And his banshee's wail – now far and broken –*
> *Murmured 'Death' as he gave the token,*
> *By the bonnie green woods of Killeavy.*

Finally we ask ourselves if the reading of Carleton has not really done something to us – if he has not interpreted for us material facts in terms of that joy which is also part of Reality. And we must admit that he has. But he has certainly performed the historian's function. He has laid the landscape and the figures before us – to interpret with the poet in us, to enjoy with the mundane part of ourselves [...]

(*The Irish Times*, 13 January 1945, p. 2)

Preface to *The Autobiography of William Carleton*

I do not describe William Carleton (1794–1869) as the greatest Irish writer, for I do not believe that there is any such thing as 'Irish' in literature. He is, however, a universal writer, as good, say, as Cervantes, but with no opening into the world. He had the misfortune to be born into pre-Victorian ignorance and his only ploy – sad indeed – was to change, or pretend to change, his historical Catholicism for Protestantism. Naturally, I have no prejudice against Protestantism, except that it appears to me to be based on everything that is weak in Christianity.

Less than half a century after Carleton's death, James Joyce would write in reply to a question about whether he intended to become a Protestant: 'I said that I had lost the faith, but not that I had lost self-respect: what kind of liberation would that be to forsake an absurdity which is logical and coherent and to embrace one which is illogical and incoherent?' Unfortunately for Carleton, a pure-bred Irish Catholic if ever there was one, he had only pre-Victorian Protestantism to give him a bead on the larger world. It is sad to see him making a cod of himself, Bible-quoting in sorrow rather than anger and handing out judgements of the 'the sixth (chapter) is theirs; the seventh is ours' variety.

Nonetheless, Carleton stuck by his Protestantism to the end, and I remember my father telling of a Franciscan preaching in our village church, who told the congregation of simple folk there how he had gone to Carleton's deathbed to get him to revert to the religion of his forefathers. Carleton only turned his face to the wall.

A great deal has been written about Carleton, by, among others, W.B. Yeats, who edited a selection of his works. Yet he remains in curious obscurity still. He wrote two books and a great deal of melodramatic trash. His two books are the *Traits and Stories of the Irish Peasantry* and this unfinished autobiography. Carleton's *Traits and Stories* contain the most authentic dialect and – if I may coin a cliché – most racy dialogue, which reads like a translation direct from the necessities of early nineteenth-century Irish life. For example, he wrote 'to put something by for the sore foot', rather than for 'a rainy day'. I heard this expression in my youth and it reminds us that most people at the time made their journeys on Shanks' pony.

Carleton spent his early years in what was then considerable comfort. This easy situation, with its 'hung' beef and flitches of bacon in the humblest kitchen, came to an end, I believe, after the repeal of the Corn Laws in the 1830s. The first of the terrible famines, which continued intermittently for the next forty years, had broken out in 1827, and the union of potato blight and new laws led to disaster. Carleton recorded the first famine, with much humour and pathos, in one of the *Traits*, 'The Poor Scholar', which reads like a short novel.

A good deal of the early adventures of Carleton recounted in this autobiography took place in my own intimate district and his name and fame are still known to the older generation. Indeed, only a few months ago, a man in a pub asked me if I ever read Carleton. And it was common to hear people speak of his affair with Pierce Murphy of Lowtown. He was indeed a descendant of that same Murphy who was the only man I ever knew to be called Eusebius – Eusebius Murphy – whose name I used in my novel *Tarry Flynn*.

Not far from Lowtown is, or was in my boyhood, the ruins of the notorious 'Wildgoose Lodge', and this place I passed many a time on my way to visit my maternal grandfather in Killaney. Its long, low walls still bore traces of the holocaust which destroyed the seventeen members of the Lynch family well over a century before. The name of Wildgoose Lodge was still whispered in my native parish of Inniskeen right up to my own time. It was believed that a large contingent of Ribbonmen took part in the destruction and I remember one October evening, when I was gathering potatoes as a boy for a neighbour, asking the man to tell me something about the business. He told me to ask my father. Another neighbour always swore by the name of one of those same Ribbonmen. When threatening to boot someone, he used to say, 'I'll raise you as high as the Van (Paddy Devaun) was hung!'

Carleton was parochial, not provincial. In this he was not unlike Joyce, though Joyce, with his legends and daring language, had a strong strain of pretension in him. Carleton instead wrote the lives of the obscure and humble, and he recorded the lives of his own people with a fidelity that preserves for us the culture of pre-Famine Ireland.

Carleton's uniqueness has been confused with a lot of bad nineteenth-century Irish writers – mainly female, such as Mrs C.S. Hall and the author of the introduction to a previous edition of this work, Frances Cashel-Hoey. She refers to Carleton's 'peasant background', but he was no more a peasant than is your obedient servant. His people had been 'driven out and compelled to be chaste', driven out to an illiteracy which they refused to accept.

Carleton tells us much about the 'hedge schoolmasters' of Ireland. These were not primary teachers, but university men without a university. They knew Greek, Latin, Irish and English – and mathematics. By training and experience, Carleton was one of them. His *Autobiography* gives us this lost world of ambition and deprivation in its most readable form.

(MacGibbon & Kee, London, 1968, pp. 9–11; this was Kavanagh's last prose essay.)

Sex and Christianity

The centenary of the birth of George Moore was celebrated this year [1952] and to honour the occasion W.R. Rodgers, who has introduced the bucklep to London literary society, where they think it wonderful, held the usual symposium on the radio.

I listened in to this programme without being bored during its whole hour run. For all that, a less good-mannered discussion it would be hard to encounter. There we had a crowd mainly of mediocrities and less, being funny at the expense of one of the few authentic writers who happened to live in Dublin – where he never belonged – for a few years.

Dublin thought him funny. It is the way Dublin has for dealing with a man of deep passion. Moore was a passionate lover of truth, of the Tao which all true creative thinkers know. He had less venom in him than Yeats, for he was, in spite of all his humours, a Catholic in all his points of view. But more so than Catholic he was what used to be called an artist. (A new name for that kind of thing is needed.)

We owe several debts to Moore: one is a wonderful portrait of Yeats, so good-natured and accurate, and the second is his portrait of the interesting times he lived in.

Far more so than Yeats he brought the mood of European letters to Dublin and for that matter to London. He wrote two books of real merit and a couple of others of a perverse merit. There are racy stories in *The Lake*. I remember 'Julia Cahill's Curse', which tells of a beautiful girl who drove men mad with love for her and how the parish priest drove her out of the country. I mention the plot because on reflection it does seem to me that somewhere in the nineteenth century, or maybe earlier, or maybe it is somewhere in Irish religion rather than in chronology, an anti-life heresy entered religion. Priests became infected with a heresy that as good as denied that they themselves were born of woman.

It was a most villainous thing. I remember an example of it myself round nineteen-thirty – how when of a beautiful summer evening, a huge crowd were dancing at Annavackey Cross on a wooden deck. As usual I was on the green bank, looking on in all my misery. But though miserable the wild rocky fields that ran away down towards Slieve Gullion looked up at me and imprinted themselves on my imagination forever. I remember the road that ran down towards Crossmaglen. On the opposite side of the road was the parish of Creggan, famous because of a Gaelic poet who lived there.

And I remember the Casadh Cam – the crooked turn – and how when the chain of my bicycle broke a companion named Boylan towed me home.

At all events, in this exciting country, the melodeons were playing and life itself was dancing when up the road on his bicycle came a little black priest who could not have been long out of college. This little man got up on the fence and ordered us to disperse, which we did; and I was ashamed of those young boys and girls who knew so little about even their own religion not to know that this little man was acting from impulses that were pernicious.

Thus ended the crossroads dance in that part of the country. Thus was ushered in the era of the commercial dance-hall with its disease-laden atmosphere. The galvanized dance-halls would have come in any case but not so quickly. The trend is in the opposite direction now, and I believe that dancing decks are becoming popular again. But if there is disease in the body of Irish society the young priests sent out by Maynooth are not free from blame.

I started off to write about George Moore. Perhaps I should forget about him and concentrate on the train of thought that his name provokes.

What makes me most interested in this heresy is the fact that in Carleton it doesn't exist and Carleton was not particularly friendly to the priests. At least he claimed to be unfriendly. In fact he was friendly enough, willy-nilly. At any rate Carleton was a faithful recorder of society, and the parish priest and curate (Maynooth men) were the soul of the party. What happened after this is the story.

On analysis the literal interpretation of the Sixth Commandment of the Mosaic Code cannot subsist with the continuance of life. A new interpretation is needed or some clarification of the position. At the present time life in Catholic society is possible because of the lax way most people interpret the Commandment.

It is important, this matter.

The catechism which I had hammered into me at school had been compiled by a Bishop of Clogher named O'Reilly, and its definition of the Sixth Commandment was 'This sin can be committed not only in the foul act but also when one looks on anything that may excite to it.' Christian marriage, divinely inspired though it be, must make its obeisance to love or lust.

Of course that catechism with its reference to 'foul act' was heretical, though I shouldn't be surprised if it is still in use.

—A casual passer-by: What about George Moore?

—Forget about George Moore, there's another week.

Before I depart from the theological scene I might make one more reference to this catechism – anent the language it used. For small children the law of fasting was defined in terms typical.

Who are absolved from fasting?

Sick people, women with child, nurses and old people of languishing constitutions.

Would the disaster which has caught up with us today have been caused more by theological heresy than by economics? Probably a mixture of the two.

But a few words about poor George Moore – who himself was subject to parenthetical fits.

He wrote two valuable books – *Confessions of a Young Man* and the trilogy *Hail and Farewell*. *Confessions of a Young Man* is memorable because of the mood, which has a rare European flavour; we feel that we are at the heart of European thought.

In *Ave* Moore immortalized Yeats. Yeats without humour provided him with the perfect subject. Lady Gregory, as Moore tells us, whispering between her teeth something about a man of genius and a man of talent coming together, had her lines crossed. Moore was at least as much a genius as Yeats.

Yeats in his come-back at Moore in *Dramatis Personae* is rather puerile. He says that Moore had a manner but no manners. Yeats apparently didn't see that Moore had a personality and a rare capacity for seeing not only others but himself. *Hail and Farewell* is the companion of *Ulysses*, in some ways a better picture of Dublin than Joyce's work.

Whenever I write about a man of genius such as Moore I feel very short-taken for something to say. There is little that one can say about a man who himself was such a sayer. Ultimately criticism is useless: the only thing the appraiser can say: this man is good, read him, or the contrary. [...]

(*Kavanagh's Weekly*, 24 May 1952, p. 7)

The Anglo-Irish Mind

Only a few days ago I was discussing the Anglo-Irish with a well-known Anglo-Irishman, their failure to take deep root in the soil of Ireland and even because of that their most useful contribution to Irish culture. The Anglo-Irish were, and are, the lookers-on. They are not part of the national conscience, but in an objective position outside it.

Somebody once remarked that (in the days when people were visiting the Soviet Union) if a man went to Russia and stayed a week he wrote a book, if he stayed a month he wrote a pamphlet and if he stayed a year he wrote nothing. Something of the same principle applies to the Anglo-Irish.

The nearer they got to the essential truth of Ireland the less they wrote about it. None of them got very near, simply because, as Lady Gregory recognized, the only short-cut to the soul of Ireland was via Rome. The Anglo-Irish are not English, much as a few of them might wish it, and there being no country called Anglo-Ireland, it follows that they are without a fatherland.

From Swift to Yeats the mouthpieces of this limbo-stranded class have had to search diligently wherever they might for the spiritual food of their creative need. Yeats was the fruit of many generations resident in Ireland, yet he was forced to adopt Ireland as his country. A people raises up a poet out of its silent necessity just as it raises a leader. Yeats was not pushed up by the under-drive of a nation; he saw that force and he allowed it to drive *him*. It was the same with Synge. Imagine the unnaturalness of Synge searching all round the world for something to write about and then finding the Aran Islands. I remember F.R. Higgins and how he would talk of a good subject for a lyric.

My theory is – and I am certain it is a sound one – that a true literature, or culture, is born unwillingly and in pain, and is never created out of the itch to write or the personal vanity of someone outside the deep womb of a people.

In a poem on the death of another poet Auden wrote a line which I remember because it showed the true poet's outlook. He spoke of his hope that the dead man had found a resting place where there was 'no need to write'.

Unfortunately to this natural terror of the mother in labour is added with us in Ireland a laziness that is quite unnatural.

Whatever else the Anglo-Irish were they were not lazy. And the fact that the writers among them were not born of the nation's deep urge has had some advantages. Practically all our archaeological scholars, folklorists, etc., have been of this class. Such affairs suited their objective outlook, being not too close to actual life which is the stuff in which true poets always deal [...]

(From a review of Richard Hayward, *The Corrib Country*, in *The Standard*, 28 May 1943, p. 3)

W.B. Yeats

It is not surprising that certain 'democratic' elements in England and elsewhere are finding Yeats a bitter pill to swallow. Yeats, though but a poor philosopher, had the poet's instinct for what is vital and masculine, and among his many personalities were to be found supporters of Fascism, Irish Republicanism and many other ideologies. Those people who find such activities to their liking will claim the poet as their own. But the fact is Yeats had no central loyalty – except to his poetry – and he wandered from philosophy to theosophy and politics, taking from each what was useful to his art. It is this absence of a central theme in the poet's life which has been his biographer's greatest problem. Mr Hone has been blamed for not attempting an assessment of Yeats as poet and man. But Yeats will not stay put. He is not a socialist like Shaw, a priest like Hopkins, or a peasant like John Clare. Wherever Yeats sensed artistic energy, there he went. About the only place in which he never sought a poetic religion was the Catholic Church; indeed, it is possible that he had a constant centre – and that was the core of Irish Protestantism which never dissolved in any of his political or artistic passions. This core seems also to be Mr Hone's only certainty; a mild dislike for Catholics and native Irish runs through his book, though not offensively so. Many people are of the opinion that Yeats was a poor man; he was, but his was a high level of poverty. One of the first bits of unreality – a pose that would appeal to Yeats – is the following relative to the poet's father:

> As eldest son J.B.Y. inherited the settled estate in Kildare, which consisted of 626 acres with a valuation of £464. This was enough on which to marry.

Just barely enough. However, Mr Hone brings us through the much more highly valued fields of the poet's experience. The pursuit of so many shooting stars and no fixed one is liable to make one dizzy, but it is tremendously fascinating. The foundation of the Abbey Theatre, his reactions to 1916 and the constant delight of his poetry are rich compensation for having to suffer the crowds of silly women and charlatans in Yeats's litany of saints. What a marvellous technician he was! He could produce magic in verse almost automatically. He was a brilliant poet, yet somehow I feel that a truly great poet would not have been all his life the mere mirror of the phases of his time but would have spoken the unchanging beauty.

This biography should be read widely in Ireland – read critically. It is a rich book.

(Review of Joseph Hone, *W.B. Yeats*, in *The Standard*, 26 February 1943, p. 2)

William Butler Yeats

The best portrait of Yeats ever produced is George Moore's in *Hail and Farewell*. Yeats disliked it at the time, yet it is very affectionate, and even at that time when Yeats was under forty, with his best work to come, Moore recognized his genius.

But there is one facet of the poet's life that few people have discussed – his desperate desire to be thought Irish and one of the People. Nobody will deny that he was Irish of a certain kind – a noble kind, his father was a wonderful man – yet he himself was always conscious of being something of an outsider.

> *Nor may I less be counted one*
> *With Mangan, Davis, Ferguson*

As Plato tells us in the person of Socrates, a man cannot desire that which he has got. Joyce had it. Joyce, as he himself says, was 'Irish, all too Irish', and his version of the Yeats sentiment is:

> *But I must not accounted be*
> *One of that mumming company –*
> *With him who hies him to appease*
> *His giddy dames' frivolities.*

Yeats took up Ireland and made it his myth and his theme. And you can see him today standing in the centre of that myth, uneasy that he doesn't belong fully. Now we can see that he does belong fully to that exciting affair with the Nation, with Pearse and Connolly and the others. But the fact remains that he never was at ease.

It was a weakness in his character in a way, the sort of weakness that you get in Hemingway with his delusions of violent grandeur, bullfights and boxing. Still, as with Yeats, it gave Hemingway the basis of a theme. My own view is that men of supreme genius have no delusions of any kind about themselves. The truth is that Yeats did not belong to Sligo and Sligo is not the 'Yeats country' as our tourist people claim. A truer Yeats country would be London, the Rhymers' Club, the Pre-Raphaelites, Arthur Symons, that world about which he tells us so fascinatingly in the Introduction to *The Oxford Book of Modern Verse*.

A great deal of his poetry of this period has Sligonian themes – 'Innisfree', 'The Fiddler of Dooney' – but the central emotion in them is that of fin-de-siècle decadence.

I am not one of those who think that a brilliant poet should be accessible to the ordinary people. No, in the words of Ezra Pound, Yeats's great friend (he was best man at Yeats's wedding), 'the lordliest of the arts and the solace of lonely men' was not created for the amusement of the ignorant man in the street. The traditional idea of the poet in Ireland is that he sings for the people. True poetry could not be created if it had to depend on the common man. The ability to recognize and enjoy the poetic content of a poem as distinct from its emotional wrapping is quite rare. Much of Yeats comes over on its Irishness. Incidentally, I think his poem on 1916 shows him at his worst. 'The grey eighteenth-century houses' are phoney and Pre-Raphaelite. In my opinion, Yeats's finest work was written when he was over fifty, up to but not including the *Last Poems*. The bawdy of the *Last Poems* is not true to the full Yeatsian life.

Having written this, something smote my conscience and I looked up the *Last Poems* and some of them are really splendid and so poetically exciting:

> *I sing what was lost and dread what was won*
> *I walk in a battle fought over again.*

There are two things in particular that are the marks of the poet – his gay youthfulness and his authority. Yeats always had both. He speaks from a height.

The condition of being young is, as Mauriac recently said, a 'state of mind'. To be old is to be dead. But can a poet die? More and more I am finding it difficult to imagine the discontinuity of that which once was. I have started a new form of literary criticism. Is he young or is he old?

I do not think that those poems in *Last Poems*, which are bawdy and noisy about wild women, show Yeats's youngness, but rather those in which he is his own serene authoritative self. In one of his *Last Poems* he writes of the world he has known:

> Beautiful lofty things: O'Leary's noble head;
> My father upon the Abbey stage ...
> Maud Gonne at Howth station waiting a train,
> Pallas Athene in that straight back and arrogant head:
> All the Olympians; a thing never known again

But was it not he who made them Olympians? Yeats was the god, the authority, the Mother Mind to whom all things could be referred. Any person possessing this myth-making quality can transform a commonplace society into an Olympian one. There were others, to be sure, who had authority, not the least being George Moore. In many ways it was through his *Hail and Farewell* that the Irish Literary Revival, Abbey Theatre, etc., became a reality. He gave it a history, a form. Movements are born of The Word. No expression, no existence. I am sure that Yeats writing

> Did that play of mine send out
> Certain men the English shot?

was not so far off the mark. He was a poet. One knew he was there.

POSTSCRIPT
Many months and reflections later

Yeats accused AE of fostering mediocrity but Yeats was far more guilty. It was Yeats who was responsible for the idea of Ireland as a spiritual entity, the idea which gave us so much bogus literature. It was a formula. If I say that Padraic Colum's Irish country poems are not the result of love-observation but are a cliché derived from Synge, I am the worst in the world.

Similarly with most of the others. The trouble with this Ireland point of view is that its exponents praise what fits their bill and it is always lies. London publishers are up on their hind legs looking for this sort of stuff.

Up till recently, this 'Ireland' had found what many of us hoped was its last resting place in the BBC pub The George, Great Portland St, London, w1. Now it seems that a new bridgehead may be established in Dublin. Frank O'Connor, Sean O'Faoláin and Padraic Colum have arrived from America, and if they manage to seize Telefís Éireann we the sensitive are in for some suffering.

Yeats, you have much to answer for.

(*The Kilkenny Magazine*, Spring 1962, pp. 25–8)

George Moore's Yeats

I fear we are getting too serious and solemn about Yeats. There is no doubt now that he was a great poet and probably the last great poet the earth will produce.

The adjective great is a bad word for it implies bad heroic art – like Rodin's and even Michelangelo's. This greatness may have its place in Palaces of Splendour, but it isn't my dish. I don't think Yeats was great in that way, and that he had enough of small simplicity in him to be truly great.

Yet I wonder had he? And do many read him with affection and gain from his work that extension of the self which poetry creates in the reader? And considering the matter with all the solemnity of a Yeats Festival, I must answer 'yes' to those questions. And 'no'.

I have no doubt that there was in him that exudance of genius which delights and corrupts its disciples.

Like Socrates, Yeats was a great corrupter.

What I was intending to write about is George Moore's portraits of Yeats in that gay and beautiful book – *Hail and Farewell.* For many years this triple volume has been a bedside book of mine, and mainly because of Yeats.

And looking in this mirror of an age, we now can see how ludicrously wrong were 'AE's canaries' about the man whose career was only about to begin.

Some Longworth longworthy forgotten nonentity to whom Moore has given a name comes out with a typical Dublinism:

> I fail to see how anybody can speak of a style apart from some definite work already written in that style. A style does not exist in one's head, it exists upon paper and Yeats has no style bad or good for he writes no more.

Well, there's wiseacreage for you.

The shock of all this and all that monstrous authority, arrogance and faith – and I am not alone in feeling that shock – is the statement made by somebody: 'But he is only 37.'

And with a career behind him. And none before: I am sure Moore was far too sharp and too rich in comic perception to believe that Yeats would write no more.

Moore gives the poet his dubious due: 'A real man of letters.'

And referring to a speech by Yeats: 'But I will no longer attempt the impossible; suffice to say that I remember Yeats sinking back like an ancient oracle exhausted by prophesising.'

'So all the Irish movement rose out of Yeats and returns to Yeats.' And 'He's only 37' renews its shock.

But the Irish movement owed almost as much to Moore, who recorded it, or rather recorded Yeats.

Yeats was a fully-born poet at a very early age and we should not be surprised to be dealing with a very adult adult and we should not be surprised at the leering sneering fools who pursued him. The majority of people like a poet to be a sweet singer, but they violently resent the terrible authority which is the theological side of the poet.

Although I realize that Yeats the man was what Moore has described him – a monk of literature, an inquisitor, a Torquemada – there was in him a phoney element.

All that rubbish about The Theatre and great actors and great actresses more so. But then he was young, in his late twenties or early thirties. And the times were provocative to a great poet. Those times that he invented.

And yet the seemingly complete portrait that Moore drew was only the beginning of Yeats's career.

I only once saw Yeats and then not very plain, and I have never been really excited by his verse. Still one cannot fail to recognize the poet in the man's behaviour: his rudeness to stupid people, his integrity that cut through personalities.

When AE asked him to listen to some poems by a protégé, James Stephens, Yeats listened and said nothing.

And when AE said how valuable a collection of poems published by Stephens would be to the young man, Yeats replied with the detachment of the poet and absolute critic.

'For you, my dear friend, the personal, for me the aesthetic.'

I think that twenty-five years later Yeats the aesthete had reservations about Sean O'Casey's quality even when he defended *The Plough and the Stars* from the stage.

But on the whole I believe Yeats a great critic. When he crammed the *Oxford Book of Modern Verse* with rubbish by his friends, he was showing his sense of values. He knew it didn't matter a damn. Or could the awful truth be that he believed Gogarty and Dorothy Wellesley were poets? Anyhow, all this attitude – and we hope it an attitude – was part of his phoniness, his compromise with society.

If I seem to be a bit wobbly about Yeats's simple greatness, it is not so much the detachment of his verse as his ability to integrate himself with bourgeois society.

There is another defect in Yeats – his dislike of ideas. He maintained that ideas were for the pulpit. It may be that he knew his limitations. Reading De Quincey's reminiscences of the Lakers – Coleridge and Wordsworth and Southey – I couldn't think of him as a man in the intellectual class of these.

Nor has he written a poem as memorable as the least of these – Southey's 'Blenheim'.

But then no poet writes for posterity except accidentally. And the worst one can say of Yeats is that he was a real man of letters. Real men of letters hardly ever produce immortal poetry. You could hardly call Shakespeare a man of letters. Pope was, in an oblique sort of way. Not Swift.

As for Yeats's Irishness I am inclined to believe in it because of the Irish angle and pattern of his love life. Nothing could be more Irish than this.

In the end he became a stage Anglo-Irishman. Blathering in the Senate about the unmean people he represented. Yet one must compliment that noble unrequited gentleman, Mr W.T. Cosgrave, for appointing Yeats to the Senate and adding therefore much to the gaiety of the nation. There is the photograph of Gogarty presenting swans to the Liffey with Yeats and Cosgrave in attendance. Marvellous comedy and evocative of a period. I have read part of Frank O'Connor's recollections of Yeats and I have not been impressed.

And who the devil are you to be impressed? my conscience cries.

Only passed the remark, I reply.

At any rate, O'Connor's views are too humble to be valuable. To describe a man or to hold a conversation with him, you must be on the same level. O'Connor is too humble.

And that is more or less all I have to say on the subject of Yeats. Except his bad influence on Irish writers because he advanced Ireland as a spiritual entity.

A common passport is not a common ground.

I know I have written equivocally of Yeats and yet I know that he was a nearly great poet.

He had compromised the ultimate integrity.

A final word on the incomparable George Moore. He was truly Irish and Catholic and European and with Joyce and Yeats deserves to be remembered equally. And I am puzzled why this delighting book has never been in my knowing the theme for a wise thesis, or brought out in paperback. I am for thinking that Moore is still out in the looney world of current (American mainly) criticism.

(*The Irish Times*, Yeats Centenary Supplement, 10 June 1965)

The Playboys
of the Western World

Nobody, as far as I know, has ever written about the Irish 'playboy' from the inside. Synge, who gave the idea a pseudo-classic permanence, was so fundamentally superficial that as a social document his play is worthless. We only see face values and if a man's face wears a smile we take it that he is happy.

The Irish talent for 'acting the cod' is very widespread. The talent is the child of poverty and oppression. It was of course the English conquerors that were responsible for the 'playboy'. They would not take us seriously and as a result we got a name for a certain kind of harum-scarum humour that I am glad to say we never really deserved. On the other hand, the flamboyant imagination that is born of faith in the next world rather than in this, has kept in us an optimism that is not a commercial asset. The world will not accept a happy philosopher. The influence of Chesterton, for instance, is much less than he deserves, simply because he couldn't be a solemn momentous humbug. To be a success in the world one should try to censor any originality that is in one.

[…] I have known many 'playboys' intimately. One of them was a jolly devil-may-care fellow who sang and drank and made himself out to be the drollest fellow alive. But underneath was a bitter heart. I met him when I was a boy, and I met him, too, in that place where every man and woman is paid the noble compliment of being taken seriously – in his own kitchen. To overhear that man and his wife discussing affairs of farm and state was a revelation. The talk was hard and to the point. His wife once described him to me as a 'street angel and house devil'. Now suppose a town visitor or a writer with no inside knowledge of the country such as Synge: he would bring away a picture of a delightful character, a man who would be a grand companion in a tavern, but not a man who could be entrusted with anything like a serious job of work. Then there was another fellow, a little fellow with a round red face whom everybody took a hand at. This 'fool' allowed this impression of him to develop until one day when he was about forty years of age he went to an auction where a shop and farm of land were being sold. The shop and farm of land were one lot and didn't my bold fellow bid on it. He was the highest bidder, but the auctioneer who thought he was using the 'fool' as a 'puffer' wouldn't knock the property down to him till my man brought out a wad of ten-pound notes – and ten-pound notes, as everyone knows, transform the biggest fool there is into a wise man. It turned out that this man had been doing some money-lending all his life, and, I am rather afraid, a spot of quiet blackmail too. After he got the shop and farm he shed his folly and his old torn coat and became a man of the world in real earnest.

I do not want to over-emphasize the cynical side of the 'playboy', but I cannot too strongly declare that practically all the acting of men of this description is done with a purpose. The laugh and the folly is the poor man's cloak of invisibility from his enemies and competitors.

I think that no sin is more to be condemned that that of putting the fool farther. It does keep them happy, but it is far better to grieve in truth than rejoice in the untrue. I myself cannot help when I meet a man – or even more so a woman – trying to awaken him to a realization of things as they are.

'People think that I'm a gay fellow,' said a man of the foolish kind to me one day after I had given him a sense of discomforting reality. 'I'm the funny fellow. I'm the funny fellow and I never had a day's pleasure in my life. Sometimes my heart does be breaking and still the people laugh.'

'Yes,' I said, 'but the fault is largely your own. Why can't you act serious and say the dull stupid things like everybody else?'

'You see the thing got in on me, it's a habit. Do you think that I never wanted to settle down and have a house of my own? Here I am, ferreting and doing a day's work here and a day's work there, living from hand to mouth, lying out drunk and no one to care a tuppenny damn whether I ever come in or not.'

My point is that there's no such thing as an authentic 'playboy'. Whatever of it there was or is is nothing more or less than the degradation of the poor. We have had novelists and playwrights like Lover, Lever, Lady Morgan and Synge, with no deep feeling for the essential dignity of humanity, who took the easy way out and just painted what was on the surface. The 'playboy' is dying out rapidly, and no lover of Ireland will be sorry. For his second name was Poverty.

(*The Standard*, 18 September 1942, pp. 3–4)

Paris in Aran

I bought the Penguin edition of the plays of Synge solely for the Introduction by W.R. Rodgers, for at a glance anyone could see that Mr Rodgers is a remarkable bucklepper. Sorry for using that word again, but it is the word that best fits this thing.

Mr Rodgers is a word-weaver, a phrase-maker the equal of any Radio Éireann writer.

There is something to be said for Rodgers' buckleppin' Irishness: he is out of touch with anything that may be called Irish and he is not good enough to live without a country.

Sometimes I am tempted to forget the Protestant friends of this paper and to cry 'What dreadful humbug Protestantism!' Then I remember all the bouncing Roman boys and I begin to wonder if stupidity and charlatanism has any particular religion.

But because of all this, Mr Rodgers is well qualified to introduce Synge: he is a Protestant clergyman, and Synge was connected with that profession.

What is the dominant note in Synge? I would say bitterly non-Irish. It all came from the basic insincerity upon which he built. A man should be true to himself first of all, for unless a man is true to himself the mould is false.

Synge never asked himself the fundamental question: where do I stand in relation to these people? Whether or not Synge portrayed the people of the West truly is not of much importance: as I say, it is the lie in his own heart that matters.

Daniel Corkery said that Synge failed to bridge the gulf between himself and the people because he was a Protestant. There is something in this but it is not all. Any man who is big enough and sincere enough is at one with every man.

Somerville and Ross were Protestants – in theory at any rate – but they evoked something valid in Irish life by their pantheism. The ditches and lanes come alive in Somerville and Ross. There is nothing as valid as that in Synge.

His peasants are picturesque conventions; the language he invented for them did a disservice to letters in this country by drawing our attention away from the common speech whose delightfulness comes from its very ordinariness. One phrase of Joyce is worth all Synge as far as giving us the cadence of Irish speech.

But what has been the most shocking has been the way that Synge's necessary mummerset was taken up by other Irish writers since.

Synge's way was the easy way; he just wasn't good enough to dig beneath the crust of the ordinary and find the romance that is not a mere invented phrase.

Returning to Mr Rodgers' Introduction I find him a marvellous follower of Synge – 'a community as rounded as the belly of a pebble one would pick up on a shore', 'the halter of hunger round their necks', 'tongue forked for praise or blame'.

Mr Rodgers says that Synge knew the Irish glens and hills as Yeats never did. I disagree. Yeats knew little of the Irish glens, hills or bogs, but he was a more sincere mind than Synge and got closer to the heart of the matter.

Synge provided Irish Protestants who are worried about being 'Irish' with an artificial country. One hates being sectarian in this matter, but it all springs from insincerity, and literature has to do with sincerity. It doesn't matter what so-called nationality you belong to.

I once mentioned this same insincerity in F.R. Higgins – the same word-weaving and phrase-making, the same unreality.

Yet in spite of his insincerity regarding himself Synge happened to be just good enough to overcome his defect to some extent. He wrote a few poems of merit, a wild kind of merit with a healthy extroversion such as

Seven dogs-days we let pass
Naming Queens in Glenmacnass

Mr Rodgers says that Synge's evangelical upbringing left his mark on him, and this is true. But when Rodgers says, 'His ascetic nature, his preoccupation with an insistence on "the truth", the living phrase, the real as opposed to the fanciful – all this was partly a legacy from his evangelical upbringing,' he is saying something that emphasizes Synge's insincerity. Synge neither took the living phrase nor the truth – that is speaking imaginatively, which is the only truth.

Synge's plays and writings would be tolerable to me if they had been set in Never-Never-Land, the Land in which the plays of Congreve and Sheridan are set, but one can never get away from the 'Irish' thing that hangs over them; we cannot forget that Synge in some way is claiming to portray real people.

All this raises an old pet argument of mine – the relationship of Catholicism to Irishness. On reflection perhaps this question no longer burns. It may well be that soon the fashion in nationalities will change: we may all begin to want to be Yorkshire or Scotch.

The average man requires a ready-made cloak with the clear pattern of his nation on it, for this gives the nonentity a distinction. For this purpose there should be lots of small nations.

As for Synge – detached from the phoney Irish atmosphere his plays are entertaining in a light way and he is a great master of mummery. Words are unnecessary, the action tells us all.

But on the higher levels of passion and sincerity he fails utterly. He is the originator of the bucklep and Mr W.R. Rodgers is one of his disciples.

There is one other item which will for some time to come keep the Irish act a living performance: as long as we remain provincial with London our metropolis there will always be a market for bogus Irishness. For the metropolis has never anything but contempt for its subservient provinces. The metropolis is not interested in the imaginative reality of provincial society: it only asks the provincial to perform. You get this metropolitan attitude in the London novel-reviewers who never fail to go into ecstasy over the fraudulent Irish novel. The authentic thing they look upon as indecent courage on the part of a man whose job is to entertain them. It was no accident that when Joyce's *Portrait of the Artist* came out in 1916 it was practically ignored by the London reviewers, as I discovered when I looked up the reviews of that time.

Donagh McDonagh, Walter Macken and of course W.R. Rodgers have brought this bogus Irishness to the London market and the result has been, and still is, that the genuine article born out of individual pride is passed by.

On the other hand, if it weren't for the artificial commodity there would be too little writing here and no such thing as Irish literature. There is no trouble turning out the conventionally Irish verse or play. I guarantee to teach any average intelligence how to compose – and compose is the word – a buckleppin' poem, play or story in a few lessons. Any man ought to be able to pump out of him extempore miles of stuff in the Radio Éireann–Abbey Theatre manner.

Since writing all this I have re-read *The Playboy* and I find – that Synge has imposed on the peasant women of Aran a psychology which is only to be found among the higher types of women. It is only the sophisticated, educated woman who has the courage to worship the hero, and I say this remembering the worship of film stars that is common among uneducated women. The repressed peasant has not the courage to go through with hero worship. Synge found Pegeen Mike among the sophisticated upper-middle-class women of Paris or Dublin and put her in an incongruous setting. From this point of view he has flattered the peasants.

(*Kavanagh's Weekly*, 7 June 1952, p. 7)

The Gallivanting Poet

Writing about F.R. Higgins is a problem – the problem of exploring a labyrinth that leads nowhere. There is also the problem of keeping oneself from accepting the fraudulent premises and invalid symbols established by the subject. The work of F.R. Higgins is based on an illusion – on a myth in which he pretended to believe.

The myth and illusion was 'Ireland'.

One must try to get some things straight about the man:

He was a Protestant.

He most desperately wanted to be what mystically, or poetically, does not exist, an 'Irishman'.

He wanted to be a droll, gallivanting 'Irishman'.

Nearly everything about Higgins would need to be put in inverted commas. All this was the essence of insincerity, for sincerity means giving all oneself to one's work, being absolutely real. For all his pleasant verse Higgins was a dabbler. It is not an easy thing being sincere; it takes courage, intelligence, and integrity. It is difficult to take seriously a man who could so consistently deceive himself.

The word 'gallivanting' appears throughout his verse.* The last thing you find in this Ireland is gallivanters. No doubt Synge made the gallivanter his theme, but for me Synge's characters and language are offen-

* One of Higgins' poems was called 'The Gallivanter'.

sive and humbuggish. The quality in Synge which excites has nothing to do with Irish peasants, and it survives in spite of their silliness.

It is well known that the sure way of making ourselves incapable of true feeling is by pretending that we have it. A true lover doesn't have to pretend being in love; on the contrary he is always pretending that he isn't in love, hoping thereby to auto-suggest the pain away. So by Higgins and his Irishness.

Somebody writing recently in the press described Higgins as a 'noble Protestant gentleman' – and I am not inclined to disagree about the final two words. The most valid aspect of the man was his Protestantism and, for all his gallivanting, his unIrishness.

In one of his poems he writes about what he calls 'Flock Mass', and throughout his work there are many allusions to Catholic ritual. If he were a really true poet he would not be always 'making out and the door shut', as the saying goes; he would have written about a Protestant church and a Protestant service – and while it might not be as droll, it would have the merit of being sincere.

You get the same thing among Irish Protestant writers in general. It is not without point that the fathers of 'Irish wit and humour' (more inverted commas, have nearly all been Protestants. They were trying to bypass Rome on their way to the heart of Ireland.

You have Lover, Lever, Lynn Doyle, George A. Birmingham and many others, all true Protestants pretending to be 'gay fellas'. Some of them, such as Lover, had genius and that makes all the difference. We hear the genius and we are not in 'Ireland' then but in the fairyland of poetry.

> *A mother came when stars were paling*
> *Wailing round a lonely spring.*
> *Thus she cried while tears were falling*
> *Calling on the Fairy King.*

Their Protestantism has been a great tribulation to Irish writers of that persuasion. Alone of modern Irish writers Yeats got there merely by being himself, by being a sincere poet. He dug deep beneath the variegated surface to where the Spirit of Poetry is one with Truth. I say this with reservations, but none the less it is largely true. O'Casey turned Communist, which is the real Protestantism of our time.

Another development of the Protestant writer's dilemma is to be found in his attempt to build up the idea of Dublin as a spiritual entity – the Dublin of Swift, Berkeley, Gogarty, Joyce, and 'Larry-the-night-before-he-was-stretched'. This was really gerrymandering the constituencies of the soul so as to segregate disagreeable elements and to provide one's own narrow outlook with a safe seat.

Most of us at one time or another have allowed ourselves to pretend that we believed in the mystique of the Nation or the City State. It is not an adult attitude though it can be amusing. Higgins is full of this nonsense. His *Deuce of Jacks* has it for theme. A man of genius can focus on a narrow facet of the soul and yet suggest the complete picture of Mankind. Fools only see that he focused on the narrow facet and they think that narrow facet the all-important. They say for instance: 'Only a Dublinman can understand Joyce.' But in so far as Joyce is a writer of genius the Dublin part of his work is of very superficial importance. Yeats wrote of names like Swift, Berkeley, Parnell, but in so far as he is a true poet these names could as validly have been Chinese.

It is not very easy to base a critical argument on the work of a man when it is so unreal, so unrelated to any values we know.

Even the man's name is doubtful. Somebody once told me that while travelling with Higgins in Meath the poet inquired of an old man regarding the great Irish family of the Higginses and the old man said: 'The name wasn't Higgins, it was Huggins, and they were an English family.' The whole point is that the name wouldn't have mattered a hoot – he could be called X Y Z – if he didn't himself think it mattered. And when he based his whole work on this heresy one can realize what a shadowy foundation and a shadowy building his achievement is.

He didn't dig.

He wrote one short play called *A Deuce of Jacks* and he wrote a couple of short stories, but when he died his principal achievement as a writer was the poems contained in his last collection, *The Gap of Brightness*.

Yet of these poems one can say very little. There is no direction in them. They give pleasure, but not the highest poetic pleasure, for the highest poetic pleasure consists in giving new direction to men's imaginations, in freeing new worlds for men. Growth, development, is true pleasure.

You get all this growth and development in Yeats. His own poems may not have the qualities of greatest endurance, but they have a vitalizing effect on the reader. He makes poets of his readers as all genuine poems do.

The nearest thing to a really sincere utterance Higgins achieved is probably 'Father and Son':

> *Only last week, walking the hushed fields*
> *Of our most lovely Meath, now thinned by November,*
> *I came to where the road from Laracor leads*
> *To the Boyne river – that seemed more lake than river,*
> *Stretched in uneasy light and stript of weeds.*

This is charming, but it lacks passion. Though he is writing about his father one feels that the poem is a composition rather than a spontaneous creation. You get this careful artificial construction in all his poems. Somewhere he writes of a cord 'knotted over a parcelled earth'. But I am afraid there is nothing in the parcel.

One of Higgins' best-known poems is his lament for Pádraic Ó Conaire, also an interesting *composition*.

> *They've paid the last respects in sad tobacco*
> *And silent is this wakehouse in its haze,*
> *They've paid the last respects; and now their whiskey*
> *Flings laughing words on mouths of prayer and praise.*

There is no impact in this. There is no urge behind it, and no grief. As poetry I must say that I get nothing out of it.

Looking through the poems I find everywhere the signs of the poet's false premises, his insincerity.

> *When sap ebbed low and your green days were over –*
> *Hedging a gap to rugged land,*
> *Bare-skinned and straight you were: and there I broke you*

To champion my right hand.

There is little vividness here, nothing to make us believe that Higgins felt the thorns of a living blackthorn bush. A good poet would not tell you about a blackthorn stick, he would show you the blackthorn. In fact this blackthorn is only a symbol of his phoney Ireland.

Just why Higgins' fake Ireland has devitalized his work may appear odd when one sees how a writer like Congreve can set the spirit dancing in an utterly fake society. Similarly with Ben Jonson and many others. The trouble is that Higgins was self-deceived by his fake world. These others rise on the wings of their fantasy above the earth where all things are born to die.

Sometimes Higgins, willy-nilly, releases the spirit of poetry from a background which has no social or national reality. It is not present in great abundance, but even a little of it is the stuff that endures. Perhaps the following is very like mere word-weaving, word-magic, but I think it is something more.

> *O were I a wife with herds,*
> *Found by the light of strange money:*
> *One nursing a speckle of fields*
> *On the mountain earth,*
> *They'd give me no sin of limb*
> *To cleanse on a Garlic Sunday –*
> *No scandal to sharpen my name*
> *By gable or hearth.*

What this means on the plane of reason I do not know, but it gives me a curious sort of pleasure.

A similar sort of pleasure is to be found in that poem about Meath:

> *Where soft grass gives the udders comeliness,*
> *Before late milking time in Meath or Carlow,*
> *Come, MacNamara, in whiskey let us bless*
> *The pastured royalties of Tara.*

What is getting me down as I write these words is the futility of all this verse, its meaninglessness. We have reached a point where we cannot continue this pleasant dabbling. A poet must be going somewhere. He must be vitalizing the spirit of man in some way. He must have dug deep beneath the poverty-stricken crust of our time and uncovered new veins of – uranium, the uranium of faith and hope, a transcendent purpose.

Now is the time for silent prayer and long fasting. Literature as we have known it has come to the end of its tether.

It can be said for Higgins that he wrote before the final disillusionment. In his day it was still possible to believe that pleasant dabbling in verse, word-weaving, white-magic, was enough.

And as I run through his poems again I find all the time the illusion of an illusion which means nothing to us. And instead of dwelling on the work of Higgins I find my mind wandering to the sincere voice of Auden, expressing the despair of his time.

> *About suffering they were never wrong*
> *The Old Masters; how well they understood*
> *Its human position.*

This may seem a deviation from the subject, though I do not think so. There you have the humility of our time, our pity.

By flinging ourselves prostrate before God and admitting our dire distress we may be admitted to a new dispensation. The best poets are those who lie prostrate before God. But poets like Higgins keep on pretending that the futile decoration on the walls is enough for the day.

Oh for the kick of Reality.

How the various verse-writers in this country can go on doodling and dabbling, unconscious of our real need, is to my mind pathetic. Chesterton made a remark which is applicable to them: 'The trouble with our sages (poets) is not that they cannot see the answer; it is that they cannot see the riddle.'

Higgins grew up in an Ireland which had only recently been invented. There were cheering revivalists (of what we now cannot say) and a general bedlam going on which gave everyone the notion that great spiritual activity was in the air. It was like the old charlatan Sequa who used to go around the country curing people of their rheumatism. The patient was brought into a tent where a band was blaring and there he was rubbed and shouted at till he forgot his pain. Home he went without his crutches only to find that the cold of the journey home had revived his rheumatism. That is what has happened to us. On the hysteria of nationalistic charlatanism we can shout away our pain no longer. We must dig. Many Irish writers came into being on the wings of this hysteria, but when the day of reckoning came they were found without a penny in their pockets, the pennies of experience.

> *She genuflects; and our new priest*
> *Looks – only to falter in the Mass;*
> *Even the altar boy has ceased*
> *And his responses, now, alas,*
> *Are not 'amen' – but towards the door*
> *He seems to sigh:* a stoir, a stoir.

That is pure Protestantism posing as Catholicism. From no theological view but merely from the view of sincerity I find this from 'Flock Mass' painful. Many Catholics have written about the Mass from the common worshipper's viewpoint, yet even when, like Joyce, they seemed blasphemous, or, like Carleton, comic, no one could doubt that they were writing from the inside. And that is the main difference between journalism and literature. The journalist tells you about something; the poet stands inside the thing and cries how it hurts him.

Again I search through these poems for something sharply felt, sharply visualized, something seen intimately, not generally, and I am being disappointed.

> *O Hawks claw-clinched and bronze-plated*
> *On your sun-splintered forts,*
> *Brave winds be your perch to blaze on*
> *The crows in our pastured slopes.*

I cannot see those hawks or those slopes. Everything is too general, not precise. He does not strike the note of a personal experience that is universal. He writes about what appears on the crust which he has not broken. No sap flows here.

In a word, Higgins did not experience vividly. One cry from the blood would be worth all this superficial stuff.

On a lower plane of criticism Higgins comes off well enough. But when I was young I read with something of enchantment things like –

> *Now that the grey wet of the road makes quiet*
> *Each step we take, ah, there can float*
> *No stir on the air, but the stir of a cuckoo*
> *Hopping its double note.*

Considering this one finds that it has vividness; the road comes alive in our imaginations. And it has magic, too, something that cannot be analyzed, something that does free the imagination. Such moments are rare in Higgins, but the fact that they are there at all makes him worthy of serious consideration.

Personally, Higgins was like his verse. He carried the gallivanting pose into his ordinary life. He pronounced poetry 'poertry' and drawled humorously. One gets weary of such posing and longs for the simple reality of a man. I hate being cruel to his memory, but I cannot get away from the thought that he never became adult and sincere.

He always had a joke for a companion. He always gave a man the pleasant answer. Perhaps I didn't know him well enough; there may have been depths of pathetic sincerity in the man which I missed. I never thought him a droll or gallivanting fellow for all his acting; and meeting an illusion always tired me.

He was to my cute, countrified way of thinking at the time a practical, slightly embittered person, one not particularly friendly to Catholicism – or to Ireland. He did love 'Ireland' of course.

He wrote three other books besides *The Gap of Brightness*. They are *Island Blood*, *The Dark Breed*, and *Arable Holdings*. Poems from all three are to be found in the last collection. His play, *A Deuce of Jacks*, appeared in the *Dublin Magazine* but was not published in book form I think.

He was a poor man all his life. He began as a messenger boy. He worked in Brooks Thomas, Dublin, and organized a strike there – which at least showed an awareness of life. Afterwards he made a living by editing a trade journal, dull work surely. In the end he was made Manager of the Abbey Theatre. He was 'educated in country schools' according to *Who's Who*, which probably means a National School education.

It may have been this background and this wearing existence that embittered him and made him clutch more tightly about him the cloak that was his pose of the gay gallivanting Irishman.

He was influenced by Yeats and by Hyde's *Love Songs of Connaught*. If he had lived he might have dared to shed the cloak and give utterance to something small, maybe, but very real – himself.

NOTE: The editors suggest that my thesis gives the impression that I think a Protestant cannot be an Irish writer, and have asked if I would disclaim such a theory.

My immediate reaction would be: Who wants to be an Irish writer!

A man is what he is, and if there is some mystical quality in the Nation or the race it will ooze through his skin. Many Protestants, doubting that their Irishism would ooze, have put it on from the outside. National characteristics are superficial qualities and are not the stuff with which the poet deals. The subject matter of the poet is the Universal and in this he is one with Catholicism. By a peculiar paradox the pursuit of the Universal and fundamental produces the most exciting local colour as well. In desiring to be 'Irish' a man is pursuing the non-essential local colour. 'Seek first the Kingdom of God and its justice and all things will be added.'

That Protestants can have the authentic local coloration is proved by such names as Standish O'Grady, Dunsany, O'Casey. But they didn't consciously desire this.

(*Irish Writing*, December 1947, pp. 62–70)

James Joyce

I find it difficult to form any particular opinion about Joyce. I have one advantage over certain others: I was never an original admirer of Joyce and so have not had the normal reaction, that readjusting of one's values which is common in regard to one's enthusiasms. It often happens in the case of a person with whom we were in love. We react violently to right the balance. I read *Ulysses* for the first time about seven years ago. Since then it has been my second-favourite bedside book.

What I think a mistake is reading deep symbolism into *Ulysses*, drawing comparisons. *Ulysses* is a very funny book and it is also a very wearying book. It is almost entirely a transcription of life. Joyce added nothing – except possibly Stephen, and he gave us Stephen completely in the *Portrait*.

There is nothing wrong with Joyce, who, as Chesterton said about someone else, is sane enough; it is his commentators who are mad.

Almost the most outstanding quality in Joyce is his Catholicism, or rather his anti-Protestantism. Joyce, through Stephen in the *Portrait*, must have done more damage to Protestantism than any modern apologist.

His reason made him a bad Catholic but, whatever the defects of Catholicism, he saw that Protestantism was a compendium of all those defects.

There was nothing in Joyce's life of noble self-sacrifice – except the fact that he went off with a penniless girl. Perhaps it was the artist in him which gave this kink to his character.

Yet I am constantly reminded of the number of writers who achieved the depths of Hell's despair simply because they happened to get a woman without the spondulecs. I could name a score of dramatic tragedies from literature and from life which could have been solved by money. O'Casey's *Juno and the Paycock* couldn't exist if the Will hadn't been botched or they had won the Sweep. Everywhere I find this problem, which most people attribute to some tremendous integrity. This may be so, for the ways of God are strange and He sometimes makes a man turn away from the door of Midas's counting-house. It has happened to myself. I am nearly incapable of not falling out with anyone who isn't as poor as myself. If Joyce had had a thousand a year would he have written *Ulysses* as he did?

Prosperity takes a lot of the bitterness out of life. It is more than possible that an affluent Joyce could not have remembered with the same awful hate that boon companion in the canary waistcoat, Buck Mulligan. And there is also Mr Deasy, whose wonderful thumbnail portrait we might have lost.

It seems to me that God, through the agency of society, manages to breed a race of artists by the process of starvation and all kinds of indignity due to poverty. Is it not on the cards that an artist can be bred artificially in this way? Or must he have the kink in him originally?

He has got to hate society, that is nearly certain.

Remember Dante exiled; Goethe crying: 'Beware of what you pray for in youth for you will get it in middle age.' Ah, yes, the story of men who, generally against their wills, were miserable.

Sometimes you get the artificial breed, who betakes himself to a mews where, on a stretcher bed, he subsists on a diet of brown bread and champagne. But these are the phonies who love society and who are loved by it. So it appears that my theory of artificial artistic insemination does not work out.

> *Art is Life squeezed through a repression.*
> *Milton, Homer, blind.*

Byron and Shelley, two wealthy men, did manage to achieve misery and sudden death.

Joyce and Eliot have a good deal in common: they are both materialists, which may be one reason why they have become a fashion. Society knows where it stands with mere matter. (I am not too sure of my argument here: society has also a deep affection for the immaterial.) What I am trying to say is that Joyce has little or none of that ethereal commodity known as inspiration. He is the very clever, cynical man who has found a formula. In the end, this introvert formula which feeds on itself exhausts its material. A true creator is always trying to be a little more than matter.

Finnegans Wake is the delirium of a man with no more to say. He has melted down even the matrix.

> *You, Cochrane, what city sent for him?*
> *Tarentum, sir.*

There is in this writing here a strange, intangible quality which helps to destroy my argument. There is something which enlarges the imagination, excites the reader creatively.

But the *Portrait of the Artist* is Joyce's testament.

And yet, as I read through some of the more violent parts of *Ulysses*, I feel that Joyce is an unmannerly child enjoying destruction. Hate and pride. It is a form of idealism. We feel that when the cities are flattened and civilization destroyed something better will arise. It is a delusion.

> *The fabled daughters of memory are all pastiche,*
> *God born clean we desire*
> *But thoughts are sin and words are soiled*
> *And Nietzchean blood is syphilitic.*

> *The children delight in levelling the city,*
> *Violently tear down the walls*
> *Screeching from the steps of a ruin*
> *Where a broken milk bottle rolls.*

('Diary', *Envoy*, April 1951, pp. 70–2)

Coloured Balloons:
A Study of Frank O'Connor

The gossip instinct has a great desire to know the private man behind the public man, though such revelations are seldom of much importance. I had better, however, put down a number of facts about the man. Frank O'Connor, our most exciting writer, was born in Cork city in the early years of this century. He went to a national school. To this national school came as a teacher a man named Daniel Corkery. The pupils who up till then had been feeding on the meaningless dope of serfs were shocked to find written on the blackboard in Corkery's meaningful handwriting:

> *Breathes there the man with soul so dead*
> *Who never to himself hath said:*
> *This is my own, my native land.*

Judged on the highest spiritual plane these lines of Scott are heretical, but they served a purpose: they awakened one man at least.

On leaving the national school O'Connor, whose father was a workingman, got a job as a messenger porter at the railway station, another of his important contacts with the mother Earth.

Shortly after this O'Connor's contacts with the healthy clay became less tangible. He became a writer at an early age – too early perhaps.

Some of his early poems which appeared in the Poet's Corner of the *Weekly Independent* are extremely adult for a young man. Here are some lines about the Táin:

> *Singers there were who went down to their graves*
> *Leaving songs immemorial behind*
> *Which scattered to the waters and the wind*
> *Were blown to shore at last by angry waves.*

In 1922 he, with O'Faoláin, took the Republican side in the Civil War, and his early stories, like O'Faoláin's, are based on those experiences. Unlike O'Faoláin's, however, O'Connor's lack the somewhat cynical objectivity which the theme demanded.

Next we find him interned. The internment camp was for him the equivalent of a university. There among his fellow internees were to be found a number of men with questioning minds, such as Mr Sean T. O'Kelly, who lent him the novels of Anatole France. During the internment a well-meaning Quaker, in an attempt to lead these men to a life of non-resistance, sent in copies of AE's newly founded *Irish Statesman*. In this way O'Connor made contact with the humanist side of letters and with Yeats. He contributed poems, stories and reviews of Gaelic plays to this paper, and these are all full of the warm imagination of young genius. But they also suffer from a serious defect which can, I think, be attributed to the influence of Yeats. Yeats created a pose of swift indifference to the common earth, and the same isolation in the thin air of 'literature' is to be found in O'Connor. To read him now was never to imagine that he had once lived in a poor street in Cork or worked at a draughty railway station. No man more successfully detached himself from his background. Yeats could carry this pose well enough, though whether or not it hasn't invalidated much of his work is another matter. However, Yeats was a poet somewhat independent of what we may call the common earth. It would not be entirely true to say that O'Connor had entirely detached himself from his background, but he dimmed it into a literary mist.

The Yeatsian pose of aristocracy suited Yeats, for the pose fitted him perfectly. It was the essence of Yeats's verse. O'Connor also attempted in his own verse the ruthless hammer-blow arrogance of the older poet.

In the meantime O'Connor became a librarian and more and more poised on the ridge-tiles of the literary house of cards – above ordinary life.

'He has his roots in the soil' is a well-known phrase and people who say it generally mean that the man was born and reared in a country place. But the real soil in which a man's roots are is the soil of common experience. You can follow the tracks of the writer whose feet are in that soil – Blake, Wordsworth, Milton, Shelley or Yeats – their clay trail is the trail we can follow. The man who wrote –

> *Tiger, tiger burning bright*
> *In the forests of the night*
> *What immortal hand or eye*
> *Could frame thy fearful symmetry?*

was writing out of the pain of living, living close to the bone. And the same is true of Milton.

> *When I consider how my life is spent.*

However high they raised their mystical heads they all had their feet on the clay earth. That is why they felt the electric shock. Can one say the same of O'Connor?

As I pursue him I am continually losing the trail. Has he a direction? His feet are too seldom on the earth for me to follow. Is he merely a high-flying entertainer? Does his work hold the mirror up to life? Does he mean anything?

All these questions can only be answered by an examination of O'Connor's work. He began as a poet and his first book, published in 1931 by the Cuala Press, comprised translations from the Gaelic. This very fact that he began as a translator is somewhat of a key to his work – that his technical and imaginative machinery is greater than his material. For, like a great actor who is useless without a theme, O'Connor is inclined to be futile when left with only his own experience. Surely nobody has ever done such exciting translations as he has. What a lovely cadence he brings to his re-creation of an Egan O'Rahilly poem. How warmly human, rooted in life, when compared with the metaphysics of Stephens' translations.

> *And a bright enchanted mist fell over the land*
> *From Cork of harbours to Galway of pearls and thrones,*
> *From root to crown there was fruit upon every tree,*
> *Acorns on oaks and clear cold honey on stones.*

Root and crown are in these verses where the writer had material sufficient for his technical skill. His own original verse, which afterwards was published in a volume called *Three Old Brothers,* is obvious, honest verse. He uses a Yeatsian technique – the adjectiveless bang, bang of nouns. But what in the hands of Yeats becomes magic in O'Connor's use of it becomes a dumb wooden mallet:

> *While some goes dancing reels and some*
> *Goes stuttering love in ditches,*
> *The three old brothers rise from bed,*
> *And moan, and pin their breeches.*

Yeats, who knew what he wanted – he wanted the touch of the earth – could write about prosier things than this and make them sound wonderful, for he could produce that verbal tension, holding a thin or obvious truth till it seemed like the wisdom of the world. The same tension is to be found in Hopkins. O'Connor has it in his prose where its value is less. As a poet he can only be seriously considered as a translator from the Gaelic. His actor's ability to give body and life to somebody else's ideas is shown by these translations.

O'Connor has written two novels but his reputation is rightly founded on his short stories. The first collection of his short stories to be published was *Guests of the Nation,* based on his experiences in the Civil War. These stories touch the earth at more points than any of his other work, and yet for all that they lack a very vivid detail. Granted that O'Connor is right in his protest against Corkery's claim that writing should be merely representative, is there enough poetic excitement and vitality in these stories to compensate for the dimness of the representation? He seems to me to fall between two stools. He is neither on the safe earth nor among the stars. What makes his work deceptive is the fact that he is very nearly on the earth. He is – as it were – about an inch from the top of the grass. We have had many writers of this kind here – from Canon Sheehan to Seumas O'Kelly. If one says that these are utterly unreal one will be wrong, for they do on rare occasions put their toes down on the earth. *Guests of the Nation* has in lieu of real blood a good deal of the treacle of sentimentality, as has Sheehan and Seumas O'Kelly and the minor ones such as Francis MacManus.

The title story in *Guests of the Nation* reveals the O'Connor to come. The main characters, two English soldiers held as hostages by the IRA to be executed, are a pair of clichéd sentimental characters – the dumb, good-natured Englishmen. They evoke our maudlin pity. What is worse, they evoke the author's pity; he himself weeps over their deaths and in this he lacks the courage and integrity of the great artist.

> I alone of the crowd saw Donovan raise his Webley to the back of 'Awkins' neck, and as he did so I shut my eyes and tried to say a prayer. 'Awkins had begun to say something else when Donovan let fly, and as I opened my eyes at the bang, I saw him stagger at the knees and lie out flat at Noble's feet, slowly, and as quiet as a child, with the lantern-light falling sadly upon his lean legs and bright farmer's boots. We all stood very still for a while watching him settle out in the last agony.

The fact that the story is told through a third party, a participant in the affair, does not excuse the author making him take sides in the tragedy. The whole thing makes us sick and unbelieving. Neither is the vivid detail which lights up the whole scene present. There are too many words, too much 'literature', and the final effect is enervation.

The house among the mountains where the hostages are being held and where they all sit around playing cards is seen only vaguely. The story gives the impression that the author had only got one look at the place and wasn't deeply impressed. The authentic note is seldom struck. Everything is partly believable in and there is its danger. I haven't got by me the stories of Carleton, but if anyone wishes to see the sharp vivid reality which convinces not only on the earth level but on the higher levels he should read those stories. O'Connor, I gather, does not like Carleton, which disappoints me, for it cannot be said too often that Carleton is by far the greatest delineator of life Ireland has produced.

In some of these stories there is a charming poetic atmosphere, but even it is always half and half. You cannot damn it without being wrong and you cannot praise without being equally wrong.

His first novel *The Saint and Mary Kate* is a charming idyll of young people in Cork city. It is lyrical in a thin way. The heroine is a sentimental character. She is closely observed and heavily documented, but the lot doesn't add up to a fully alive human being. Once again you have that inch, which is as bad as a mile, between its dangling feet and the earth. You can discern the characters moving vaguely beneath the literary skin. In so far as our straining eyes can pick out the landmarks this is something of a revelation of life in Cork – or anywhere. What I enjoy about *The Saint* are the too occasional episodes into which the author has put without stinting prudence the essence of his experience. The hero says, and he is expressing the naïve innocence of every young boy:

'... if I kissed you it would mean I was going to marry you.'
'No, it wouldn't,' she retorted promptly. 'You could kiss a girl without marrying her.'
'I couldn't,' he said between his teeth.

This is absolutely enchanting, pure O'Connor and so, pure everyman. It is equal to the scene in Carleton's 'Denis O'Shaughnessy Going to Maynooth', between the young Denis and his girl. So gay and so happy. Unfortunately there is a lot of descriptive stuff in the novel, a desperate straining to give us all the facts about the girl.

'There's something I wanted to ask you, Bridie love,' said Mary Kate coaxingly, feeling the table behind her with her hands and lifting herself on to it.

There is delayed-action in this. It hasn't the directness that one finds in the greatest writing. It is hardly to be wondered at that O'Connor is an admirer of Jane Austen, whose delayed-action tricks give such an illusion of cunning, subtlety and delicious wit, and whose brilliant handling of what isn't worth handling has such an appeal for the middle class who delight in brilliant technique with the minimum of reality.

Trying to follow O'Connor's indeterminate trail among the active cultural forces I find him attempting to get his feet on the earth for a number of years. He becomes director of the Abbey Theatre, author of plays; and nowhere more than here is his lack of acquaintance with common earth more evident. Just when one is looking forward to his having a great career he leaves the earth altogether. He was under the influence of Yeats at this time; one man's integrity is another man's compromise; and so it was with O'Connor. In spite of his unearthly pose Yeats had a real sense of direction. At times he may have appeared to temporize, but on the fundamental issues he always brought the sword of judgment down without fear. He flung the Fays out when they sought to seize the Theatre for the actor and in general his sense of direction was perfect. O'Connor has a poor sense of direction, and a very dim consciousness of purpose. He seemed to carry a Yeatsian pose which did not fit. He was not himself. He was not on the ground. He has written and spoken a good deal of what seems unsound about the theatre – temporizing with ideas of actors and audience. A man with a philosophy is ruthless, tyrannical. He must never be in doubt. O'Connor is nearly always in doubt. The sum of his travels in the active cultural life of this country has been futility. His trail, which I have tried to follow, is a footprint here and there, going round in circles.

Now let us return to his main line, the short stories. He has hardly ever written a story that is not entertaining. He has hardly ever written a story that does not bear some resemblance to reality. But as in his novels and other work there is a 'kitchening' of the material, a tentativeness. He is a showman, getting the laughs where he can, but from the more serious point of view purposeless. His second collection of short stories, called *Bones of Contention*, has a number of very enjoyable pieces. 'The Majesty of the Law' is a burlesque as brilliant as O'Kelly's 'Weaver's Grave'. An old man who has cracked a neighbour's skull is waiting to go to jail to spite a neighbour whose 'wake, wandering, watery eyes' are looking down on the scene. This is the best of comedy, and like the majority of comic writing it is detached – from Life. The main character is a lie, the sort of good-natured myth which makes good-natured fools open-mouthed, uncritical, say: 'Aren't these Irish charming?' The author is in that particular mood which most of us have experienced to our spiritual cost in which we are being corrupted by our audience. On such occasions a mob's collective lie is in our mouths.

I have heard O'Connor compared to Chekhov. No two writers could be more unlike. Chekhov's genius is the cutting edge of sincerity ruthlessly piercing through the crust of the ordinary. His courageous poetic mind is never the slave of his audience. One can see it in all Chekhov's work – the continual surprise which vexes so many people who want a writer to run true to form. O'Faoláin is much closer to the Chekhov mentality. It is interesting to note that Chekhov comes across to us entirely on the strength of the cutting edge of his mind; the magic of his language is naturally lost in translation. Translation is a good test for the reality of a work.

One of the best stories in *Bones of Contention* is 'In the Train'. This is about a group of people who are returning from a court trial:

> 'Ah, Delancey is a poor slob,' the Sergeant said affectionately.
>
> 'Oh, yes, but that's not enough, Jonathan. Slob or no slob he should make an attempt. He's a young man; he should have a dinner-jacket at least. What sort of wife will he get if he won't even wear a dinner-jacket?'
>
> 'He's easy, I'd say. He's after a farm in Waterford.'
>
> 'Oh, a farm! A farm! The wife is only an incidental, I suppose?'

There you have O'Connor 'on the cod' with his characters. I feel as I read that he has never allowed himself to be involved in the lives of these people. He is an outsider even more than Synge was in this thing. It is the prudent mind carefully spreading the material thin. This is pure fiction, an invention. Relating it to life, what would the crude unliterary self in us say? We would say that it was great fun but meant nothing as a revelation of life.

'First Confession' is a popular story, but sentimental. I would say that O'Faoláin, even when he appears anti-clerical, is much nearer to the Catholic mind. Throughout all O'Connor's stories I am being continually mesmerized by the easy hum-hum of the narrative. Sometimes he says things which may shock, but they are artificial shocks as when he takes pleasure in the weakness of human beings. The creative shock of truth revealed is a different thing. His next collection of stories is *Crab Apple Jelly*, and it is a very jelly-like book.

One of the stories is called 'Bridal Night' and is about a girl who went to bed with a madman to cure him:

> 'And isn't it a strange and wonderful thing? From that day to the day she left us there did no one speak a bad word about what she did, and the people couldn't do enough for her. Isn't it a strange thing and the world as wicked as it is, that no one would say the bad word about her?'

I agree that the action of the girl does throw some light on human nature, but the reactions of the people to her, as O'Connor presents them, are just nonsense. It is too abnormal, a 'special' case. Dostoevsky's supposed abnormalities are merely intensities of the normal, but here we are dealing with the aberrations of disease. This story seems phoney and in keeping with the Synge-like style. The principal story in this book is the 'Long Road to Ummera', a frightfully sentimental account of an old woman's wish to be buried in her native place.

> Always in the evenings you saw her shuffle up the road to Miss O's for her little jug of porter, a shapeless lump of an old woman in a plaid shawl faded to the colour of snuff that dragged her head down on to her bosom ...

That is really the limit of treacly sentimentality. She just sickens me. As sticky as Marie Corelli.

Another story is about a pious old fraud and what the New Teacher thought about him:

> 'Extraordinary man,' said Sam, nodding his fat head, 'extraordinary blooming man, making a will like that.'

'He was,' Johnnie agreed a bit doubtfully. 'Of course, he was always very religious.'

'He was,' said Sam drily, 'particularly with Children of Mary.'

'That so?' said Johnnie, as if he had never heard of a Child of Mary before.

I am afraid I find an implied sneer, an insincerity, in this. A great poet never sneers. He may show people sneering but he does not take part in it as the author of this seems to take part. You cannot satirize fraudulent piety unless you stand on some dogmatic centre of truth. This is necessary even as a hypothesis. In so far as O'Connor has a centre it is in his unholy laughter, which is fairly constant.

It would be hard to overpraise the skill with which the stories in O'Connor's latest book, *The Common Chord*, are composed. Yet, these sexy stories are utterly unreal. How often as I read did I wish that the author could have thrown in a few spadefuls of the earth's healthy reality – roots, stones, worms, dung. In this patch intelligence could grow. It will be observed that the greatest writers never take themselves seriously – only their work. O'Connor takes himself seriously but his characters lightly. A Calvinistic leer grins from every page. O'Connor's Nora Lalors, Tim O'Regans, etc., are not people but silly 'attitudes' which are to be found less in Ireland than in a war-hysterical England, and their intellectual level is that of the gossip columns of the *Daily Mirror*.

Passing an interim judgment on O'Connor I find that he is a purveyor of emotional entertainment, and that he has surrendered to this minor role. There is tension in his mind, but most of this tension is expended on the construction of the container so that there is little left for the contents. He is like a powerful engine drawing a light load. The same is true of many writers who have achieved great contemporary fame – Joyce is a good example. Every generation produces fine technicians, designers, entertainers. But time destroys the tension of the wrapping paper, which their contemporaries mistook for inner excitement, leaving the dusty contents to be blown by the wind.

(*The Bell*, December 1947, pp. 11–21)

My Three Books

[…] Some good books have appeared within the past year or so, for instance *Kon-Tiki*.* But will *Kon-Tiki* be remembered in twenty years? I doubt it. The pressure of new generations of books is very intense.

Kon-Tiki was a good adventure story and yet something is missing in it – inevitability. The Kon Tiki expedition was a dilettante's expedition, but the pursuit of the White Whale in *Moby-Dick* was inevitable. It is one of my three, or possibly four, books. The other two, with the third fighting for its existence, are *Gil Blas*, *Ulysses* – and Knut Hamsun's *Wanderers*. I have read all these books scores of times and they are always new. When having a cup of tea I bring down my *Moby-Dick* and prop it against the typewriter and read as if for the first time:

> Days, weeks passed, and under easy sail, the ivory *Pequod* had slowly swept across four several cruising-grounds: that off the Azores; off the Cape de Verdes; on the Plate (so called), being off the mouth of the Rio de la Plata; and the Carrol Ground, an unstaked, watery locality, southerly from St Helena.
>
> It was while gliding through these latter waters that one serene and moonlight night … a silvery jet was seen far in advance of the white bubbles at the bow. Lit up by the moon, it

* Thor Heyerdahl, *The Kon-Tiki Expedition by Raft across the South Seas*, translated from the Norwegian by T.H. Lyon (London, 1950).

looked celestial; seemed some plumed and glittering god upris-
ing from the sea. Fedallah first descried this jet. For of these
moonlight nights, it was his wont to mount to the main-mast
head and stand look out there, with the same precision as if it
had been day ...

There is something of the mystery of the sea in this that is not in *Kon-
Tiki*. *Moby-Dick* is only incidentally about the sea and fundamentally
about the soul. Melville had the courage of the true poet; indeed he was
a very great poet and *Moby-Dick* is one of the great epics of all time.
Some critic has said that it shares with *Ulysses* the fame of being one of
the two greatest works in English prose fiction.

Ulysses, too, is only incidentally about Dublin and fundamentally
the history of a soul.

Shallow writers, that is writers without the courage to be true to
themselves, are afraid to drift from the main plot, the external story is
of no value except as the frame for a man's own reality.

Proust had this courage too.

The same critic who called *Moby-Dick* one of the greatest works in
English prose fiction also referred to *Moby-Dick*'s symbolic meaning.
The White Whale is the spirit of evil. Symbolism of this kind when it
is authentic is never deliberate; it is willy-nilly in all great works: it is in
Hans Andersen and only slightly in *Ulysses*, but it is there just the same.

Melville, the author of *Moby-Dick*, wrote a few other books after his
masterpiece, but they were ignored. *Moby-Dick* was that one book
which is supposed to be in every man. There should be no professional
writers. A man writes his one great book and is thereby led into the
field of professional letters. He is expected to keep up an output.

The friendship between the author and Queequeg, the Indian, is
one of the most beautiful in literature. And yet one wonders if there is
such a man as Queequeg, the simple unspoiled child of nature. There
isn't, but there is the ideal.

Now, as I before hinted, I have no objection to any person's religion, be it what it may, so long as that person does not kill or
insult any other person, because that other person don't believe

it also. But when a man's religion becomes really frantic: when it is a positive torment to him; and, in fine, makes this earth of ours an uncomfortable inn to lodge in: then I think it high time to take that individual aside and argue the point with him.

And just so I now did with Queequeg. 'Queequeg,' said I, 'get into bed now, and lie and listen to me ... hell is an idea first born on an undigested apple-dumpling; and since then perpetuated through the hereditary dyspepsias nurtured by Ramadans.'

But it is the sea, for all that, that is the hero of Melville's book. There are vast expanses of ocean and thousands of fish in Thor Heyerdahl's book, but Eternity is in Melville's. Melville's horizons are limitless.

When gliding by the Bashee isles we emerged at last upon the great South Sea: were it not for other things, I could have greeted my dear Pacific with uncounted thanks, for now the long supplication of my youth was answered: that serene ocean rolled eastwards from me a thousand leagues of blue.

The great merit of Melville's book is that it enlarges the world for us: it brings us through the ivory gates into the expansive world of the imagination. The world is still large. We can find the same expansiveness in a small field. To get to know even a small field is a lifetime's exploration.

I remember myself standing on the top of a hill and looking east up a valley a mile distant from Swanzy's Bog and I sometimes promised that one day I would visit that distant place which I remembered walking through in childhood. But other places called: I owed a visit to the corner where there were stepping stones across the stream at the junction of four fields. Part of my life was there, the happiest part. On many a summer's day I had sat in that corner taking a rest after cutting bolthans (ragwort) with an old scythe. That would be the month of July. How lazy I was too. And yet – how it breaks the heart to contemplate that time! I was complete, grown-up, and yet I was lost in the fog. No man knows the curve his destiny takes. Yet my destiny seems so commonplace, but it is not.

I can feel the hard, sun-baked earth under me. I can see the wiry grass that grows on the scrugan in Caffrey's field. Those fields are there still, and the deep sunken stream that gave us such trouble is there still and the view through the hedge of the plain of Muirthemne right out to the Irish Sea at Annagassan. If only I could go back and be a little more awake and aware.

There is no going back.

The happiness in that life consisted in its unconsciousness. When we are unconscious we are close to the Eternal. We have to shut our eyes to see our way to Heaven. *Moby-Dick* is an evocation of the sea and of that unconsciousness to which I am referring. It was written out of the blind life.

My other two or three books seldom stir me as *Moby-Dick* does. There is nothing in *Gil Blas* but light entertainment: it is a picaresque story, an adventure of a young man. There is really nothing to it – incident piled on incident – and yet we are intoxicated. I have read *Gil Blas* at least a hundred times. I am a bad example for book buyers. [...]

(*Kavanagh's Weekly*, 28 June 1952, p. 7)

Auden and the Creative Mind

Reading the poems of Auden, I am led to consider the quality called creativity. Nobody writing today has this quality in more abundance than Auden.

What is it?

It is a sort of drug produced by the fusion, in a peculiar way, of ordinary things and events. The poet is born-not-made to the extent that no one by taking thought can produce in himself this synthesizing nature. I learned, or was made aware, from reading Auden that the great poets never teach us anything. The great poets are those who burn in the smithy of their souls the raw material of life and produce from it this erotic-creative essence. Shakespeare, Homer, Cervantes, Dickens, Swift and Joyce provide us with an orgy of sensation and nothing else or more.

There is wisdom in Shakespeare but it is incidental. Almost any kind of the crude material of life can be burned to give us this intoxicating thing. With the great writers we are in a constant state of excitement, like gamblers waiting for the result of a race. In fact, it is the very same thing as gambling, sex or drink – on a higher level. Not only do such writers not bore one but one becomes suspicious of the speed with which they whirl us from point to point of excitement. It might, therefore, be argued, as possibly Plato did – though I haven't read him on the subject – that the poet is immoral. For all the poet does is to explode the atoms of our ordinary experience. He takes our lives and stimulates the drab things and when this comic performance is over it is probable that the world is a little the worse for wear. To some extent the life of the sensations must eventually result in a wearing down of energy; and it is true; but there is a great deal of energy in the world, and this is the age of the gambler, as every age is the age of everything, and we want excitement.

Auden, like all the great ones, is all sensation, all pictures, action:

> *Make your home*
> *With some glowing girl; forget with her what*
> *Happens also. If you ever see*
> *A fuss forming in the far distance,*
> *Lots of police, and a little group*
> *In terrible trouble, don't try to help;*
> *They'd make you mock and you might be ashamed.*

In this poetry the poet doesn't come to teach us anything or to add anything to life. He is amoral, like Homer or Shakespeare.

There is one possible defect in this poetry from which the very greatest may not have suffered. It is entirely earth-born and there are no (or very few) intimations of anything more. Although all great poets progress on the energy of the sensations, and essentially offer us little or nothing else, they are healed after the orgy by a religious passion and purpose. They attempt something more than this earthly thing.

James Stephens, though a very inferior poet, or not a poet at all by true standards, was nevertheless a perceptive critic. His criticism of Auden in a conversation was that Auden was bounded by mortal walls. He didn't project. He had the power of earth-bewitchment but not prophecy. Where there are no gods – no God, indeed – there is ultimately dissatisfaction. Stephens illustrated this point with a ballad which he sang for me in the Monaco restaurant in Piccadilly a couple of years before he died.

> *She died of a fever and no one could save her*
> *And that was the end of sweet Molly Malone –*

That, too, would be the end of the Auden poem. But the ballad goes further:

But her ghost wheeled the barrow through streets broad and narrow
Crying cockles and mussels, alive! alive O!

The trouble, however, with those who attempt the prophetic, the didactic, the responsible is that they are not down among the bewitching
earth. They are not earthed and they do not come alive.

A great poet is a monster who eats up everything. Shakespeare left
nothing for those who came after him and it looks as if Auden is doing
the same. Yet this may not be quite so. It looked that Joyce had eaten
up his age and Eliot seemed as if he had laid waste a good deal of land.
Yeats, too, had the synthesizing power but not to the same extent.

My father upon the Abbey stage
His beautiful mischievous head thrown back

doesn't come to a flame. He had the secret but not enough experience.
Auden could take a thing as banal as that and make it a sensual drug.

Blind on the bride bed the bridegroom snores,
Too aloof to love. Did you lose your nerve
And cloud your conscience because I wasn't
Your dish really?

He touches nothing that he does not make an excitement:

Eternal truths: 'Teddy Peterson
Never washes.' 'I'm not your father
You slobbering Swede.' 'Sulky Moses
Has bees in his bush.' 'Betty is thinner
But Connie lays.'

Those critics who misunderstand the nature of the creative mind would
say that this material is rubbish and they would be right. But their attitude would be that of a man who would judge a fire not by its heat or
by the fact that it was alight at all but by the largeness, the importance
and the respectability of the lumps of unburnable stone or wet wood

that were piled up in the grate. And so you have in every country the so-called conservative side who think that they can impose responsibility on something that is intangible. No matter how good the fuel seems it is useless if it isn't lighted. It would be better if Auden's material were of a more durable kind – perhaps. But is Shakespeare's any more durable?

> *Can you not see? or will you not observe*
> *The strangeness of his altered countenance?*
> *With what a majesty he bears himself;*
> *How insolent of late he is become*
> *How proud, how peremptory, and unlike himself?*
> *We know the time since he was mild and affable;*
> *And if we did but glance a far-off look*
> *Immediately he was upon his knee.*

Even without the almost modern sensationalism of the word 'affable' the thing that comes through is exactly what comes through in Auden and in the *Pickwick Papers* and in *Gulliver's Travels* and in Homer.

That verse from Shakespeare, which is taken at random, is typical of Shakespeare. It was not that he deliberately chose to entertain his auditors, but obviously due to his having such a high degree of bore-ability himself he would be incapable of boring others. So he piles event on event, no inactive phrase is tolerated. The average idiotic critic who wishes to prove that Shakespeare as an entertainer is in the company of the vaudeville performers, which is all the critic can rise to, does not understand the universal nature of creative excitement – which hardly needs to be said. But it is a fact that the vulgar fool does try to equate his boring activity with the arcane fantasy of the poet. The poet's kind of entertaining is a rare commodity and is not I fear very intense in the later plays of Eliot, though it was in his earlier poems.

It is never found in what is called Tragedy, though it appears throughout all those plays of Shakespeare which may be wrongly called Tragedies. Shakespeare, like all great writers, only wrote comedy. For comedy is detachment, the view from above. *The Divine Comedy*, as far as one can gather from bad translations, is not comedy, and therefore not poetry. Boccaccio's pseudo-comedy is not it either. An interesting example of a tedious writer is Shaw. His dull theses plod along on their allegedly important legs. Shaw is all lies, because he never saw his subject from above. He hadn't the poet's comic detachment.

It is, however, not necessary to criticize a man for something he didn't possess, but to draw attention to those who did. Shakespeare and Auden in common give the impression that they have found a formula and that they could employ ghosts to turn out their particular line till there would be no need for another poet for a long time.

There is a good deal in this point, for part of genius is his discovery in a world we all thought bankrupt of rich veins of gold. There is something of the prospector's luck about a great poet's success. Wordsworth is a good example, too. In such conditions it is only pride which restrains the poet's contemporaries from expressing their jealousy and rushing in to take a share of his stake. Yeats, until his old age, worked a precious and very narrow vein of ore. It was only towards the end that he saw the potentialities of mass production; and he had not the raw material of experience to keep such a mass-production plant going. Yeats had the misfortune to come at a bad time, in the wake of Victorianism. His material was a weary parochial thing, Irish nationalism. Yet he had a good deal of the voracious appetite and digestion of the great poet. Still, it is more than likely that the appetite sharpens the instinct for life and the food thereof.

He would have abandoned the anaemic world of petty nationalism and followed his stomach's leanings if he had been great. Part of his minor microcosmic mind was his advice to Synge: 'Go to the Aran Islands and express a life that has never found expression.' Yet right beside him was the great anonymous heart that had never found expression, and which Joyce discovered. I think it may be said that there is no luck in a great poet's discoveries; it is the call of his hunger.

After Shakespeare the greatest discoverer is Dickens. It always seems after the discovery has been made and exploited that it was very obvious, a thing due to an accident of circumstance. Dickens discovered orphanages and poorhouses, a world of oppressed children and all sorts of bizarre characters formed by the incoming tide of industrialization. But it was not the uncontrollable tide of industrialization coming in which twisted into fantastic caricature these creatures, but Dickens' creative mind. Dickens wasn't a humanitarian. He wasn't a social reformer. He merely found his material. *The Pickwick Papers* is supposed to be some sort of a picture of Merrie England, but its real validity is in the mad activity which never gives us a respite from excitement. Dickens was as amoral as Shakespeare or Auden.

The same is true of Swift, who also had no message but only energy. One of the great poets who is detached from this earth-bewitchment is Blake. He is as a result cold and more of a philosopher than a poet. He didn't possess the amoral, selfish, greedy mind which feeds on children to produce monsters of energy which as he saw is 'eternal delight'; and his seeing of which proves that he hadn't got it, for we only see what is not ours. Pope has the wild energy, too. The *Essays on Man* and *On Criticism* purport to be moral poems but they are nothing so; they are a series of delighting sensations, as is the case with Swift and the rest of the true race of the poet. *Don Quixote* is another orgy, and Homer.

Till the publication in a modern idiom of the Penguin Homer and Cervantes, those of us who were unable to read these works in the original were often led to believe that Homer and Cervantes were responsible, philosophical men who in their efforts to instruct us were willing to drag their arguments through long stretches of boredom. But now that we have seen these works in a fresh new light we see that they are quite without morality or a didactic purpose. Just delight, sensation.

But is this world of the poet, this world of sensation, not likely to wear itself out, like all earth-turned emotions, if there are no reinforcements of hope and faith coming up from the silences to refertilize the wasteland?

Shakespeare lived on the capital of Christianity, Cervantes within it, and Homer had his gods coming every day with fresh reserves.

Eliot has seen this problem and has turned to a form of Catholicism. Auden, too, is bent in a similar direction. The trouble often with the thing we call upon to reinforce us is that it destroys in us what we wanted to save.

But we need the religious passion and purpose to prevent the orgy from eating away the heart of man. Returning to a consideration of Auden, I once again see how authentically he is in the tradition of the great poets, how close to Shakespeare he is. And it also occurs to me how much this is the age of the gambler, the age which lives on sensation. All the modern writers whom the world has made its heroes have this intoxicating quality – Joyce, Auden, Sartre, Connolly as a critic. They are the men who speak for the neurosis which is always with us, the Original Sin. Disease is the sign of life.

> *Every evening the oddest collection*
> *Of characters crowd this inn:*
> *Here a face from a farm, its frankness yearning*
> *For corruption and riches; there*
> *A gaunt gospel whom grinning miners*
> *Will stone to death by a dolmen;*
> *Heroes confess to whores, detectives*
> *Chat or play chess with thieves.*

Auden knows the perils of the orgy, and in 'Let His Weakness Speak' he has done so:

> '*I heard Orpheus sing; I was not quite as moved as they say.*
> *I was not taken in by the sheep's eyes of Narcissus nor by whining*
> *Echo; I was angry with Psyche when she struck a light.*'

There is the voice of a great poet.

(*Envoy*, June 1951, pp. 33–9)

Some Reflections on
Waiting for Godot

The existentialists declare
That they are in complete despair
Yet go on writing.   —Auden

To those of us who cannot abide the theatre, with its flatulent pieties, its contrivances and its lies, *Waiting for Godot* is a wonderful play, a great comedy. I do not set out to interpret *Godot*, merely to say why I like it, which is probably the only valid criticism.

Take a play like *The Bishop's Bonfire*, which was well received in Dublin. There you have the old unhappy shibboleths paraded; the theme of 'Ireland' as a moral reality, and the last refuge of the weak, the theme that our failure to ramble out into those flowery lanes of liberty, which O'Casey is always talking about, is due to forces outside ourselves. In O'Casey's case the restrictions of religion are the villain of the melodrama. All of us who are sincere know that if we are unhappy, trying to forget our futility in pubs, it is due to no exterior cause, but to what is now popularly called the human condition. Society everywhere today and its beliefs are pastiche: there is no overall purpose, no large umbrella of serenity.

This world-wide emotion has seeped through national boundaries. It flowed into Ireland many years ago, but the 'Ireland' writers continued as if nothing had happened. Now and again one noticed their discomfiture; why, they seemed to be asking themselves, was no one giving them any heed?

These 'Ireland' writers, who are still writing, of course, could not see that the writers of Ireland were no longer Corkery and O'Connor and the others, but Auden and George Barker – anyone anywhere who at least appreciated, if he could not cure, their misfortune. Saying this is liable to make one the worst in the world, for a national literature, being based on a convention, not born of the unpredictable individual and his problems, is a vulnerable racket and is protected by fierce wild men. A national literature is the only thing some men have got, and men will not relinquish their hold on the thing that gives them a reason for living.

It is because of its awareness of the peculiar sickness of society, and a possible remedy suggested, that I like Beckett's play. The remedy is that Beckett has put despair and futility on the stage for us to laugh at them. And we do laugh.

I am not going to say that *Godot* is a great, illuminating, hope-creating masterpiece like *King Lear*. But then, that is the present condition of humanity. Beckett is an honest writer. Academic writers and painters are always ready to offer the large illuminating symbol; they give us gods and heroes, and they write and paint as if society were a solid, unified Victorian lie.

I know that I am not being very direct in my statements about *Waiting for Godot*, but that is part of this play's importance. It both holds a mirror up to life and keeps reminding you, if you are interested in sincerity, that the reason you couldn't endure the theatre hitherto was that it was tenth-rate escapism, not your dish at all. Having seen *Godot*, you begin to see that, for one who can enjoy, say, a poem like –

> *My love lies in the gates of foam,*
> *The last dear wreck of shore**

there is nowhere to go in the evening except to the pub [...]

(*The Irish Times*, 28 January 1956, p. 8)

* From Lord de Tablay, 'The Churchyard in the Sands'

The Bones of the Dead:
Reflections on the Gaelic Language

Sir,

In every country inarticulate frustration uses whatever weapons are handiest against the creative writer. For a quarter of a century the most potent weapon against the writer in this country has been the 'revival' of Gaelic as a written language. Men with such Irish names as de Valera and Blythe talk of it as the 'badge of nationhood' and have the audacity to speak of writers named O'Connor, O'Faoláin, O'Donnell, O'Flaherty as 'Anglo-Irish' writers. Another weapon is also being used – the weapon of the safe arts of painting and music.

None of these attacks would be so very dangerous if the writers themselves did not fail to see the position as it is. The position is: The Gaelic language is no longer the native language; it is dead, yet food is being brought to the graveyard. The attempt to provide a safe alternative culture in the shape of painting and music is nothing more than the old nineteenth-century Dublin of silly opera expressing its emptiness again.

Therefore, let me put down a few uncultured peasant facts about the old language. It can never be revived as a spoken language, not to mention a writing language. However much we have loved the creature when it was alive we must be realists and accept that it is dead when it is dead. Let the frustrated and inarticulate continue to lay food beside the corpse.

Drive your cart and your plough over the bones of the dead.

End this inability to make up our minds whether we are to keep the corpse of a language propped up with pillows, bringing it food, accepting its authority, or to bury it decently. Every decision, as Chesterton says, is a desperate decision. Now, although the old language is dead so far as speaking or writing it goes, something of its spirit could without compromise be saved.

It could be taught for half an hour in the schools every day so that children might find the poetry in the names of places, in their own townlands. This is as much as can be hoped for without injury to the cause of reality.

Two or three events have recently given me new hope in the essential soundness of the native heart.

Speaking to a priest who teaches in a secondary school, he told me that the change of attitude on the part of the parents to the teaching of Gaelic was amazing. He did not like it. Through the children he could learn that the parents of these boys were simply sick of the humbug revival of Gaelic. They had endured the farce long enough. This is the solid sense which must delight the heart of the creative writer.

Another story which shows the return to realism is the story that a prominent ecclesiastic wrote to the head of a Catholic school where Christian doctrine was being taught through the medium of Gaelic and ordered that the children be taught through their mother tongue. What, he asked – and he was right – could children know of Christian doctrine taught through a language with which they were only vaguely acquainted?

These two things have cheered me immensely as they must cheer all sensible people. The core of reason is asserting itself. I think a political party which had the courage to lead this new – and old – commonsense would have a great future. Or must politics here be forever based on sentiment?

One often hears people saying that if Carleton had written in Gaelic – which he knew even better than English – or if Dan O'Connell had used it as he might, the language would have been saved. In our own day too, Liam O'Flaherty, a native speaker of the tongue, wrote in

English. Did these deliberately let down the language? Those who say so do not understand that the creative writer has in him a feminine passivity. He is not so much a positive thing as an instrument played upon by the vital consciousness of the people. There is a kind of amoralism about him which accepts the force of life without question. Anyone who has written seriously knows that one of the supreme tests of the vitality of a subject is to try to write it down. It is the same with a language. If the subject of the language is dead or dying it will come to pieces in the writer's hands. Therefore it is not to be wondered at that all the movements, literary and political, which have had a vital impact on the people of this country used English as their medium.

What the writers must realize and express is the fact that language is not particularly a badge of nationhood. The language a man speaks has very little to do with his outlook and character. What do words matter to a lone ploughman in a field?

PATRICK KAVANAGH

(Letter to *The Bell*, January 1948, pp. 62–4)

Literature in the University

[...] A university cannot give a man the unlearnable quality which makes a great writer – and no one should be interested in anything else [...] 'Dare to be true, nothing can need a lie,' said Shakespeare.

To have the courage of being yourself is to be truthful. You will be an iconoclast and considered a maker of wild statements, but every true personality in movement is iconoclastic. The usual iconoclasm you get among undergraduates is not the true article which springs from a man expressing the only thing he has in him to express – his unique personality; but it could be good practice.

To want, as so many do in a superficial way, to express themselves is quite a different thing from true expression of personality. They rush off to become actors or things like that, hoping or believing that the beat of publicity releases their true selves.

How the essential personality is released is a mystery really, but by going to a university and stumbling on some remarkable mind the way might be pointed out.

A good man cannot tell you the right way; he can only tell you the ways that are not right. He can tell you what is dead or was never alive, and that you are to bring no conventional offerings to the graveyard. You might even meet some experienced man who could tell you how to deal with the sneering enemies of promise.

By one brave gesture a man may be saved.

One of the things it would be necessary to teach in Ireland is that the pygmy literature which was produced by the so-called Irish literary renaissance is quite worthless.

But it would be a mistake to concentrate on the negative too much.

It is essential, as I said at the start, to consider nothing but genius; for anything less is no good. The aim of a good deal of literary and academic criticism is to raise up the mediocre, to get people to believe that the tenth-rate is in some way the respectable. It takes courage not to praise the tenth-rate, for as soon as it is known by society that you are one of these mediocrity-admirers they know that you're 'all right' – a serious traditional man deserving of a stake in the country.

There are few geniuses in the world at any time, for the world could not stand more than a few, for though they do, in a remarkable way, ennoble they are at the same time a destructive element. They have voracious appetites for living and the ordinary man who comes into contact with one of these monsters will find himself, and his personality, getting thinner and thinner –

Unless he accepts. Society as a rule hates the great poet because he eats up all the emotion; he is the cuckoo bird in the nest. But society in behaving like this is immoral. The bees make a queen at the expense of thousands of sterile workers.

That is the apparently sad position. If there is a genius or two at large in society, the moral thing to do is to accept him and to accept your own sterile fate.

But immorality is something you cannot eliminate. To have the fortitude and the faith to be willing to be nothing is one of the best ways of being something.

But the world of today, with so little faith and so many petty tensions, so much social development with which the majority do not know what to do, is never done searching for the easy way out that is not an exit at all. And so you have schools of acting, painting, writing, all claiming to teach that which cannot be taught. These three trades can be taught, of course, but the people are not interested in a trade – they are looking for self-expression; and in that they make their mistake. They only find bitterness, and spend the best part of their lives trying to prove that what they were capable of being taught is the only duty.

This neurosis is particularly violent in a small society such as ours. In England, where there is better opportunity for emotional expression, a versifier who realized – as any man's instinct must make him realize if it is so – that he is mediocre would not go on versing.

For instance there is John Arlott, who wrote a number of excellent poems but gave up writing verse, he told me, simply because he wasn't good enough. There are none of the versifiers who have been churning out bad light verse here who would be as good as Arlott.

That was a moral as well as a wise decision. It is much nobler to bring the gifts of society to a great poet such as Auden than trying futilely to land a spit in his face. And you get that here and also in other similar mean circles among those who are not satisfied with being nothing – not glad to admire the God- and Earth-created glory of a great genius.

So it is that the warmest friends of the poet in society are the women whose nature is surrender and worship. The unwise male tries to project and strains most pitifully when he is completely impotent.

There were some sad examples of this in Ireland during the time when Yeats, who was by no means a very great poet, was living here. He was 'haw-hawed' at regularly from the back benches. I can, as I have suggested, see the reason or lack of it – the hysteria – for this. Why expect the sterilized to admire the monster who has robbed them of their life, their little life? Yet, as admirers they could have saved themselves.

This willingness to admire the good would be a real function of a university; and out of it good would come, and release for the admirers.

It may be said outright what is implicit in my theme – that you cannot learn to be a genius either in a university or out of it.

It might be that universities open a man's mind to his own potentialities, but if the potentialities are there it is almost certain that they will find a way out; they will burst a road. I scarcely believe in the theory of the 'mute inglorious Milton'. There might well be mute Bowens or Priestleys or Blundens, but hardly a Milton, a Shakespeare, an Auden.

Yet, though the university cannot make a genius, a man who goes to a university is often likely to meet some strange awakener of genius who might put him on the right road, save him a lot of trouble.

Poetic genius, which is the only kind of genius, has never been properly defined. Arnold, a well-meaning bore, described it as a criticism of life, which in its dull way is not bad. It is an intoxication of the spirit. There is a good deal of talk about the ennobling nature of great poetry, but I am not sure if this is true. The catharsis of tragedy, which follows the drunken spell, is the poet trying to bring you back to your senses – trying, one might say, to undo the damage he has caused.

The one thing which is the material for genius and which is not only not teachable in a university, but might well be the opposite, is the capacity for experience. There is no poetic thyroid extract which keeps you growing, experiencing.

In fact, there is liable to be a lack of ordinary fresh food for experience in the university. But even this is not all the truth, for if a man has the original appetite his sense of smell will lead him to experience.

I might even illustrate my theme with views of my own life. I may say that I have never been to school, but I have never felt that I was in any way hindered from doing what was mine to do, or saying my say; and I have never felt, as some people say un-universitied men of genius feel, any discomfort or inferiority complex because of it. And I would say that any man who felt such a puerile emotion could not possibly have that detachment which sees both the grandeur and the insignificance of man in the world, which is the most important quality of poetic genius.

I may say here that I hope no one will think that this view, this universal view, is capable of caring for its own self. In other words, I am not trying to equate myself with genius and at the same time I am not trying to do the opposite. I am just detached.

Some sentimentalists suggest that a country background is a better one than a sophisticated university one. I disagree with the notion that the background means a thing to the creative mind. A background is no more important than the back curtain of a stage. Experience takes place on the stage of life.

It might be thought that Joyce is dependent on his background, but the quality in his most successful book, *A Portrait of the Artist*, that queer intoxicating synthesis, operates in defiance of mere events and facts. In the coarser world of O'Casey, because he hasn't got a true poetic genius, the background is important.

Synge, though one may criticize him for a certain coarseness born of his Protestantism, the loutish superiority of a mediocre ruling class, which he might have outgrown, had this creative intoxication, though he would never be really good. The gaiety of the *Playboy* is not dependent on its Western background. Synge was a minor poet, but an authentic one, as distinct from minor people who have no poetic merit.

What may be called the Abbey Theatre school of writers had practically no merit beyond the background. The repertoire of this theatre is in general not above what I would call good racy sentimental journalism, the level of such a paper as *Ireland's Own*, a journal which few people see nowadays but which was literature for rural Ireland in my youth.

Synge had a touch and so in a few of his pieces had Frank O'Connor. 'In the Train' has the poetic intoxication but, unfortunately, these few authentic writers lacked the slow solemn humus of pity and terror which gives full satisfaction to the soul of man. When you have heard them out you are weary, you have been devitalized rather than the contrary.

With the exception of Yeats's work practically none of the verse which was written in Ireland during the present century has had any poetic merit – which is the only merit worth considering in a poem. Some of the verse had other merits which however had more to do with politics than poetics.

None of the verse-writers who are at it just now have any poetic quality at all. This is not surprising when one is dealing with a commodity as rare as poetry. And if you deliberately limit your field of vision to something called 'Irish' it must follow that you're going to have a lean time.

True criticism collapses within the national field and instead of the poem being considered as a poem it is considered as a political pamphlet, an essay in prosody or something like that.

One must never be so foolish as to expect a Phoenix hour, a literary movement in an area much too narrow for one great genius to move. There are a few young people – or at any rate one young person – who has recognized the intolerable nature of political boundaries when dealing with a universal thing. There is a graduate of this university,* Anthony Cronin, who, if he has it in him, will be unlikely to be led down the national cul-de-sac. But once again there is no real need to say this; for if a man has the poetic nature in him he will take this universal view which is ultimately so personal and so gay.

The rest of the world should be satisfied by loving God, by praising His works, and the greatest work of God on this earth is the dancing flame of the poet's imagination.

The wickedest thing, and universities might try to teach this, is to try to deny it, to try to protest that what is dead is alive.

To bring food to the graveyard, that is the artistic sin. Genius is the only thing worth considering. The next best thing to being a genius is to recognize him and praise him and ignore everything else. And to do our best to cut down the nets which mediocrity flings to hold back the soul from flight [...]

('Diary', *Envoy*, July 1951, pp. 65–71)

---

* University College Dublin; this essay is based on a talk given there in 1951.

Parochialism and Provincialism

[...] Parochialism and provincialism are direct opposites. The provincial has no mind of his own; he does not trust what his eyes see until he has heard what the metropolis – towards which his eyes are turned – has to say on any subject. This runs through all activities.

The parochial mentality on the other hand is never in any doubt about the social and artistic validity of his parish. All great civilizations are based on parochialism – Greek, Israelite, English [...]

In Ireland we are provincial not parochial, for it requires a great deal of courage to be parochial. When we do attempt having the courage of our parish we are inclined to go false and to play up to the larger parish on the other side of the Irish Sea. In recent times we have had two great Irish parishioners – James Joyce and George Moore. They explained nothing. The public had either to come to them or stay in the dark and the public did come. The English parishioner recognizes courage in another man's parish.

Whenever you have had parochial courage here it was always an aggressive courage, not the taking-for-granted kind.

[...] Advising people not to be ashamed of having the courage of their remote parish is not free from many dangers. There is always that element of bravado which takes pleasure in the notion that the potato-patch is the ultimate. To be parochial a man needs the right kind of sensitive courage and the right kind of sensitive humility. [...]

(From 'Mao Tse-tung Unrolls His Mat', *Kavanagh's Weekly*, 24 May 1952)

A Goat Tethered outside the Bailey

[...] For a man in Ireland to have the label 'poet' attached to him is little short of a calamity. Society, when it has established a man as a poet, has him cornered within narrow limits. If he looks like having too much scope in his little corner he will be still further narrowed by having an adjective in front of 'poet' – such as Country poet, Catholic poet and so on. He becomes a sort of exhibit, not a man in and of the world. If he happens to be a dilettante without a passionate faith he will enjoy this position, but if he is a genuine poet it is an indignity and something much worse. Therefore, I announce here and now that I am speaking as a journalist. I have resigned from being a poet and I hope that my resignation will be accepted.

As an example of what the poet is not we have only to go to the Irish Tradition. There is an Irish Tradition though it is not absolutely special to Ireland; it derives from attitudes that are common throughout society everywhere but it is so strongly defined here that it can be called an Irish Tradition. I am fully aware that, in the words I once heard in a comic film, society here is 'agog with indifference' regarding poetry. That is accepted. At the same time it is a thing to be regretted if we have a true concept of what the poetic mind really is.

In so far as the poet is thought of in Ireland, the idea is that he is either an uproarious, drunken clown, an inspired idiot, a silly schoolgirl type, or just plain dull. He is in no way to be taken seriously.

The Irish ideal of a literary genius – weak, charming and a challenge to nobody – is in the image of that celebrated synthetic tramp, Pádraic Ó Conaire, with his goat tethered outside the Bailey.* I find it hard to pass from this image without saying that Ó Conaire, choosing the disreputable life, is the direct opposite of my idea of the poetic genius. The poet does not seek misfortune; the poet does not pursue experience – experience pursues him. The poet does not go searching for beauty or intensity; these things happen to him. But that is a long story.

The logical collateral of these ideas regarding the poet is that poets are quite common in Ireland. They are never mentioned except in batches of a dozen or more. Fourteen hundred are reputed to have been present at the famous Assembly at Drumceat, and not so long ago, in one of the Irish papers, I saw a list of modern Gaelic geniuses, which for a moment deceived me into thinking it was the list of chief mourners at the funeral of some noted patriot or industrialist.

It was a patriotic gesture. For patriotism does include belief in the importance of literature. Yet poetry has nothing to do with patriotism, nor is it interested in any special language; it is universal.

For those of us who believe that the poetic spirit is of some value, this patriotic enthusiasm is a bad thing, for it sets up as admirable, from motives that are not pure, something that cannot possibly be the authentic thing. The authentic thing, if it happened to appear, would be crushed.

This has happened and will continue to happen unless we change our attitude. Even allowing for unfavourable circumstances, it is remarkable that in a thousand years Ireland had not produced a major poet or, indeed, a good minor poet. There was no audience for the poet's high dignity. I will return to this theme later but, in the meantime, let us consider what a real poet is.

The poetic view of life is a view based on a true sense of values and those values must be of their nature what are called unworldly.

Furthermore, a man may be a poet in prose as well as in verse, or in merely talking to the people. To narrow the poetic spirit down to its

* Pádraic Ó Conaire (1882–1928), Irish-language writer of novels and short stories, spent the last fourteen years of his life wandering around Ireland, drinking heavily and sometimes living rough. Kavanagh's barb presents him as an urbanite with rustic pretensions, a middle-class poseur drinking in what was, in the early 1950s, a posh Dublin pub.

expression in verse is equivalent to narrowing religion down to something that happens on Sundays.

A good idea of the nature of the poet is to be found in E.V. Rieu's introduction to his translation of the Four Gospels. He remarks of St Luke: 'St Luke was a poet. I do not mean by this that he embroidered his narratives, but rather that he knew how to distil truth from fact.' Rieu goes on to refer to Luke's 'poetic insight into reality' and to his realization of the part played by woman in the revelation of the Divine Idea.

That is the poetic mind.

If I happened to meet a poet – and I have met poets – I would expect him to reveal his powers of insight and imagination even if he talked of poultry farming, ground rents or any other commonplace subject.

Above all, I would expect to be excited and have my horizons of faith and hope widened by his ideas on the only subject that is of any real importance – Man-in-this-World-and-why.

He would reveal to me the gay, imaginative God who made the grass and the trees and the flowers, a God not terribly to be feared.

This may seem awfully solemn. It is anything but.

It is a curious and ironical fact that for a man to show himself at all seriously concerned with the one thing that matters is to have himself looked upon as somewhat eccentric – unless, of course, he keeps that seriousness in an airtight compartment.

Society generally is suspicious of the imaginative sense of values because, as Professor Whitehead pointed out in his *Adventures of Ideas*, of the anarchic nature of the speculative mind. It cannot afford to be openly barbarous, and so you have the setting up of false gods of the imagination – people who believe in what they call Art, art of the film, art of the ballet. But one must not allow oneself to be inhibited by too precise analytic definition.

Roughly, two classes of people abhor the imaginative sense of values. There is the sound businessman whose solid worth finds expression in the trivialities of the newspaper, and there is the literary mediocrity who must deny the existence of Parnassus if his little dustheap of biographies and novels are to mean anything.

The sound man of the world never reflects. Not to reflect is what is considered sanity. Yet, without this reflective centre man is a savage and will not be long revealing his savagery if you touch the hollow beneath the conventional dress of respectability. And that touching or stripping of the hollow heart is what the poet willy-nilly does, and is the thing which makes him hated by the world. In every poet there is something of Christ writing the sins of the people in the dust.

As I have said, one of the Irish ideas of the poet is of the uproarious clown. I have hardly ever heard an Irish admirer of Gaelic or of any poetry speaking of the poet that he didn't give the impression that he thought it all a great joke.

Another idea of the poet is of a man who at the drop of a hatpin would run off with another man's wife. In the Gaelic mythology it is the priest's housekeeper who gets abducted, and this gives rise to terrible heresy which rocks Christendom. Now, I do not say that some genuine poets have not lived the wild life, have not run off with other men's wives, but I do say that it is entirely contrary to the poetic nature. It is a bourgeois concept of rebelliousness.

The note of the poetic mind is a moral one, and it is this moral quality which the world cannot stand, for it is a constant reproach to inferior men – and inferior men, let me explain, are men who are committed to inferior things, who lack the courage to pronounce a judgement in defiance of their own petty vanity. The world loves the wild, uproarious fellow who is made in its own image and will when it comes to the test take him to its bosom and confer upon him all the worldly privileges. Display a touch of this kind of irresponsibility and you're home and dried. The world knows it is not genuine.

To some extent this view of the poet is mediocrity fighting back, trying to establish a corner in commonsense. As I suggested, it is not confined to Ireland.

Chesterton met it and in his fascinating book, *Orthodoxy*, replied to the notion that there is some relationship between genius and insanity. Chesterton said: 'The facts of history utterly contradict this view; most of the great poets have been not only sane but extremely businesslike, and if Shakespeare ever held horses it was because he was much the safest man to hold them.'

Perhaps it may be said that I have been labouring this Irish idea of the poet too hard, that there does exist in this country a public which accepts all I have to say, a public which has goodwill and a sincere, moral point of view. The fact that I believe there is such a public is the reason I am saying these things; for we can only preach to the converted. In other words, the poet is himself no more than the voice of the people. It is the pressure of a people's need for a voice which is his power.

After all these high claims for the poet you might be pardoned for expecting him to utter high and stupendous truths. But that is not the way of truth. Truth is very disappointing; we expect it to come transfigured and are inclined to ignore it when it comes simple and humble.

(*The Bell*, September 1953, pp. 27–33)

The Poetic Spirit

It is an embarrassing thing to be put in the role of a prophet. Prophecy does not consist in forecasting events, but in faith, and in being able to sit at the heart of that faith and explore its infinities. Prophecy is personality; it is a man giving the essence of himself. A prophet lying at the heart of the emotion burns himself up, and he comes out of the orgy in a state of shame and collapse.

That is why he needs the protecting love of devoted disciples, otherwise an audience. He needs around him a group which has hitherto prevented the development of a poetic passion in Ireland. But today such a group is beginning to appear. The people who rely on the ingredients of nationalistic local colour are fighting a rearguard action. But today in 1957 large numbers – which is to say about two per cent of the population – know only too well that the spiritual adrenalin which the poet produces is not to be found within nationalistic formulae.

The audience is evidence of immortality. The audience knows when its poet has arrived and it is willing, collectively and individually, to submit. The audience is Blake's cut worm.

The poet's arrogance and authority are hated by vain fools who will not submit to the will of God and be themselves. As a result you have counter-poetic movements. Class hatred sets up vulgar little gods. The mean and vain cannot reach the poet's unapproachable soul.

The poet's soul seems so intimate, so immediate, so easy to approach, but around it is an invisible protecting area. And the malicious envious man seeing this rare thing unprotected dashes towards it and, when repulsed, is astonished and angry with hate in his heart. The soul is hurt but it remains intact, poised in all its Parnassian authority.

The ordinary non-poetic man has a high degree of insultability, because he has no central security. The poetic man can be wounded but not easily insulted.

The poet's secret which is not a secret but a form of high courage is that he in a strange way doesn't care. The poet is not concerned with the effect he is making; he forgets himself.

The immoral man will not accept. The poet teaches man worried about his position and his validity to cease to worry and then he will have a valid position.

Parnassus is a point of view. In the presence of the Parnassian authority we are provincials nowhere.

There is no hatred to equal that aroused by a man with the Parnassian faith. The malicious and envious rally round their false god, and when that false god of his nature disintegrates they create another. This is the counter-poetic movement which has always been strong in Dublin. Those who set up those false gods do not love them. No man ever loves a false god. The object in rallying around the false god is to wound the true god. The malicious are always looking for a 'poor man's poet'.

Malice is only another name for mediocrity. No man need be a mediocrity if he accepts himself as God made him. God only makes geniuses. But many men do not like God's work. This is another of the things the poet teaches: that every man has a purpose in life if he would submit and serve it, that he can sit with his feet to the fire of an eternal passion, a valid moral entity.

One of the principal reasons why the human male will not accept the small but unique genius that God has made is vanity regarding woman. A woman who has not been corrupted by ideas of actors and fiddlers and painters has the ability of the poet to see only the cowardly little self hiding behind the mask of a giant, and the man is in a worse state than ever.

Insincerity is boring. Masks are boring. We all seek the simple reality of a man. The poet – and I mean poet in the widest sense – is non-boring because he is himself; he is volatile, immediate and full of gaiety. Woman cannot abide boredom from a male.

There is this other thing too, which provokes jealousy.

> *Test of the poet is knowledge of love*
> *For Eros is older than Saturn or Jove*
> —Emerson.

(*Creation*, August 1957, p. 49)

Nationalism and Literature

Let us start with naming. Naming things is part of a poet's function. I did some naming once. It was an exhibition, or rather collection of copper jewellery [...]* Several people looking at the pieces of jewellery commented on the aptness with which the artist had faithfully interpreted in the work something called – I have forgotten – perhaps 'The Temple of Romance'. The remarkable thing is how the article that precedes a name comes to look like its name, for an unnamed thing has little life in the mind.

Regarding myth-making and myths in general, I note that a well-known French scholar priest is coming here to demolish the Anglo-Saxon myth. According to this man's theory the whole legend of an Anglo-Saxon culture is nothing but legerdemain. The legend is there just the same. It cannot be demolished, any more than that singular Gaelic figure St Patrick, as portrayed on banners and cards, can be demolished, or rather multiplied. A myth is necessary, for a myth is a sort of self-contained world in which one can live. As literary critics live in theirs, discussing family intimacies.

Ireland as a myth which could protect and nourish a body of creative artists is rather unique. One of the reasons why it has failed again and again is that nationalism is seldom based on those sincerities which

---

* In December 1957 and 1958, for £3 a time, Kavanagh named each of the pieces of Lunia Ryan's wrought-gold jewellery displayed in the Petite Salon at the Brown Thomas department store in Dublin.

give any truly spiritual force its power. Good work cannot survive in an angry atmosphere, and without being too boringly insistent on the value of truth, I can only say that it is the most entertaining type of communication.

The reasons why work produced by a Celt receive praise or blame have on the whole had little or nothing to do with aesthetics or truth. Mind you no man more than yours faithfully can enjoy the native sentiment in ballad tune and story. As I have said, myths are indestructible, but what I should like to point out is that myths do not work and the Irish myth is one of them. Of course the Russians had a myth. Dostoevsky in exile at the casinos of Europe is never done lamenting his absence from Russia. But of all patriotic myths the only one in my opinion that came alive and worked for the author was Joyce's myth of Dublin. Why it sustained him is that he never stopped to think, you might say. Once we stop to think the illusion is gone. In the case of a poet's mythology the all-embracing fog must remain impenetrable. We must not be able to escape from it. In certain circumstances the only way to succeed in this is to accept failure and by so doing realize that failure is something in the mind.

A myth like a theme of which it is part is a lucky break. When it's over and done with we must dismiss it at once.

I know a few writers who live in Ireland who have not cottoned on to the fact that Ireland as a myth is no use. When Dr Johnson said that patriotism was the last refuge of the scoundrel, he was once again right on the mark. In all formal patriotic activity there lies the seed of something that is not the seed of virtue. There have been many fine patriots but there must be some inherent defect in the whole business, seeing that men of little or no principle can readily weigh in with it and be accounted fine men.

Regarding the mighty corpus of English literature, this seems to me largely divorced from England the nation, the often scoundrelly nation. Some poets have praised Cromwell and a great one was his secretary and another one his cousin, but for all that the protective atmosphere which fed the English poetic world had little to do with politics or patriotism. Love of the land and landscape is of course a different kettle of potatoes altogether. Constable, Wordsworth, Clare, most of them were great patriots in that sense. It seems at first blush that English poetry grew to its splenditude in a myth void, that it was entirely individual. But there was a myth and a true one.

This curious myth has to do with faith in one's own judgement and the courage to pronounce it. Wherever there are a number of men with that faith and courage you have a myth-making society. Even today in London a man may be talking to another in a pub. As they speak they are accompanied in their consciousness by many others who are not present at all. It is this sort of family thing that alone can make a society happy. For some reason or other this source of strength has never been lost in England. It goes on quietly unconcerned, undeceived by the latest reports on anything. As one goes on in the country, knowing exactly who is down in the valley sowing turnips or levelling the potato drills and who is not, and what they are all thinking about.

It is this kind of parish myth regarding literature that has been totally lacking in Ireland. Instead we have this national thing which is no use to anyone. Is Synge the voice of Ireland? Has Ireland a voice? I believe it has a faint, odd voice, difficult to establish. Indeed Carleton is our native voice:

> *But who is he that lingereth yet*
> *Killeavy, O Killeavy!*
> *The fresh green sod with his tears is wet*
> *And his heart in the bridal grave is set,*
> *By the bonnie green woods of Killeavy.*

And I am always so glad that notwithstanding anything one may say, nobody will ever read Carleton. You can praise or blame this great writer without involving anyone. Not that I wish to involve anyone, though I will admit I never could endure the verse of James Stephens, who was very friendly to me.

The thing is that here in Ireland we have a Celtic hinterland of Festival towns deeply committed to the national myth. At these festivals you have – well you ought to know what you have. But a man is the worst in the world if he ventures any criticism. And what can one do? It is all the great days of the Abbey, *Cradle of Genius* was what a film on those great days was called. If one says that Synge wasn't a genius and so on you are instantly up against patriotism. I believe that the 'Theatre' is largely a journalistic property. You have only to glance at the space devoted to amateur theatricals in the papers to understand this. Not that I mind myself. My ambition was at one time to get on to the amateur stage in some play by perhaps J.B. McCarthy. I was full of Ireland then. And when all is said and done one might be full of worse things. Particularly down in the country you just cannot postulate high and mighty ideas. There was a time when my great ambition was to get published in *The Weekly Independent* or *Ireland's Own*. On one occasion there was a prize of half a guinea, and here I was routed by an effort sent in from a 'Care of' address. This was:

> *I think that I shall never see*
> *A poem lovely as a tree*

I mention this to fix the Irish position. Let it not be thought that I began at the high level of *Ireland's Own*. It was indeed a great day for me when I had a piece accepted and printed without any address and needless to say unpaid for by the *Dundalk Democrat*. I was quite convinced that everyone in Ireland would see it. I feel this may possibly have something to do with that voice of Ireland mentioned before. I don't suppose we have produced many poets of the best talent, but there was something and that something was not unconnected with the ballads and poems that used to get printed in these local newspapers. Those old Gaelic poets, by the way, of whom we hear quite a lot were as genuine as one could expect them to be. There was no doubt the usual percentage of true poets amongst them. But I fear there was no proper society in which they could flourish. There was no faith.

However, to return to the Irish myth, the unworkable one, this only got going properly about fifty years ago. Keegan Casey, for instance, with his 'Rising of the Moon':

> *O then tell me Shawn O'Farrell*
> *Where the gathering is to be*
> *In the old spot by the river*

Right well known to you and me …
I bear orders from the captain
Get you ready quick and soon
For the pikes must be together
At the rising of the Moon.

Or such anonymous songs as

It was early early in the Spring
The birds did whistle and sweetly sing
Changing their notes from tree to tree
And the song they sang was old Ireland free.

It is odd that we got a myth like that going here, much as America got one in which literature could flourish a century ago. You had Longfellow, Melville, Bret Harte and so forth, all derived, I regret to admit, from the English tradition as spread from New England. Today you have a sort of International writing crowd, not involved in myths indigenous or otherwise. And yet –

I suppose that judged in the cruel light of top-class literary criticism, a poet like Mangan comes out pretty badly. But to those involved with the local sentiment Mangan made a profound appeal.

Roll forth my song like the rushing river
That sweeps along to the mighty sea
God will inspire me while I deliver
My soul of thee.

At one time Mangan immensely moved me with

I walked entranced
Through a land of Morn;
The sun, with wondrous excess of light,
Shone down and glanced
Over seas of corn
And lustrous gardens aleft and right

Even in the clime of resplendent Spain,
Beams no such sun upon such a land;
But it was the time,
'Twas in the reign,
Of Cáhal Mór of the Wine-Red hand.

I almost begin to believe in the myth of Ireland as a spiritual reality.

(*Nonplus*, October 1959, pp. 74–9)

Violence and Literature

A while ago I was asked by a military man to write something for a military journal about poets as soldiers. It was a journalistic gimmick that did not greatly appeal to me, but eventually the idea sent me on a tour of inspection through the deep valleys of my ignorance. It is on such tours that we begin to realize how much we are capable of knowing, there being a curious relationship between ignorance and knowledge, a mutual dependence.

Poets it is true have been everything. One could just as well write on poets as beggars, poets as football kickers. But poets as soldiers brings me to the quite scholarly-respectable theme of violence in literature, that violence whose heart is tenderness, not the other kind. For if we are violent it should not be for the sake of violence, but for other incurable reasons. Many writers make a practice of being violent because they are weak and have failed. Others worship violence because they feel more manly that way.

Take Belloc, for instance, and Roy Campbell. Belloc was a war correspondent in World War I and wrote about strategy and things of that kind. Campbell fought on the Franco side in the Spanish Civil War but ... The only valid violence is that which we cannot avoid. Putting on the agony, any kind of agony, is silly and a form of weakness. It must come to you and you must be helpless.

Who now were the great poet warriors? Cervantes ... Byron ... David. David the King of Israel was a real warrior if ever there was one.

There is no detachment whatever in David and when he laments he is not ambitioning poetry. He is simply saying what he feels:

> Tell it not in Gath, publish it not in the streets of Askelon lest the daughters of the Philistines rejoice, lest the daughters of the Uncircumcised triumph. ... From the blood of the slain, from the fat of the mighty, the bow of Jonathan turned not back, and the sword of Saul returned not empty.

This poet of the Old Testament was not speaking idly. The word was life to him and death in some cases to others. It is what another group of phonies are trying to invoke artificially ... what they call commitment. They want to be committed, to be part of the struggle, to drink pints of bitter in bars, trying to prove they are he-men. But let them be. David the poet and soldier and prophet bears out that idea of the hero as he who is immovably centred. Or according I think to Cocteau, everything that is not believed remains decorative.

Looking for Cervantes the soldier I came upon Cervantes the wonderful war correspondent and later Cervantes the storyteller with profound insight regarding the nature of women as the repository of unconscious wisdom. I know no more moving study than this of the mystique of Woman and her role in life. It is impossible to read it without tears.

There is an idea that the poet is effeminate, an idea derived somewhat from Palgrave and his much-dipped *Golden Treasury*. To be a complete poet, or indeed man, one must have some of the knowledge instinctive to the feminine mind. Cervantes had this in abundance. All the best writers have. Those who postulate the aggressive point of view, as for instance Hemingway, are less than the best, are weak, like Gabriele D'Annunzio, the Italian poet who seized Fiume some years after World War I.

It is true that of recent times many men who took themselves to be poets avoided the draft, on that well-known rule that the first duty of a gentleman is to avoid getting into the hands of the police or into danger, you might say. There is something to be said for this attitude but then again he that loses his life shall gain it, or at least he that tosses his life into the gamble of some great conflict may get a new life back. I am not enamoured of that life drama that goes out not with a bang but a whimper; indeed I find myself constantly regretting that I took no part in World War I.

A short while ago I mentioned this in a sonnet.

Christmas someone remarked is almost upon us
And looking out of my window I saw that Winter had landed
Complete with the grey cloak and the bare-headed sonnet,
A scroll of bark hanging down to his knees as he scanned it.
The gravel in the yard was pensive annoyed at being crushed
As people with problems in their faces drove by in cars
But I with all this solemnity around me refused to be bunched
In fact was inclined to give the go by to bars
Yes there was something about that winter arrival that made me
Feel younger less of a failure, it was actually earlier
Than many people thought. There were possibilities
For love, for South African adventure, for fathering a baby
For taking oneself in hand, catching on without a scare or
Serving through a world war, joining up at the start of hostilities.

As it was I served through no war and never until perhaps too late understood the true meaning of violence. I am afraid there has been always in Ireland a most unpoetic tradition of caution. Early on the Gaelic poets amused themselves in peacetime by killing rats with satires to keep themselves in practice for serious events. But their evil eye, exemplified by that antique Mills bomb, the brain ball, by which Conall Cearnach put a long, slow end to Conor McNessa in that famous foray between Ulster and Leinster, had apparently been lost by the time it was most wanted. Cromwell had the poets on his side. Not that I laugh at the power of a curse or the evil eye. The ancient Gaels were right there. A lie is a terrifying business, looking so much more reasonable than the truth, for truth often takes time to make itself apparent. Nowadays, of course, at the outbreak of war, poets are drafted into what is called Information, one of their main jobs being the manufacture of lies injurious to the enemy.

The minstrel boy to the war is gone

There is no getting away from that, though I must say I find it hard to understand how D'Annunzio gathered an army to seize Fiume.

Let it not be thought that I am advocating aggression. Only when I think of my own fantastic caution, allowing myself to be pushed around in case some atrocious job went slipping, I can't help feeling that the spirit, the fighting spirit is all. There is hardly a day I don't kick myself for not kicking others. Indignities are indeed a part of experience, a great part, but as Yeats nearly said: 'Too great a sacrifice can make a rag of the heart.'

As for violence, violence and literature, I suppose Byron must be considered the finest example of the warrior bard. He gambles everything on the altar of life … his vast property, his wife's money, the wife herself, and any other woman who happens to be knocking about. It all seems splendidly generous to me.

A land of slaves can ne'er be mine
… Dash down yon cup of Amnian wine

How right he is. We should be throwing our bread on the waters. We should dare greatly.

I do not much believe in the art of war or the profession of arms. The poet is quite out of place in the current political game. He would be an object of suspicion and ridicule to the common run of military practitioners. But war has at times been the only resort for the spirit in travail. Byron died as he lived, nobly. I do not believe Roy Campbell did this, though he has a very lovely sonnet on another noted fighter, the Portuguese poet Camões.

Camões, alone, of all the lyric race,
Born in the black aurora of disaster,
Can look a common soldier in the face:
I find a comrade where I sought a master:
For daily, while the stinking crocodiles
Glide from the mangroves on the swampy shore,

He shares my awning on the dhow, he smiles,
And tells me that he lived it all before.
Through fire and shipwreck, pestilence and loss,
Led by the ignis fatuus of duty
To a dog's death ... yet of his sorrows king –
He shouldered high his voluntary Cross,
Wrestled his hardships into forms of beauty,
And taught the gorgon destinies to sing.

Campbell has also given us a translation of the work of that other swift violent man, St John of the Cross, towards whom this tour of inspection has, I see, been tending all along. For his Dark Night of the Soul embraces the whole idea of true violence, the abandon of love.

(*Nonplus*, October 1959, pp. 80–3)

On Poetry

Part of the Palgravian lie was that poetry was a thing written by young men and girls. Not having access to Ezra Pound, who showed that the greatest poetry was written by men over thirty, it took me many years to realize that poetry dealt with the full reality of experience.

Part also of the lie was that poetry was very sad –

Our sweetest songs are those that tell of saddest thought.

This is not true. Our sweetest songs are those that derive from that gay abandon which is the keynote of the authentic Parnassian voice. The abandon is not the riotous braggadocio which is often associated with the poet. The true abandon and gaiety of heart spring from the sense of authority, confidence and courage of the man who is on the sacred mountain.

It is essential to consider nothing but genius; for anything less is no good. The aim of a good deal of literary and academic criticism is to raise up the mediocre, to get people to believe that the tenth-rate is in some way respectable. It takes courage not to praise the tenth-rate, for as soon as it is known by society that you are one of these mediocrity-admirers, they know that you're 'all right' – a serious traditional man deserving of a stake in the country.

Poetry is what it says. The thought shapes the language. At its purest all the didacticism is burned away, and you get that impalpable beauty which pertains to the divine –

Absent thee from felicity awhile.

The wicked critic, instead of telling his audience to lift the child in its arms and enjoy its smiles, tells it to ask why it has eyes and what causes the smile.

One can never get away from the idea of the Audience in discussing the poet. The audience stands outside the hotch-potch of lies that is the world of journalism and politics. In London the journalist has no influence on literature. In England there has always been a traditional audience, a word-of-mouth audience. That audience cannot be bought, is uninfluenced by financial success or failure.

Great men are not concerned with whether or not their work is involved in the ephemeral. Only bad, silly writers are worried over such matters. They hope that a 'mighty theme' will save them, because they do not know that the only permanent thing is the soul, and what has happened to it.

Art McCooey, a late-eighteenth-century poet, is known for a poem he wrote on Creggan graveyard. But as is the case with so much that passes for poetry in Ireland, it is whimsical. He does not, as the true poet does, name and name and name with love the obscure places, people or events. To the poet, what is loved is worthy of love. A better poet than McCooey was Evelyn Shirley, a nineteenth-century landlord from south Ulster, and he wrote no verse at all as far as is known. But in his *History of Monaghan* he names and names and names in the true poetic fashion. He recorded the history of the obscure fields, graves, forts and families, with all the Parnassian disregard for any supposed public. He had an audience, no doubt, of a few of his friends.

There is only one Muse, the Comic Muse. In Tragedy there is always something of a lie. Great poetry is always comic in the profound sense. The only plays of Shakespeare which are less than comic are the alleged comedies. *King Lear* is the pure incantation of the Comic Muse. Comedy is the abundance of life.

O, reason not the need: our basest beggars
Are in the poorest thing superfluous:
Allow not nature more than nature needs,
Man's life is cheap as beast's –

(From 'Poets on Poetry', *X*, no. 2, March 1960, pp. 66–7)

Part IV

Diary, June 1950

The problem of writing a diary for immediate publication is the problem of releasing oneself without that loss of dignity which would not be the revelation of a man's heart but of his soul. Give a man a mask, said Wilde, and he will tell you the truth. So it is that most diaries and autobiographies are a form of fiction. Pepys' diary is an authentic one; but the most intimately revealing of diaries is the one that James Joyce, through the character of Mr Bloom, projects. There you have everyman as God sees him. How interesting the memoirs of famous public men would be if they put down their real thoughts, feelings, doings. We may not all be constantly thinking of the frills on a woman's petticoat, but if that is not the symbol of our private silliness something equally undignified is. No man is a hero to his valet. I am not too sure of that, but it is certain that no sane man is a hero to himself. A man may have moments when he is lifted out of the prison of the body to something heroic. On account of this Bloom is a one-sided character. The best medium for releasing our private selves, the heart's cry, is verse which can give nobility to intimacy. It speaks for all of us: Coleridge –

> *This soul hath been*
> *Alone on a wide, wide sea:*
> *So lonely 'twas, that God Himself*
> *Scarce seemed there to be.*

And Blake –

O what is Life and what is Man? O what is Death? Wherefore
Are you, my Children, natives in the Grave to where I go?
Or are you born to feed the hungry ravenings of Destruction,
To be the sport of Accident, to waste in Wrath and Love a weary
Life, in brooding cares and anxious labours that prove but chaff?

Stephen Spender in an essay on Yeats drew attention to Yeats's never having cried the passionate cry. He was constantly autobiographical, but it was all writing on the veil of Public Importance – which is never of any importance. You never fall in love with anything in Yeats because his private world does not enlarge into a world for everyman. He does not evoke pity, passion or anger, and for all the burden of his native country in his work no poet could be more outside what we may call the Irish consciousness, and this is because he is too detached, too careful, too prudent to be human. He wrote ballads which he foolishly hoped would be popular with the people, but the people sensed this artificial note. Yeats wrote at a consistently high level but one single scream of the heart that pierces heaven he could never reach. For this reason he leaves me cold and leaves me in much doubt about his ultimate survival. Yeats belongs not to Sligo or to Ireland but was a child of the Victorian myth. He was the last Eminent Victorian. Yet it is impossible for us to read some of his later poems without bowing to his magical technique, and feeling that he is dining at last with Landor and Donne. [...]

I was talking about diarists.

If I were writing a true diary, which I have not been for various reasons, it would be entirely personal, and if it were to have value that personalism would have to be capable of enlarging itself into the diary of everyman. How right de Valera was when he said he looked into his own heart when he wanted to find out what the people of Ireland were thinking and feeling.

I am sure that this personalism has a system of telepathy which communicates all round the world.

What would my diary for today be?

Day in June, 1950:

It is almost midnight and I am sitting alone before my typewriter in my room wondering whether I should surrender to my natural and sinful sloth and go to bed.

I have been reflecting on my friendlessness in a society where everyone gives the impression of wanting to be friendly. I am sure that no one has ever been more sympathized with than myself. Yet it is a case of 'water, water everywhere nor any drop to drink'.

Who has ever sympathized less with his suffering fellows than yourself, Patrick Kavanagh? Yet you think the neighbours should be worried as to whether or not you die of loneliness and hunger. Nobody has ever invited you out although they know you are constrained to live alone. Why should they care? Some of them claim to be interested in art and letters, are to be seen at all sorts of Exhibitions and Openings, but they really don't care for these things. You should wake up to the fact that your death would be no more to the majority of your acquaintances than a further sensation. Tell me of anyone's death which would be more to *you*. You are as selfish as a cat.

Yes, I agree with you. But why do they want a man to go on writing? Why do they blame me for letting them down by writing so little? The other day a woman lamented to me and said: 'Terrible pity the way you are throwing your life away.' But why should I not be happy this evening, out swimming, or at the Phoenix Park Races, instead of sitting here hammering the typewriter?

How do you know they are happy? You know that Thoreau was right when he said that the masses of men lead lives of quiet desperation. Most of these 'happy' people would give a good deal to possess the pleasures of the mind which are open to you.

My view on that is that the pleasures of the mind are there for anyone who will pay the price. The price is loneliness and poverty.

You have endured much less of either than you pretend. You have never been hungry in your life – and everyone is lonely. See the millions of lonely women in the world. What about that woman who keeps writing you the passionate anonymous letters twice a week? I tell you, you are the luckiest man I know.

Lend me ten bob.

If you wanted to make money you could make it, as Ethel Mannin has told you. You have a touch which can make you the most popular writer this country has produced.

I partly agree, but something always prevents me realizing it.

A defect of character, my friend; you've had it since you were not (as country phrase had it) 'two hands over a hen'. It is hard to define this defect of yours, which is actually the source of your attraction. It is an innocence of heart but it is a feckless quality too. It produces pride, covetousness, lust, gluttony, envy, anger and sloth. It is a great pity.

Yes, but in arguing with me you seem to suggest that this defect can be cured. *Can* it be cured? I have tried but it is always there bleeding my life away.

Original Sin, in that wound is all growth. It is there the Tree of Good and Evil is planted. Consider these trees.

Actually I find the defect less than it was before you began to talk.

That is because for the first time in about two weeks you have sat down and used your mind and not gone to bed to luxuriate in wicked dreams.

Work, that's the cure for your disorder.

You are a proper bourgeois. I heard one speaking the very same things to me a few days ago. He said I should be glad of my state, and not be constantly running away from it, into pubs or wherever I could find distractions to make me forget.

Good on you, as the fella said to the ballad singer; you're showing a fine improvement. A little more of that tension and you'd have less time to criticize a sincere man like Clarke who has written many verses of excellent merit and who as a critic is far less sycophantic than many of your so-called friends. He is a sharp critic and writes a nice prose too.

But how am I to get immediate money?

Didn't I say, work? If you work all the other things will fall into your lap. You needn't tell me that you couldn't have married on account of poverty. Several women to my own knowledge have quite recently been most approachable. None of them had a great deal of money but all had character or they wouldn't attempt to approach you. Any of them would have helped you through for the next two years and if after that you couldn't keep her you deserve to be in the state you are, O idle monster! There is also the BBC, which is quite friendly to you, and there are scores of journals in America if you weren't too damned lazy. Ah, Kavanagh, I'll never make a man of you. Stick to your typewriter.

Don't mind that call at the door asking you out to the pub to waste *your* time and *his* money.

You're a slave-driver.

Nothing to what I will be if I get half a chance. This is the first time you've listened to your conscience since – I can't help using country expressions – since God was a gassan.

I'm tired; I want to go out.

Stay in; there's just the chance that your hard work will earn you something you've been hoping for. Everything comes to him who works.

This is terrible.

Another June day:

I have been returning to the writing of verse. It has been a long time since I last wrote verse.

ANTE-NATAL DREAM

I only know that I was there
With hayseed in my hair
Lying on the shady side
Of a haycock in July.

A crowd was pressing round
My body on the ground
Prising the lids of my eyes –
Open and you'll be wise.

The sky that roared with bees,
The row of poplar trees
Along the stream struck deep
And would not let me sleep.

A boortree tried hard to
Let me see it grow;
Mere notice was enough –
She would take care of love.

A clump of nettles cried:
We'll saturate your pride
Until you're oozing with
The richness of our myth

For we are all you'll know
No matter where you go –
Every insect, weed
Kept singing in my head.

Thistle, ragwort, bluebottle,
Cleg that maddens cattle
Were crowding round me there
With hayseed in my hair.

Now for bed:

That was a harmless sort of a day's writing you did yesterday.

I was writing other things.

You were not; you spent an hour studying the racing page of the paper, and time and again I have told you that this behaviour is a terrible waste of time. Didn't Mr Leopold Bloom whom you mentioned earlier come to the conclusion having listened all day to punters' talk that guess-work it came to in the long run? Give that up whatever you do. As a result of your betting you can't pay for lunch, but the loss of time and nervous wearing is the worst.

I am not quite satisfied with this diary.

It is excellent. You have managed to reveal yourself at many points without self-pity or loss of dignity. You have succeeded in looking at yourself from the outside.

I haven't lacked discretion, have I?

Well, the mask has been thin in spots, but generally no. And you've told no lies to yourself or to your readers.

('Diary', *Envoy*, June 1950, pp. 75–82)

School Book Poetry

One of these days I intend making an anthology – for myself – of school book poetry, the poetry that helps to form our tastes. Not always bad taste either.

I read somewhere how for many people the imaginative landmarks in their lives were popular songs – 'Ah, yes, that was Nice in 1927!'

For me, when I read 'Eugene Aram',* I am back in my native place, aged about sixteen with all my dreams sealed in the bud.

> *He told how murderers walk the earth*
> *Beneath the curse of Cain.*
> *With crimson clouds before their eyes,*
> *And flames about their brain,*
> *For blood has left upon their souls*
> *Its everlasting stain.*

There I am walking a lane peeping through the privet hedge into the field of turnips. The mood and atmosphere of the time comes alive in my mind. The comfortable worry of the summer fields is upon me. All the bits and pieces that furnish Imagination's house come up by magic.

'Locksley Hall' and I am several years younger, about twelve:

* 'The Dream of Eugene Aram', by Thomas Hood.

Comrades, leave me here a little while, as yet 'tis early morn,
Leave me here, and when you want me, sound upon the bugle-horn.

I had been thinking of getting a collection of the old school books (but they are not so easy to come by) for their covers would add to the evocative impulse. 'Eugene Aram' was in a bright yellow cover, 'Locksley Hall' in a blue. They had a particular smell too.

In the meantime I have found a good substitute. This is the new edition of the American anthology – the anthology to end or make superfluous all other anthologies – *The Home Book of Verse.* Four thousand large pages. Almost everything good and bad that I had in my school books is here.

Bret Harte's 'Dickens in Camp' –

> *Above the pines the moon was slowly drifting,*
> *The river sang below;*
> *The dim Sierras, far beyond, uplifting*
> *Their minarets of snow.*

And that was me in the virginal time before I had ever thought of writing a verse. A strange time, too, difficult to visualize, for a man who afterwards became so deeply involved in verse. How strange a thing like that happens to a man. He dabbles in something and does not realize that it is his life. There is nothing deliberate or conscious about my beginnings. It all happened like an accident. With most other verse writers of whom I have read there was usually a literary background or some roots somewhere.

If roots I had they were in the school books. When I read –

> *Often I think of the beautiful town*
> *That is seated by the sea*

I am walking through a field called Lurgankeel away down towards a shaded corner; it is an October evening and all around me is the protecting fog of family life. How shall I live when the fog is blown away and I am left alone, naked?

Longfellow was far from being a bad poet. In his naïve way he took a short-cut to immortality; for as Chesterton has said it is 'the awful judgment of the mob' that in the end matters. Whatever will live must touch the heart of the mob in some way. Contemporary fame is eclectic. It is for this reason that I cannot see the work of Yeats surviving. He was exciting to his contemporaries but there is little in his work that appeals straight to the heart.

A very good poet is Kipling, who is represented in the giant American anthology. His 'Maxims of Hafiz'* very nearly says something to everyman – though never quite:

> *My Son, if a maiden deny thee and scufflingly bid thee give o'er,*
> *Yet lip meets with lip at the lastward. Get out! She has been there*
> *before.*
> *They are pecked on the ear and the chin and the nose who are lacking*
> *in lore.*

That, needless to say, was in none of my school books. It is to the school books I must return for my virginal youth, for a winter morning in a desk near the fire, near the map of Scotland with my head dipped into a new satchel sniffing the wonderful memorable smell of new canvas.

> *I have you fast in my fortress*
> *And will not let you depart*
> *But put you down into the dungeon*
> *In the round-tower of my heart.*
>
> *And there will I keep you forever,*
> *Yes, forever and a day,*
> *Till the walls shall crumble to ruin*
> *And moulder in dust away.*

(*Kavanagh's Weekly*, 10 May 1952, p. 8)

* 'Certain Maxims of Hafiz'

From Monaghan
to the Grand Canal

I have been thinking of making my grove on the banks of the Grand Canal near Baggot Street Bridge where in recent days I rediscovered my roots. My hegira was to the Grand Canal bank where again I saw the beauty of water and green grass and the magic of light. It was the same emotion as I had known when I stood on a sharp slope in Monaghan, where I imaginatively stand now, looking across to Slieve Gullion and south Armagh. An attractive landscape of small farms and a culture that hadn't changed in a thousand years. A hundred yards away from me I could observe primitive husbandry where Paddy Nugent was threshing oats with a flail in a barn.

Yes, indeed.

But something disturbs my imagination.

I am thinking of a term which was much in use in the early days of my life in Dublin, just under twenty years ago. He has roots in the soil, they used to say. I was one of those who had an unchallenged right to claim roots in the soil, but I was an exception and the rooted-in-the-soil theory gave birth to a vast amount of bogusry – in Ireland, writers like Michael McLaverty, and in England, H.E. Bates and indeed Thomas Hardy. Could any man be more remote from the simple elemental folk of Wessex than Hardy?

Roots in the soil meant that you knew about people living close to nature, struggling for survival on the small farm, and you had a practical knowledge of animal breeding.

But of course roots in the soil have nothing to do with these things. What are our roots? What is our material?

Real roots lie in our capacity for love and its abandon. The material itself has no special value; it is what our imagination and our love do to it.

Lying at the heart of love we wander through its infinities.

The world that matters is the world that we have created, just as we create our friends. In making friends or a myth the material is sometimes of account. Some people will not stay made as friends; you mould them to your heart's desire, and when you are absent they change their shape.

Writers whose gimmick is roots in the soil produce a very violent article. The Seven Deadly Sins of Pride, Covetousness, Lust, Envy, Anger, Gluttony and Sloth loom large in those novels. But real elementalism is a more tawdry thing, resentful, mean and ungenerous. The majority of men live at a very petty level.

The society and place out of which I came was not unattractive. No man ever loved that landscape and even some of the people more than I. It was a barbaric society not appreciably different from an old-fashioned Dublin slum. Our manners were the same. But there was the landscape and the sense of continuity with a race that had come down the centuries.

I loved that country very much in spite of its many defects, and I had no messianic impulse to leave it. Everything that I did as regards acting or doing something was done against my natural feelings. Perhaps it is that basically we realize that all action is vulgar, that only the contemplative matters.

Watching the potato buds coming up, living the old pattern, what was there of spiritual values that could not be fitted into that context? And yet, having sown a couple of acres of barley in May, I walked off. I felt that I shouldn't have done it, that I was acting by some untruthful principle that had been created. It is indeed that untruthful principle that besets all of us in most of our activities. We can be taught only what we know. When you try to teach someone something they have not experienced, they do not hear.

I think that coming from the society and background that I have come from was disadvantageous to me in some respects. The worst respect was that one accepted as the final word in painting and letters the stuff that was being produced in Dublin. Another disadvantage was that the basic ingredients of the society in which I grew up were football and the smoky, sweaty dancehall. Football is not too bad but as the dancehall is one's only contact with social life, it was tough on a man of sensibility. It was simply impossible to love a galvanized dancehall and the atmosphere both physical and moral which prevailed there. Literature could not be made out of that material as Carleton made literature out of the many thrilling dances which are to be found in his *Traits and Stories*. Earlier I did find some imaginative and comic material in dances given to celebrate a wedding. The ear caught many of those delectable idiocies that people produce when in a state of excitement.

I remember a neighbour giving such a dance explaining that they weren't going to have any intoxicating drink. 'Their fill to eat and drink of currant bread and tay, and what more do they want?' A phrase like that was sure to gain currency in the ironic country where there were many intelligent and amusing people.

When I came to Dublin in 1938 the dregs of the old Literary Revival were still stirrable. The Palace Bar was crowded with two or three dozen poets and their admirers. I do not wish now to be satirical about these men. I am speaking about them now as part of my literary pilgrimage mainly because I have been provoked into it by some articles in a recent issue of *Studies*. Here the Movement which I thought quite discredited was being talked about. When I came to Dublin, Yeats was dead. Yeats was a poet and he invented many writers. He invented Synge and Lady Gregory and he was largely responsible for F.R. Higgins. As George Moore wrote: 'The Irish Literary Movement began with Yeats and returned to him.'

During my early years in Dublin the virtue of being a peasant was much extolled. This peasant derived naturally from the roots-in-the-soil theory. Knowing nothing better I accepted it and flaunted my peasantry in their somewhat spivvier genealogies.

Poor Higgins tried hard to play the peasant with bad poems about blackthorn sticks. The ballad was the peasant's poetic form. I suffered sore at ballad-mongering sessions before I realized that this form of torture was no different from the self-expression of any bore from the golf bore to the architect and cricket bore. Ballad singing is all right for the singer, but will he ever stop and give the others an innings?

I was the established peasant poet. Far from the poet being a peasant – if there is such an article outside the Russian novel – he is the last word in sophistication. All his life's activities are towards the final fusion of all crudeness into a pure flame. The keynote of the poetic mind is an extreme subtlety.

All this stuff about roots in the soil, peasants and balladry was no doubt the degenerate family of the preRaphaelites, coupled, by the time I came to know them, with the left-wingery of the International Brigade of the Spanish Civil War. The magazine *Ireland Today* brought this element in and I cannot deny that I subscribed my quota of 'working class' jargon to the magazine. Somebody recently embarrassed me by reminding me of a poem I had printed in *Ireland Today* about a servant boy. O my goodness! Well, we live and sometimes learn.

With a small society lacking intensity like this, one needs a coarse formula, if we are to have any body of writing. And that is what we have had for the past fifty years.

I cannot help saying that as far as I can see and as far as I have experienced, there has never been a tradition of poetry in Ireland. One can feel this lack of belief all the time.

And now raising my eyes to the horizon I am again looking across the small fields of south Monaghan and south Armagh, and wondering did any of the Irish writers who claimed to bring realism instead of the old sentimentalities ever express the society that lies within my gaze, with the exception of my own small effort in *Tarry Flynn*?

I am not suggesting that being true to life in a realist way is the highest function of a writer. As I have pointed out already, the highest function is the pure flame from the material.

The writers who wrote about Ireland in the new 'truthful' way proved to be no truer than the popular sentimentalizers such as Kick-ham and Canon Sheehan; they all seemed off-truth. This is not sur-prising, for most men who attempt to write about a particular society are deluded as to their qualifications for the job. For example, Mr Peadar O'Donnell has written novels about Donegal. It seems at once his country, but is it? Similarly there is a group who write about Gal-way and another about Cork and another about Kerry. Yet another school believe that in Dublin with its unique clichés and way of life is a ready-built bandwagon on which to ride to literary success. Any critic whether from Dublin or Soho can see that this stuff is just noisy empti-ness, completely unfunny.

It took me many years to work myself free from that formula for liter-ature which laid all the stress on whether it was Irish or not. For twenty years I wrote according to the dispensation of this Irish school. The appraisers of the school all agreed that I had my roots in the soil, was one of the people and that I was an authentic voice. I wrote, for exam-ple, a terrible piece about –

> *My soul was an old horse*
> *Offered for sale in twenty fairs.*
> *I offered him to the Church – the buyers*
> *Were little men who feared his unusual airs.*

One can at once see the embarrassing impertinence and weakness of it, the dissolute character whining. But it was the perfect Irish formula and English publishers loved it. Nothing would satisfy them but to put it first in the book. There has always been a big market in England for the synthetic Irish thing. Even Shaw, who was a bogus Irishman, had to do a bit of clowning.

Another villainous maw opened for things Irish-and-proud-of-it is the American literary market. The stuff that gets published as Irish in America is quite awful. One of the great, roaring successes of American publishing a couple of years ago was a novel by a Brian Moore about some Irish girl who had a vast number of illegitimate children. In re-viewing this book (and books of this kind) none leaned further back in referring to its compassion, its humour and its many other qualities than the Catholic papers. They seem terrified that they will be outdone in the liberal-ethic race. A dreary dust of left-wingery, a formula which excludes all creative thought, lies over the vegetation. They feel, I suppose, that literary and thought politics, like all other politics, is the philosophy of the possible. What's the use in being different if you can't get your words printed? Still.

In Ireland one is up against the fact that very few care for or understand the creative spirit. You can come across by being specifically Irish in manner and spirit, but when you attempt to offer them the real thing it's no go.

When I started to write what I believe is the real thing three years ago, there was not much response, except possibly from Stephen Spender who described it as 'violently beautiful'.

Previously I had been concerned with Ireland and with my ego, both of which come together often enough. Imagine the dreadfulness of:

> *It would never be spring, always autumn*
> *After a harvest always lost,*
> *When Drake was winning seas for England*
> *We sailed in puddles of the past*
> *Chasing the ghost of Brendan's mast.*

M.J. MacManus, writing about this, described it as wonderful poetry but bad history. If a thing is untrue it cannot be good poetry. When the editors of *The Oxford Book of Irish Verse* wanted something of mine they worked on me for this poem, and in the end, owing to my need for money, I let them in. But how appallingly this poem accepts the myth of Ireland as a spiritual entity.

Then one day as I was lying on the bank of the Grand Canal near Baggot Street Bridge having just been very ill in the hot summer of nineteen fifty-five, I commenced my poetic hegira. Without self-pity to look at things.

> *To look on is enough*
> *In the business of love.*

To let experience enter the soul. Not to be self-righteous. To have a point of view which is a man poised with a torch. Whoever wants to light a taper may; the torch-bearer does not mind. The light was a surprise over roofs and around gables, and the canal water was green stilly.

> *Commemorate me where there is water,*
> *Canal water preferably, so stilly*
> *Greeny at the heart of summer. Brother*
> *Commemorate me thus beautifully*
> *Where by a lock niagarously roars*
> *The falls for those who sit in the tremendous silence*
> *Of mid-July. No one will speak in prose*
> *Who finds his way to these Parnassian islands.*
> *A swan goes by, head low with many apologies,*
> *The bending light looks through the eyes of bridges*
> *And here! a barge comes bringing from Athy*
> *And other far-flung towns mythologies.*
> *O memorial me with no hero-courageous*
> *Tomb but just a canal-bank seat for the passer-by.*

This sonnet was inspired by two seats on the bank of the Canal here 'Erected to the memory of Mrs Dermot O'Brien'.

> *The main thing is to be free*
> *From self-necessity.*

On the road of my hegira I began to reflect with astonishment how poor as technicians the Irish school of poets and novelists have been. Real technique is a spiritual quality, a condition of mind, or an ability to invoke a particular condition of mind. Lack of technique gives us shallowness: Colum's

> *O, men from the fields!*
> *Soft, softly come through –*
> *Mary puts round him*
> *Her mantle of blue.*

A charming sentiment undoubtedly, but all on the surface. Technique is a method of being sincere. Technique is a method of getting at life. The slippery surface of the cliché-phrase and -emotion causes a light skidding blow.

I discovered that the important thing above all was to avoid taking oneself sickly seriously. One of the good ways of getting out of this respectability is the judicious use of slang and of outrageous rhyming. Auden in a radio lecture a year or so ago mentioned this and made a special reference to Byron's *Don Juan*. The new and outrageous rhymes are not to be confused with the slickeries of Ogden Nash. I draw attention to my rhyming of bridges with courageous.

Another bad thing about the Irish school was its dreadful sadness and lack of comedy. People who are unsure of themselves cannot afford to break out into uproarious laughter or use a piece of slang. You may find a small number of readers who cotton on to the technique, but large numbers of people will look with contempt at you and say what a pity it is that he lacks schooling. This can be depressing.

To write lively verse or prose, to be involved with Comedy, requires enormous physical and mental power. Energy, as Blake remarked, is eternal delight. The more energy is in a poem or prose work the more comic it is. Melville's *Moby-Dick* is a tremendous comedy, borne along to its end on the wings of its author's outgiving faith in his characters. Melville loved everything on that ship. And what a great poet in prose he was! We laugh inwardly in our souls with Melville.

Laughter is the most poetic thing in life, that is the right kind of loving laughter. When, after a lifetime of struggle, we produce the quintessence of ourselves, it will be something gay and young.

But to be undull is dangerous. Dullness as a cultural asset is most valuable. One remembers that old school friend meeting Johnson after many years and his saying rather sadly that he might have been a great success but 'cheerfulness kept breaking in'.

I have my own trouble with humour. A work that is inspired by the comic spirit has much to contend with, for a work that is inspired by the comic spirit has a sense of values, of courage and rectitude – and these qualities are hated immemorially.

Why they should be hated is not difficult to understand. A man in offering the small unique thing that is the most the greatest possess, eliminates completely the gassy fiction by which the majority live.

The notion of being one of the people is part of the general myth of roots in the soil. Analyzing the thing now I see or feel that I always had some sort of kink in me. It is this kink which makes a poet, I believe. As Colette observed, it is not what a poet writes that makes him one, but this other thing. 'Rectitude', Cocteau calls it. To have absolute rectitude in any field is to be an eccentric. You are not in step. Perhaps it is a form of pride and selfishness born of the realization that telling lies is a bore. In high company or low pub this rectitude is a constant quality with a poet. Being fated to live with this terrible tyrant of truth has often driven the possessed to violence, rage and, as in the case of Dylan Thomas, drink.

I am not sure if this kink of rectitude is on the whole beneficial to the man possessed by it; it makes a poet of him, but is it really necessary? It is this kink which makes people say, 'Why are you so damned difficult? We are anxious to help you.' And so on.

A trouble with the poet is that he is not a professional writer in the usual sense. Most of his hours are spent living. He can gulp out all he has to say in a short time. After a lifetime of experience, as Rilke pointed out, we find just a few lines. It is because of the minute quantity of that poetic essence that is in the best men that I do not regret having developed late and very slowly. If you read about English poetry you will find that the poets spent most of their time in taverns – Ben Jonson at the Mermaid, Dryden in Will's Coffee House. It takes a lot of living to produce a little experience. We remember Tennyson's remark, quoted by Carlyle, 'I am the greatest poet since Shakespeare; unfortunately I have nothing to say.'

The poet is a poet outside his writing, as I have often argued. He creates an oral tradition. He does something to people. I am not sure that that something is always good, for it is a disruptive, anarchic mentality which he awakens – and if we pursue him far enough we will be inclined to agree with Plato that the poet is a menace.

There is however not much danger of his menacing Dublin or, I imagine, Ireland generally.

Voltaire said that doing a thing was the only reward worth while, and Cézanne put that idea into practice when, having painted a picture, he left it behind him in a cottage or perhaps flung it into the bushes.

For a period of about a week a year ago, I wrote some poems to the new light and since then I have been sustained by them. If most of them have not yet been published, I do not mind. I am sending them out sparingly, as I want to 'kitchen' them.

But maybe now I am talking too near my ego.

It was a long journey for me from my Monaghan with my mind filled with the importance-of-writing-and-thinking-and-feeling-like-an-Irishman to the banks of the Grand Canal in nineteen-fifty-five, the year of my hegira.

(*Studies*, Spring 1959, pp. 29–36)

Suffering and Literature

I had been thinking of doing an essay on The Tragic Muse with some special relevance to my own experiences, which have over the past number of years contained a great deal of misery, at least as much and probably more than Dante's. Dante was only thirteen years wandering among and eating off rich friends before he got a house of his own.

Let it not be thought that I am presumptuous and conceited in comparing my lot to Dante's. Indeed from what I have been able to discover of Dante in various translations his intensity is too much for me and the great mystical cosmos he brings us tires me because of its lack of humaneness. One cannot live or feel all the time at that heat. It may be that in the original Italian the *Divine Comedy* is a comedy, yet somehow I imagine it is not, or Dante would not have referred to it as such. Anyhow the *Divine Comedy* is a very celebrated work and has been admired by a good many critics including Ezra Pound. But one must not be afraid of great reputations or terrified by great works, for the best that man can do is within the comprehension of the majority of intelligent men. There are no Great Men, or to put it another way a man is Great when he is not great or attempting to deliver some enormous message, as it seems to me Dante is trying to do in his Great Work. He took himself too seriously, a thing that is repugnant to my point of view, for that kind of taking oneself seriously is taking oneself unseriously. His real defect as a poet is his belief in the importance of Public Life. A really great man should always be of no public account. Dante was a Public Man in Florence and when he had to beat it out of his native city he took it very badly. He speaks of the saltness of the food that is eaten at another man's board and the steepness of the stairs. These can be great agony for the spirit, it is true.

But there is yet another point in Dante's cry about his misery during those years. A poet should not and does not become the slightest bit ashamed or loth to receive any gifts that anyone offers. This is the modern mood at any rate. The only thing that will madden him is if such gifts are insufficient to enable him to live in comfort if not in luxury. James Joyce lived mainly on and off Harriet Weaver and his spirit did not suffer for it. I agree that this sort of living is poor substitute for having lots of money of your own, but one is not humiliated as is the third-rate writer who lives by his pathetic rubbish. And a good poem is its own panacea.

Perhaps it was because I was incapable of writing such a good poem that much of my life has been at least as tragic as Dante's. I know and will put no tooth in it that the society and traditions of Dublin are unfriendly to the creative spirit. It is only that many people here are completely off beam regarding the creative spirit. I came to Dublin and stayed. I suppose that was my tragedy. I have however survived it. And it would be less than fair if on looking down on and over these last ten or twelve years I did not say that although the areas of suffering, even starvation, are substantial they are still only streaks in the general pattern.

That I did meet evil cannot be denied. I got very ill, but some may say that it is hard to kill a bad weed. When I was in hospital and the rumours of my early demise were floating – they floated back to me – a couple of patriotic chaps decided to do me proud in death. They would have me waked in state in the City Hall. Lying in state it would be called. But there were good people too, every sort of kindness has been showered on me by good people. For such love the only possible repayment seemed, at the time I was sick, to die. Anything else would have looked like cheating. However, I did that little bit of cheating and afterwards went on to accept all goodness, generosity, love as it came my way. We should be taught to accept.

Then there is yet another view that continually stares at me as I consider my life. What right has anyone to expect anything of anyone?

When one has one's health it is possible to live any old how.

Ah yes to be sure, to be sure, to be sure, we are now caught in the barbaric mood as we almost always are. The only things that matter are eating and drinking. There are no arts. We are all animals whose highest function is eating potatoes and cabbage, and beef if we can get it. That is the dénouement we arrive at when we logically think through the mazes of Dublin and Irish society. Probably of all societies, though in England and other countries it may be a little different. I came to Dublin. All we learn from experience is the way from simplicity back to simplicity. But at times it seemed a long, long and useless journey from the black hills of Shancoduff ...

> *My black hills have never seen the sun rising,*
> *Eternally they look north towards Armagh.*
> *Lot's wife would not be salt if she had been*
> *Incurious as my black hills that are happy*
> *When dawn whitens Glassdrummond chapel.*

I can see the neighbours now, each in every detail. The sun is shining on a particular grass.

> *My hills hoard the bright shillings of March*
> *Till the sun searches the last pocket.*
> *They are my Alps and I have climbed the Matterhorn*
> *With bundles of hay for three shivering calves*
> *Under the Big Forth of Rocksavage.*

> *The sleety winds rustle the rushy beards of Shancoduff*
> *While the cattle smugglers sheltering near Fetherna Bush*
> *Look up and say: Who owns them hungry hills*
> *That the waterhen and snipe must have forsaken?*
> *A poet! then by heavens he must be lean,*
> *I hear and is my faith not somewhat shaken.*

So you can see I did not have to go on pilgrimage through the valley of suffering. The poem is one of my earliest, also one of my best, but I never knew it then. I hadn't the courage of my simplicity, and such simplicity as remains with me has not come out of subtle, complex, useless journeying. Those hills were sharp, crooked and triangular, the triangularity providing the most efficient system for drainage.

Shancoduff is the name of a townland, and whenever you get the duff (or dubh) in a townland's name it means that the land faces north. It was sour land, lime-deficient, but then in my time there was a lot of mystery about land. Lime was looked upon with suspicion as something that enriched the father but robbed the son. Yet there is something very health-giving even in talking about soil. In days past girls who were anaemic were put to do a day's anything they liked, which involved walking over dry clay. Nonetheless, mowing with a scythe is undoubtedly one of the most slavish occupations, if you're doing it every day. I have a number of photographs taken for publicity purposes of me in action with that noble implement. But then again the song of a scythe being sharpened in some invisible hollow blends beautifully with the creak-creak of the corncrake. Out of this idyllic world I came into a useless struggle, merely as it turned out taking a long road home.

To revert a while to tragedy, I do not feel that a wise man expects any favours from his fellow men. To be wise one recognizes that in this world, except in the case of very virtuous people, it is every man for himself and the devil take the hindmost. That at any rate is the pattern of society in a country as recently poor as Ireland. Allowing for this I am sorry to have to record that there actually are people in this society who hate any man who is exceptional and who gloat over his misfortunes. Like that sardonic idea of the body of yours truly being laid out in state and draped in the flags of the United Nations above in the City Hall along with the statues. All the same I find it terribly hard to build a tragic tale out of my life and hard times. There is only one period in all those years that lies sick on its back, as I those years lay sick, and that was the year 1954, when I lost the sense of taste. To have no sense of taste is to be practically incapable of eating. My main source of wealth those days was three guineas a piece which I got from 'Sporting Prints' – short articles on sporting matters for the *Irish Press*. They were anonymous, which meant that the readers could take them seriously. To me athletics was always a second love and I had all the enthusiasm of the mediocre, believing as much in the virtues of the high jump as a bad novelist believes in 'The Art of the Novel'.

Well, it has been a long road, and maybe I've been too lyrical about it. I am constantly afraid of being unfair. Indeed I have found no technique that might adequately deliver me from certain bitter experiences. The evil thing. The leer that hurts the soul. Yet such is the nature of the world that the loyalty of bad people can be very great, and a man may travel far and be well looked after in their company.

But what of it? Who would exchange that defeated thing for the joy and happiness of the good, seeing that one implies the other?

(*Nonplus*, October 1959, pp. 85–9)

Autobiographical Note

My beginnings were so peculiarly humble and illiterate that I have never dared to write about them. I dislike talking about myself in a direct way. The self is only interesting as an illustration. I can begin only when things are moving into the comedy of humility.

I used at about the age of twelve to make up ballads in my head and these I sang to the neighbours. They were useful ballads telling about football matches, dances, etc. More than thirty years later I heard one of those ballads being sung. It was about a wedding dance which a number of men tried to crash:

> *Farrelly climbed in by the window*
> *But Dooly fell back with a souse*
> *And the singing and shouting was terrible*
> *Around the half barrel of stout.*

My misfortune as a writer was that atrocious formula which was invented by Synge and his followers to produce an Irish literature. The important thing about this idea of literature was how Irish was it. No matter what sort of trash it was, if it had the Irish quality. And that Irish quality simply consisted in giving the English a certain picture of Ireland. The English love 'Irishmen' and are always on the lookout for them.

So it was that, in the sign of this horrible constellation, I wrote a dreadful sort of stage-Irish autobiography called *The Green Fool* (1938).

I have never been able to live it down. My second greatest misfortune was that I came to live in Dublin. This was at the start of the Hitler war. My lot was cast in the midst of a crowd of the usual kind of lying journalists. Never in touch with anyone who would give me a line on the situation. One quality the school demanded of me was that I express peasant life. I was the authentic peasant. Several other Dublin bards were contending for the peasant title but I don't think any of these ever deposed me. Through hopping and trotting in the end I woke up.

I wrote a novel, *Tarry Flynn*, which I am willing to say is the only authentic novel of life as it was, and is, lived in rural Ireland. One must not hesitate to tell the truth even when it is in favour of oneself. The Pilot Press, which published *Tarry Flynn* in 1948, went broke immediately and the novel was remaindered at a shilling. It is now hard to get.

Then it dawned on me that the whole school of Irish writers and poets had nothing but 'Ireland' to offer. So I started a campaign to destroy the school. That campaign succeeded and the 'Irish' thing has fled either to America or the BBC.

But my real awakening came later, in 1955 and 1956, and most of the poems in *Come Dance with Kitty Stobling* were written in that period. I wrote all these new ones in an orgy of energy in about a week. It takes colossal energy to write a good poem and I have only the one lung; the other one had the misfortune to contract cancer and had to be removed in 1955. That's about the size of it for the present.

(Untitled in *Poetry Book Society Bulletin*, no. 25, June 1960, p. 1)

On a Liberal Education

A fund is being established to enable young Irish
creative artists to further their liberal education.

A liberal education? To enable the net of lies. To arrive at simplicity by
the shortest route. To laugh uproariously but with good nature at all
propounders of the liberal cliché. To laugh uproariously in the middle
of a half-finished poem. To be true to one's own judgement when every
journalist says the opposite. Certain kinds of smarmy humanitarians
should also be laughed at – the Rev. Michael Scott and Albert
Schweitzer for example. Yet not to be hard about it, not to make a philosophy out of it. To love all things in literature and life that are gay and
happy and to suspect all things that are gloomy and sticky with a purpose and people that are concerned with improving man's lot. I take a
moment off here to say that we should also be able at the earliest possible age to see behind the gloomy concern of the various kinds of
patriot and worker in good causes to find out if the cause of the gloomy
concern is a frustrated pea-sized ego.

When I was on my way to where I now stand – wherever that may
be – I encountered many aspects of The Lie. And no man was ever
more wide open to corruption.

I do not feel too bitter over all this; in fact I am always in danger of
bursting out laughing. And that's another thing: the majority of people
will never forgive you for being comic about the dull little things by
which they try to beat the artistic rap.

The Irish Literary Revival as it was called was responsible for many damaging lies. The 'peasant poet'. Having one's roots in the soil. They were all claiming to have their roots in the soil and to be peasants as well – Colum and Corkery and T.C. Murray, Brinsley MacNamara, Frank O'Connor, F.R. Higgins. Yeats was a troubled man because he couldn't achieve peasantry. In his last poems he did manage to move his mount over to the greener going on the stands side, if I may use the lingo of the racing game.

It was borne in on me from all sides that I was a peasant and a ploughman to boot and that anything outside the peasant in the ploughing field would not carry the authentic Irish note. So sadly I turned my ploughshare into a pen and in 1936 produced a slim booklet called *Ploughman and Other Poems*. In spite of all the liars around me there are things in that little book which are uncontaminated. However, there must have been enough of the authentic peasant note for I got a front-page spread in one of the Dublin newspapers. At the time I couldn't make out why I found that newspaper piece so wounding and offensive. It was an attitude very common in Ireland. I learned in time.

'What do you think of him?' said a man to me in 1957 about a prominent Irish businessman.

'A decent fellow but too fond of poetry' was what I replied. Or so this Boswellian friend told me later. He thought it a witty reply. It is a sharp one with much meaning. Journalists and businessmen and nearly everyone in Ireland loves the Muse and won't stop pawing the sweet wee thing.

> *I turn the lea-green down*
> *Gaily now,*
> *And paint the meadow brown*
> *With my plough.*

Then there was the all-over lie that was Ireland. Some men of genius have helped to support this lie – Yeats and Joyce in particular.

Because Joyce is passionately obsessed with Dublin, many fools imagine that it is Dublin confers the virtuous glory and not the obsession. Yeats too made Ireland his theme. But the work of Yeats which is deliberately Irish in this way sounds awful phoney. Irishness is a form of anti-art. When you meet one of these artists you discover he has no passionate faith in art. The tentacles of allusion which he throws out are aimed at no Promethean theft. A prominent Irish painter recently declared that he and not Jack Yeats was in the apostolic succession of art. If he had said he and not Matisse.

Ireland as a theme like every other formula was something within the reach of the average mediocrity. In spite of what may be said, O'Casey is loved in Ireland because however he attacks he always accepts the theme of Ireland. To deny Ireland as a spiritual entity leaves so many people floundering without art.

> *My soul was an old horse*
> *Offered for sale in twenty fairs.*

That was more of it. The idea of a poet offering his soul in fairs is quite repugnant to the whole nature of the poet. But the Irish persons love it. Loved they also –

> *It would never be spring, always autumn*
> *After a harvest always lost,*
> *When Drake was winning seas for England*
> *We sailed in puddles of the past.*

This is painfully Irish but I must confess. A good critic is one who enthuses over your good points and ignores your bad ones. The Irish critics always enthused over my bad points.

I think too it might have been possible for me to have remained in my native Monaghan and achieved simplicity and the technique which is part of that learning if I had been taught the score. The technique of reserve above all.

I feel that for a moment the mood I have evoked may give the impression that I think what happened to me is very important and that I am important. Nobody is important. Nobody is major. We get to our destiny in the end.

Small as life, not large as life is the proper phrase.

Journalists and university lecturers are another hazard for the liberal education seeker. They do not speak from a raised rostrum but from a hole in the ground. The good liberal education will lift a man up from that hole in the ground.

You will hear them speak of 'the giant figures' of the Literary Revival – Synge, Yeats, O'Casey. And 'major writers' like Frank O'Connor and Paul Vincent Carroll. Remarks of this kind might be likely to frighten the advancing scholar who if he had anything of the poet in him with the poet's arrogance would be just the opposite of the 'hole in the ground' talkers. A certain sort of humility is one form of The Lie.

It is smallness that gives power. Smallness and obscurity and insignificance. I do not however think a man should seek those three cardinal virtues of the poet. If he is one they will be conferred upon him by a grateful press and the other voices of ignorance and The Lie. One big English Sunday paper used to avoid mentioning George Barker's name under the belief that this was bad for him. But of course it is hard to achieve this sort of obscurity. To pursue the matter a little further, a man of unique genius in any field will be a man whose name you are tentative and shy about mentioning. Nobody has heard of him. You are speaking in a vacuum. Yet it is good for the soul to practise such courage.

This business of having one's roots in the soil is another thing. Roots in the soil means roots in experience, in love. The roots in the soil that I was told about was knowledge of the accepted formula. The last word in embarrassment in this field that I know of is to be found in Joseph Campbell.

> *I have gathered* luss
> *At the wane of the moon,*
> *And supped its sap*
> *With a yewen spoon.*

The principal reason for the existence of powerful bodies of supporters of the off-creative thing is the apparent need for all members of the male (human) sex to project themselves. The search for identity, it is called. It is the desire to be somebody. It is awful to be a nobody in a crowd.

This problem was solved in Ireland by diluting the Pierian Spring one part in ten thousand lies. In the past poets proliferated all over the place and even today there are a goodly number.

To satisfy this human need many art movements have been started. The Irish Literary Revival was essentially one of these. To vary the metaphor, a debased coinage to let everybody have plenty of money.

Thirty or so years ago Dr F.R. Leavis of Cambridge, aided and abetted by Ezra Pound and T.S. Eliot, launched what came to be known as the New or Higher Criticism. More recently the Angry Young Men, and more recently still in America there has happened the Beat Generation. People in a more desperate plight in their efforts to beat the artistic rap just go berserk with beards and canvases or go hacking in fury at blocks of wood.

An American, Jackson Pollock, literally threw a pot of paint in the public's face and became a great art name in America. The limit of pathos or bathos was surely reached when an art exhibitor in London poured tar on canvas, set a match to it and there was a work of art.

But to understand all is to love all and the man on the hunt for liberal learning is on the hunt for understanding and the love that goes with it. As I have hinted in the earlier part of this essay, this understanding is not going to make a man happy, far from it. Understanding people and feeling for them and laughing naturally and uproariously at their concern with what is not really important is like prying into a mean room. But of course love can go farther and understand understanding. Yes, yes, yes.

On the way towards the final understanding the thing is to know the score as regards the various movements and the different individuals who are not in movements.

Take the New Criticism first.

I know many supposed literary men who are impressed by it and who get bogged down in its intricacies. They haven't the over-all view, they haven't a world in their mind.

The Leavis criticism was criticism as a thing valid in itself and independent or nearly of the original work it purports to deal with. This surely is a form of synthetic insanity. In criticizing by the New Critical canon anything goes, anything you say about any work is as good as the next man's opinion. In writing about Hopkins' *Falcon* some speculated that this referred to Christ the King and others that it was the King of England and so on and so on and so on. It was a wonderful idea. I call it artificially induced paranoia. As anybody who has the misfortune to know paranoia or persecution mania produces in the sufferer an inability to stop writing or talking as the case may be. A man once rang me up and asked me to meet him in a Dublin restaurant: he had something he wanted to show me so that I might speak to some editor about it. He warned me, as I entered the café and asked him if he was the man, to speak low; he was being watched.

Then he slowly drew out of a large briefcase a foolscap MS about three inches thick in single-spaced typing. It was not the whole story of his woes from the time he was sacked as a town clerk of an English town to that present moment … it was a précis of the story of his woes.

The New Critics have been able to induce this disease artificially and so you have this fantastic verbal diarrhoea, most of which comes from American universities. One of them will turn out a dozen books while you'd be saying F.R. Leavis.

And not only have they induced the verbosity, they have also other symptoms: they bring personal relations into the argument. I once knew a well-known N.C. who refused to come to a party because I'd be at it.

The liberal learner should be given a few names to memorize. In America Hugh Kenner, R.P. Blackmur, Lionel Trilling; in England, besides the revered founder William Empson, Donald Davie; and in Ireland Denis Donoghue.

It would also be necessary to add that many of these have a lot of real talent, especially an architectural talent, the ability to construct even when the edifice they are constructing may be of little value to mankind.

When one has learned about these prolific critics one can understand what the opposite side is. The side of small output. The side that realizes with Rilke that all the best of us has to say is 'after a lifetime's experience a few lines'.

Advising a young creative artist to go to America might appeal to some people. There are many Fellowships which enable a young person to go to America. Yet though America is a most fascinating place socially, it is disappointing from the creative view.

With the exception of two little magazines as far as I know – *Poetry Chicago* and a new one, *The Fifties* – there is practically no publication in the United States that will print anything that is not the liberalistic formula or touched with it. This dreary philosophy lies like a dust over the vegetation. *The Commonweal*, edited as a Catholic weekly, leans backward to appear straighter than *Partisan Review*.

The universities and colleges of the United States have all their faculties of creative writing and I cannot imagine a more baneful influence. No standards. No courage to make standards.

In *The Fifties*, the first number brought out in 1958, there is a feature not unlike one I ran in *Kavanagh's Weekly* which I called 'The Old Foolishness', just mere quotation of foolish sayings. Quoted ironically is an extract from an article in another magazine, 'The Writer as Teacher'. It is not unfunny and it tells us something about the American cultural scene.

> A recent survey showed that nine thousand poems were written in classrooms last year, two thousand of them directly on blackboards. [As compared with only seven thousand written in other places.] The same survey showed that over five hundred poets stopped writing in universities last year as against only two hundred who stopped writing elsewhere; moreover 21 poets committed suicide in the universities last year as against only 2 who committed suicide elsewhere. No one can deny that the writers are in the universities. Now at last poetry has a home; a spiritual home in the spiritual life of the universities. This spiritual life is growing greater every year; last year for instance our poets spent a total of twenty-eight thousand afternoons listening to their students' problems.

This appears to show an Irish influence. The Assembly at Drumceat had 14,000 poets I think.

The main thing that is wrong with America from the creative point of view is the absence of a humus of repose. In the whole of the United

States there are only a few writers of conventionally high talent. John Steinbeck is coarse stuff without that simple rectitude that makes a work of art. Old Robert Frost, who was given honours in Oxford and here a couple of years ago, writes dull prosy verse. Dead stuff, I would say.

Richard Wilbur constructs artificially like Thomas Kinsella in Ireland. No inspiration. No life. No gaiety. Very popular with the masses of people who worship or pretend to worship what is within the grasp of the mediocrity. From the occasional whiffs of originality and poetic courage that come to me through such little magazines as *The Fifties* and *Poetry* I can see that the dust bowl has not entirely conquered the States.

Some people are of the opinion that going to France or Italy is a cultural education, and in so far as the visible is concerned it could be so called. But love is love and love of everything. Standing on the side of a hill in Monaghan, an indifferent landscape of crooked lanes and little humpy hills covered with whins, I found love, the kind of love that purifies, a sort of Divine love. Yes –

The fields that heal the humble.

In more recent years I have begun to love the visible rather than the ideological. I can look for long at a scene. When I was in Rome last I could not do that. I was mentally too strong and arrogant. When one gets physically weaker and so also mentally weaker one enjoys the static pleasures of looking and listening. It was while recovering from a serious illness in the hot summer of nineteen fifty-five as I lay on the bank of the Grand Canal that I learned the pleasures of being passive. The green still water, the light around gables. There are two seats on the canal bank 'Erected to the memory of Mrs Dermot O'Brien'.

O commemorate me where there is water,
Canal water preferably, so stilly
Greeny at the heart of summer. Brother
Commemorate me thus beautifully
Where by a lock niagarously roars

The falls for those who sit in the tremendous silence
Of mid-July. No one will speak in prose
Who finds his way to these Parnassian islands.
A swan goes by head low with many apologies,
Fantastic light looks through the eyes of bridges –
And look! a barge comes bringing from Athy
And other far-flung towns mythologies.
O commemorate me with no hero-courageous
Tomb – just a canal-bank seat for the passer-by.

It was however a long journey and a dark travail from the little fields of Monaghan that might have saved me had I got the right education and would have accepted it to that July afternoon on the Grand Canal beside Baggot Street, Dublin. Surely the purpose of a good education is to prevent one from squandering one's life in useless suffering. Then again is any suffering useless and is there any way home but through it? I didn't get a liberal education laid on to be absorbed in a couple of years. I got it in the end.

So our seeker after a liberal education is still in Dublin. Certainly he has to get out. I suspect he will be sent to France or Italy because I am sure that the administerers of the fund are convinced that France, Italy or Spain will do the trick. The disreputability of the Continent of Europe is in a way respectable so long as Art is involved. Going to London on the other hand is hardly a thing one of our art patrons would wish to fork out money for. To give a young man a wad of notes with which to stand drinks to poetic loungers in a Soho bar would be even less respectable. And yet I am convinced that the chief place today where the poetic faith is to be found is in some of the bars and clubs and cafés of Soho and also in other spots. You get enthusiastic and sincere people in all sorts of outlying districts. But the main concentration is in the Soho district.

The bar or the club or the café with its groups of the poetic faithful is the only place in which a young creative artist can further his liberal education. The only good way to gain admission to such a group is to have talent, to have done something that any one man of the true artistic faith, one of those who will never tell a lie, will like.

The three or four hundred pounds which the fund will provide for our young creative hopefuls will be a useful ice-breaker. Then again the idea of a young man throwing drink into ... But one must face the facts. A man from Ireland with a thick roll will be heard coming at London Airport, and unless most of the boys are abroad as they often are there will be a fair muster. I would therefore suggest to the Arts Council that someone must be given the job of observer in Soho to report when the fullest muster is likely to be present. This is not meant to be facetious; the best poets and painters today live a great deal of their time in bars, and a man with a roll of fivers is a godsend. Whiskey is terribly dear in England and is supplied in what one man has called the 'smallest measure ever moulded for the lips of man'.

Of course there are the groups of industrious mediocrities ...

Living, and living in pubs at that, is part of the poet and painter's work – his experience. The usual mediocrity with his regular output never gestates; he is always dribbling something not life out of him.

We come now to another aspect of the liberal education, another aspect of the corrupting influence that a strong creative character can have on a young man who has not got that diamond hardness that is the poet's. I do not refer to any ordinary corruption. A man's spirit is broken in a different way and he becomes a mere parroter of the master's words and opinions. In many ways there is not much remedy for this and it is possible that a liberal education ultimately consists in copying a selected master. There are only a few originals. This is not a happy condition. I have no answer to it and it may be that there should be no answer to it.

The purpose of a liberal education is to learn to be simple. We begin by being simple and then for years plough through complexities and affectations to come back to where we begin.

All that trouble and here I am again.

(*X*, vol. 2, no. 2, August 1961, pp. 112–19)

Writer at Work

I have seen a few of the pieces you have published on 'The Writer at Work'. I only remember one vaguely and it was very wild and wonderful – about Life. Life.

I have a fair share of experience of talented writers and I have never caught any of them working. With Anthony Carson I have shared the same roof plenty of times and damn me if I've ever seen him put a word down. The general impression of him in my mind is of a large man with a half bitter in his fist, striding over and back a bar-room floor. Not far away is George Barker, leaning against the bar with a whiskey in his fist. When the bar closes taxis are ordered and away with the lot of us to someone's flat.

Carson and Barker between them have published about eighteen books and each with 'his uniqueness'.

The position is this: Being pregnant with celestial fire is similar to pregnancy of the flesh. Poets, whether in verse or prose, don't have to wear maternity gowns to show that they are in an 'interesting condition'. It takes only a short time to give birth if you've anything to give birth to. Poetic pregnancy is very rare and the poet's living it up in pubs, and so forth, is only waiting. Ladies-in-waiting. Poets-in-waiting.

I'll tell you a bunch of writers that you will surely catch at work: John Wain, D.J. Enright, Donald Davie, Elizabeth Jennings, Graham Hough, etc., etc. Without mercy they keep at it.

But they're fooling nobody. Just dull people.

I do remember when I actually did work. With my cup on the table before me, at nine in the morning I sat in front of the typewriter and I wrote like the devil till about twelve. I wrote a few novels at the time after the Hitler war, but did not ask anyone to publish them yet. The whole secret of writing is energy and a gay mind. Writers like Wain and those others and their kind whom I have mentioned have a coarse sort of energy, but it is not the gay energy of the poet. They are experts in the business of boring.

Boringness is undoubtedly a form of energy without feeling.

I object to nationalism, particularly Irish nationalism in letters, because of the harm it does, the false values it postulates. The world is a small place these days and the poetic spirit is in a weak condition everywhere. There is nothing worth mentioning in the great United States. You have a lot of trashy playwrights, fifth-rate poets like Tennessee Williams, and twelfth-rate like Arthur Miller. The theatre is journalism (forget about Shakespeare and Goldsmith, Congreve and Sheridan) and America is a great place for journalism. Broadway is just another projection of the *New York Times* and the *New York Daily News* (wonderful paper the *Daily News*, no plays in New York as good as that journalism). But the point is if you cannot write, write a play.

A lot of Celts here in Éire have cottoned on to this fact. And please don't laugh and think me funny. The fact is that in the whole world to-day there aren't a dozen writers worth discussing. In America you have Robert Lowell (mainly as a translator or re-creator) and in a thin way William Snodgrass. Kerouac's *On the Road* is a lively report on the United States. Gregory Corso is not so bad either. There are only one or two small publications in America that will publish anything that isn't dead and I'm sorry to see that telly is putting many of them out of business. The *New York Times* lifts poems from various sources, but does not pay for them. The honour is enough.

That's about all I have to say though I suppose I might be expected to make some comments on the Celtic situation.

There is the Censorship (now belonging to the pre-war (Hitler) period). Frank O'Connor after his return from the USA banged right into it, not knowing that that jag is as much a joke in literary circles as the Liberal Ethic. The small large towns of Ireland are full of this class

of stuff and the advanced peoples there think me very backward in not
knowing among other things – the damage the censorship does to Celtic
Irish writers, the greatness of Synge, and other Protestants who give expression to the Spirit of Ireland on British telly and steam wireless.

Nothing damages any writer except his inability to write gay lively
stuff, the stuff that will cause pain to your liberal who will see at a
glance that it isn't Art.

Art is what's a-wanting.

(*St Stephen's*, Trinity Term 1962, pp. 27–8)

Collected Poems: Author's Note

I have never been much considered by the English critics. I suppose I shouldn't say this. But for many years I have learned not to care, and I have also learned that the basis of literary criticism is usually the ephemeral. To postulate even semi-absolute standards is to silence many lively literary men.

I would not object if some critic said I wasn't a poet at all. Indeed, trying to think of oneself as a poet is a peculiar business. What does it feel like to be a poet?

I am always shy of calling myself a poet and I wonder much at those young men and sometimes those old men who boldly declare their poeticality. If you ask them what they are, they say: Poet.

There is, of course, a poetic movement which sees poetry materialistically. The writers of this school see no transcendent nature in the poet; they are practical chaps, excellent technicians. But somehow or other I have a belief in poetry as a mystical thing, and a dangerous thing.

A man (I am thinking of myself) innocently dabbles in words and rhymes and finds that it is his life. Versing activity leads him away from the paths of conventional unhappiness. For reasons that I have never been able to explain, the making of verses has changed the course of one man's destiny. I could have been as happily unhappy as the ordinary countryman in Ireland. I might have stayed at the same moral age all my life. Instead of that, poetry made me a sort of outcast. And I was abnormally normal.

I do not believe in sacrifice and yet it seems I was sacrificed. I must avoid getting too serious.

I belong to neither of the two kinds of poet commonly known. There is the young chap who goes to school and university, is told by lecturers of the value of poetry, and there is the other kind whom we somehow think inspired. Lisping in numbers like Dylan Thomas, Burns, etc.

Looking back, I see that the big tragedy for the poet is poverty. I had no money and no profession except that of small farmer. And I had the misfortune to live the worst years of my life through a period when there were no Arts Councils, Foundations, Fellowships for the benefit of young poets.

On many occasions I literally starved in Dublin. I often borrowed a 'shilling for the gas' when in fact I wanted the coin to buy a chop. During the war, in Dublin, I did a column of gossip for a newspaper at four guineas a week.

I suppose when I come to think of it, if I had a stronger character, I might have done well enough for myself. But there was some kink in me, put there by Verse.

In 1942 I wrote *The Great Hunger*. Shortly after it was published a couple of hefty lads came to my lonely shieling on Pembroke Road. One of them had a copy of the poem behind his back. He brought it to the front and he asked me, 'Did you write that?' He was a policeman. It may seem shocking to the devotee of liberalism if I say that the police were right. For a poet in his true detachment is impervious to policemen. There is something wrong with a work of art, some kinetic vulgarity in it, when it is visible to policemen.

The Great Hunger is concerned with the woes of the poor. A true poet is selfish and implacable. A poet merely states the position and does not care whether his words change anything or not. *The Great Hunger* is Tragedy and Tragedy is underdeveloped Comedy, not fully born. Had I stuck to the tragic thing in *The Great Hunger* I would have found many powerful friends.

But I lost my messianic compulsion. I sat on the bank of the Grand

Canal in the summer of 1955 and let the water lap idly on the shores of my mind. My purpose in life was to have no purpose.

Besides *The Great Hunger* there are many poems in this collection which I dislike; but I was too indifferent, too lazy to eliminate, change or collect. For these and other reasons I must offer thanks to Mr Martin Green who made the collection.*

(MacGibbon & Kee, London, 1964, pp. xiii-xiv)

---

*John Montague's editorship of the *Collected Poems* was kept secret from Kavanagh, who would have objected to a younger Irish poet making a selection from his poetry.

Self-Portrait

This is not a completely true self-portrait, and its lack of truth is not due to its shortness. For years I have tried to find a technique through which a man might reveal himself without embarrassment. There are two fairly successful examples of this technique – *Don Quixote* and Joyce's *Ulysses*. Sancho Panza and Mr Bloom are the private lives of two public men. I have found that only in verse can one confess with dignity. We have all done mean and ugly things and nearly always these sins should be confessed because of the damage they have done us. Even the most apparently revealing autobiographies (some, like Pepys' *Diaries,* in code) do not expose too much.

My life has been a failure till I woke this morning, which is the 24th August, 1963. I saw a wonder question-mark:

> *There is to-day*
> *And tomorrow.*

I echoed Carlyle:

> *So here hath been dawning*
> *Another blue day,*
> *Think wilt thou let it*
> *Slip useless away.*

Probably yes. But continuation is everything.

PATRICK KAVANAGH

SELF-PORTRAIT

I dislike talking about myself in a direct way. The self is only interesting as an illustration. For some reason, whenever we talk about our personal lives they turn out to be both irrelevant and untrue – even when the facts are right, the mood is wrong.

English publishers and newspapers are mad for personal data, especially about people from Ireland. They love Irishmen. America is now even worse. And the unfortunate peoples of my island home lap up all that vulgarity when it is dished out to them.

The quality that most simple people fear – and by simple people I mean terrified, ignorant people – is the comic spirit, for the comic spirit is the ultimate sophistication which they do not understand and therefore fear.

When, under the evil aegis of the so-called Irish Literary Movement, I wrote a dreadful stage-Irish so-called autobiography called *The Green Fool*, the common people of this country gobbled up this stage-Irish lie. When, years later, I wrote *Tarry Flynn*, which I am humble enough to claim is not only the best but the only authentic account of life as it was lived in Ireland this century (a man shouldn't be afraid to tell the truth even when it is in favour of himself), the principal people who enjoyed this novel were literary sophisticates; its uproarious comedy was too much for the uneducated reader. I am not trying to boost my wares. I am merely trying to illustrate a position. And I would say now that that so-called Irish Literary Movement which purported to be frightfully Irish and racy of the Celtic soil was a thoroughgoing English-bred lie. Anybody can write tragedy. The English reviewers went crazy about the poetry of O'Casey's Juno, whereas in fact we only endure that embarrassment for the laughs in Captain Boyle.

I am supposed to be self-portraying myself and I hope I am so doing. I can tell all about my background and upbringing without being very original. And it is there the lie comes in. I would have to show that my background and my childhood adventures were out of the common just as journalists do when they report on foreign countries. I remember reading a journalist on a visit to Greece who made the illuminating disclosure that the Greeks were very fond of conversation.

But if the place and the experience weren't different what the devil was he doing out there?

My childhood experience was the usual barbaric life of the Irish country poor. I have never seen poverty properly analyzed. Poverty is a mental condition. You hear of men and women who have chosen poverty, but you cannot choose poverty. Poverty has nothing to do with eating your fill today; it is anxiety about what's going to happen next week. The cliché poverty that you get in the working-class novel or play is a formula.

My father, being a shoemaker, was probably less poor than the small farmer classes. What was called the 'dropping shilling' kept coming in. But as for the scraidíns of farmers with their watery little hills that would physic a snipe, I don't know where they got any money. But the real poverty was the lack of enlightenment to get out and get under the moon.

I am afraid this fog of unknowing affected me dreadfully. But, as I have suggested earlier, all this is of little importance.

Whatever tradition of semi-civilized living existed in Carleton's time, it was not there in mine. I fell between two stools.

Round about the late nineteen-thirties a certain prosperity came through, and foolishly enough that was the time I chose to leave my native fields. I had no messianic impulse to leave. I was happy. I went against my will. A lot of our actions are like that. We miss the big emotional gesture and drift away. Is it possible to achieve our potential grand passion? I believe so. Perhaps that has been my weakness.

I came to Dublin in nineteen-thirty-nine. It was the worst mistake of my life. The Hitler war had started. I had my comfortable little holding of watery hills beside the Border. What was to bate it for a life? And yet I wasted what could have been my four glorious years begging and scrambling around the streets of malignant Dublin. I could have done my smuggling stint. I could never see my own interest. I could never see love on bended knees begging me to come. I was always in the fog. When I came to Dublin in 1939 the Irish Literary affair was still booming. It was the notion that Dublin was a literary metropolis and Ireland, as invented and patented by Yeats, Lady Gregory and Synge, a spiritual entity. It was full of writers and poets and I am afraid I thought their work had the Irish quality. The conversation in Poets' Pub had the richness and copiosity that H.W. Nevinson said all Dublin conversation had. To me, even then, it was tiresome drivel between journalists and civil servants. No humour at all. And, of course, they thought so much of poetry they didn't believe in the poet ating. I am not, I assure you, complaining, merely stating a few ridiculous facts. It was all my fault. What was I doing there? Wasn't I old enough to know the differ? Shouldn't I have cottoned on? Ah well, we live and we sometimes learn.

Now, part of my poverty-stricken upbringing was my belief in respectability – a steady job, decency. The bohemian rascals living it up in basements and in mountain hideouts horrified me. If I had joined them and endured them they'd have taken me to their bosoms. But I couldn't do it. Instinctively I realized that they were embittered people worshipping the poor man's poet. Their left-wingery was defeat. But the key to prosperity was with that sort of enemy and still is. When I think of the indignities I endured in the cause of respectability I can kick myself. And me with health and strength to dig ditches, or to leap them anyway with a sack of white flour on me back. The Monaghan–Armagh–Louth border was not a severe test for a true stayer carrying top weight. I can kick myself for all the people I didn't kick then. Sometimes when walking along a Dublin street I might well be noticed making wild, vicious kicks at emptiness and scringing my teeth at the same time. Thinking over the matter in the light of hindsight, I realize it would not have been easy for a man of sensibility to survive in the society of my birth, but it could have been done had I been trained in the technique of reserve and restraint. A poet is never one of the people. He is detached, remote, and the life of small-time dances and talk about football would not be for him. He might take part but could not belong.

A poet has to have an audience – half a dozen or so. Landor, who said he esteemed ten a sufficient audience, was very optimistic. I know about half a dozen and these are mainly London-based. It may be possible to live in total isolation but I don't understand how. The audience is as important as the poet. There is no audience in Ireland, though I have managed to build up out of my need a little audience for myself. The real problem is the scarcity of a right audience which draws out of a poet what is best in him. The Irish audience that I came into contact with tried to draw out of me everything that was loud, journalistic and untrue. Such as:

> *My soul was an old horse*
> *Offered for sale in twenty fairs.*

Anthologists everywhere keep asking for this. Also asked for is another dreadful job about Mother Ireland:

> *It would never be spring, always autumn*
> *After a harvest always lost.*

Thank God, I control the copyrights in these poems and nobody can use them. What the alleged poetry-lover loved was the Irishness of a thing. Irishness is a form of anti-art. A way of posing as a poet without actually being one. The New Lines poets of today have invented a similar system.

They are also sympathetic to the Irish thing.

No young person today would think of coming to live in Dublin as a metropolis. A new awareness is in the air. A couple of years ago I remember a young chap accosting me in a Dublin street. He was from the southern part of Éire and he was on his way to Rome – to take up the poetry trade. He was right too. At least something might happen to him there, a rich woman might take a fancy to his poetry and keep him in the decency and comfort which are a necessity of the poet. I pause here to emphasize that I have no belief in the virtue of a place. Many misguided persons imagine that living in France or Italy is the equivalent of a liberal education. French in particular is the language of art. Still, Dublin hasn't the possibilities for getting hitched up to a rich woman, and this is about the only way a true poet can remain true and keep up an adequate supply of good whiskey.

And now it's around 1955 and I am wandering around Dublin when I run into a poetry-lover.

'How are you getting on at all?' says he with much pity.

The instinct to do a day's good deed has always been a weakness with me, so I reply, 'Terrible.'

'Poor fella.'

'Sure what can I do?'

'And you're not writing any poetry these times. I never see anything by you in the *Irish Times*. The flash is gone. I say, the flash is gone.'

'I suppose so.'

'A terrible scandal that the Government doesn't do something for our Irish poets. There's forty or fifty major poets in this country today and if I had me way they'd all have a civil list pension. Peadar has been working for that this many a year. Is the health all right again?'

I cough hard and send him away happy. I won't be long in it and that City Hall booking for my lying-in-state can be taken up. And that was interesting too. When I was above in the Rialto Hospital, and the report of my impending demise spread, two well-wishers decided to do me proud in death: they would have me waked in the City Hall. A journalist friend of mine brought me the news as I lay in hospital at the end of a real tether, which was attached to the bottom of the bed, and to rise sitting you pulled on the rope. It must have been disappointing that I didn't oblige.

I fear that the mood I have been evoking may give the impression that what happened to me is important and that I am important. Nobody is important. Nobody is major. We get to our destiny in the end. I am not in the least bitter over all this. In fact I am always in danger of bursting out laughing.

I merely state the facts. Of course I do not blame some of these people. I had been assailing the myth of Ireland by which they were managing to beat the artistic rap. I had seen and shewn that this Ireland thing was an undignified business – the trade of enemies and failures.

The English lower orders and their voices, the popular journalists, wanted a certain image of the Irishman, one that would make them feel better, but of recent years a small group of Irishmen in London founded an enclave which did not tolerate such blackguardism. Some of those newspapermen were very humble if they happened to be allowed into that company, and they knew their place better than to write about them. That is indeed one thing to be said for English newspapers, they hardly ever gossip about poets – only actors and film and telly stars. I love reading that stuff, the handouts telling us of the stars and their affairs off the set. All supposed to be real-life stuff.

For a number of years I was a film critic. I attended the Irish Film Society shows of a Saturday and wrote as enthusiastically as the next man about the marvellous Italian film – the photography, the direction and the director, a man of superb genius.

That was before I learned the difficult art of not caring, of having the courage of one's feelings. But it did take me quite a while before I came out with the terrible disclosure that I thought of most of these foreign films what George the Third thought of Shakespeare – poor stuff, but one mustn't say so.

I burned my way through the film critics' world till in the end I was unable to say another word. If I had been able to stick it out I would probably today be a maker of films or a director of telly shows, or even one of those suave chaps who talk on telly and who are all noted for an excellent head of hair and who all have the same smiling face, the same age too, frozen at thirty-nine. See what I missed and see what the public missed. And there's where it was.

Among the other things I missed, one I regret was refusing the offer of Reuters to go in as a reporter with the Second Front. And look at the fellow who wrote *The Longest Day*.

Once again and as always, I was showing my cautious, respectable mentality. Instead of letting it rip. This has been a great defect in my nature. On the other hand I know of quite a couple of very fine poets in England who avoided the draft, one by pretending to be bonkers. But every man to his fancy. I was a different class of animal. I should have done something.

Another great experience I had was my law case, hereinafter to be known as The Trial or Trial and Error, mostly error. Curious thing is that an event so seemingly large at the time disappears in the perspective of a few years. What seems of public importance is never of any importance. Stupid poets and artists think that by taking subjects of public importance it will help their work to survive. There is nothing as dead and damned as an important thing. The things that really matter are casual, insignificant little things, things you would be ashamed to talk of publicly. You are ashamed and then after years someone blabs and you find that you are in the secret majority. Such is fame.

Of my early Dublin experiences I have little of value to offer. In the frosty winter of 1946 I went around trying to sell a contraption for attaching to furnaces to conserve the heat which was scarce those days. I spent a fortnight tramping the frozen streets, my contraption rejected and denounced by all sorts of janitors. Eventually, in the furnace (not the bargain) basement of a Grafton Street store, the boss foreman made a complimentary remark about my article as shown in the illustrated folder. I couldn't carry the machine, which was a hundredweight. Twenty-five pounds was the price, but he said there wasn't a whit the matter with the idea if it came at a fiver. 'Worth about a fiver for a trial,' he said. Morality triumphed over commerce. I said, 'It's not worth five shillings never mind five pounds; it's a complete fraud.'

In those days in Dublin the big thing besides being Irish was peasant quality. They were all trying to be peasants. They had been at it for years but I hadn't heard. And I was installed as the authentic peasant, and what an idea that was among rascals pretending to have an interest in poetry. Although the literal idea of the peasant is of a farm labouring person, in fact a peasant is all that mass of mankind which lives below a certain level of consciousness. They live in the dark cave of the unconscious and they scream when they see the light. They take offence easily, their degree of insultability is very great. I have written:

> But I, trained in the slum pubs of Dublin
> Among the most offensive class of all –
> The artisans – am equal to this problem;
> I let it ride and there is nothing over.
> I understand through all these years
> That my difference in their company is an intrusion
> That tears at the sentimental clichés.
> They can see my heart squirm when their star rendites
> The topmost twenty in the lowered lights.
> No sir, I did not come unprepared.

Which brings me to something that I might say is the very heart of the matter of human contentment or as near as we can get. This is the secret of learning how not to care. Not caring is really a sense of values and feeling of confidence. A man who cares is not the master. And one can observe this in the matter of simple singing in the rain or in a pub. The fellows who around Christmas sing in pubs are not just chaps enjoying themselves. Enjoying themselves has nothing to do with it. They are expressing themselves. This is their art, their reason for existence. And they are usually very humble and ashamed of their own selves, for they always assume the part of some singing star or other. No wonder I squirm. I do not blame them; few people have the courage to be themselves. And when they do appear themselves it is all put on with spadefuls of bravado. It took me many years to learn or relearn not to care. The heart of a song singing it, or a poem writing it, is not caring. I will sing now and give the poems later:

On Raglan Road on an autumn day I met her first and knew
That her dark hair could weave a snare that I might one day rue.
I saw the danger yet I walked upon the enchanted way
And I said let grief be a fallen leaf at the dawning of the day.

In the beginning of my versing career I had hit on the no-caring jag but there was nobody to tell me that I was on the right track:

My black hills have never seen the sun rising,
Eternally they look north towards Armagh.

There are two kinds of simplicity, the simplicity of going away and the simplicity of return. The last is the ultimate in sophistication. In the final simplicity we don't care whether we appear foolish or not. We talk of things that earlier would embarrass. We are satisfied with being ourselves, however small. So it was that on the banks of the Grand Canal between Baggot and Leeson Street bridges in the warm summer of 1955, I lay and watched the green waters of the canal. I had just come out of hospital. I wrote:

Leafy-with-love banks and the green waters of the canal
Pouring redemption for me, that I do
The will of God, wallow in the habitual, the banal,
Grow with nature again as before I grew.

And so in this moment of great daring I became a poet. Except for brief moments in my very early years I had not been a poet. The poems in *A Soul for Sale* are not poetry and neither is *The Great Hunger*. There are some queer and terrible things in *The Great Hunger*, but it lacks the nobility and repose of poetry. The trouble, as I may have mentioned earlier, is that there are so few who would know a poem from a hole in the ground. It is possible on the other hand to recognize a poet, for the animal is recognizable. The main feature about a poet, if you ever happen to meet one – and that's a remote chance, for I can't be everywhere at the one time – the main feature is his humourosity. Any touch of boringness and you are in the wrong shop. Beautiful women, I am glad to say, are capable of recognizing the baste. Recently a man was presented to me as being a great poet. He wrote in Irish. I expressed me doubts and the introducer said: 'How can you tell when you don't know the language?' That was a sore one, but I was able for it. I said, 'I can't bawl like a cow but I'd know a cow if I saw one.'

That a poet is born, not made, is well known. But this does not mean that he was a poet the day he was physically born. For many a good-looking year I wrought hard at versing but I would say that, as a poet, I was born in or about nineteen fifty-five, the place of my birth being the banks of the Grand Canal. Thirty years earlier, Shancoduff's watery hills could have done the trick but I was too thick to take the hint. Curious this, how I had started off with the right simplicity, indifferent to crude reason, and then ploughed my way through complexities and anger, hatred and ill-will towards the faults of man, and came back to where I started. For one of the very earliest things I wrote, even predating 'Shancoduff', started this way:

Child do not go
Into the dark places of soul,
For there the grey wolves whine,
The lean grey wolves.

In that little thing I had become airborne and more; I had achieved weightlessness. And then I heard about having one's roots in the soil of being a peasant. And I raged at Monaghan and the clay and all to that. But poetry has to do with the reality of the spirit, of faith and hope and sometimes even charity. It is a point of view. A poet is a theologian. Arts councils and the like love to believe in the poet as a simple singer piping down the valleys wild. When Shelley said that poets were the real legislators of the world he was right, although he may not have fully understood his rightness. A poet is an original who inspires millions of copies. That's all education consists of – the copying of a good model.

Reverting at that to my public career, I must mention that adventure when I edited and wrote *Kavanagh's Weekly* in 1952. We had no ads – a distinction that looks like overtaking many other papers before the century is out. I wrote almost the whole paper including the poems, letters to the editor, etc. Why do people engage in such madness?

But recently looking up the files I read something that has relevance here. On 'School Book Poetry' I wrote – quoting Longfellow:

> *There are things of which I may not speak*
> *How strange things happen to a man.*
> *He dabbles in something and does*
> *Not realize that it is his life.*

That was what I wrote then. And yet I had not yet been born, as I believe I afterwards was, though perhaps some folks may not agree. It doesn't matter. Anyhow, I did arrive at complete casualness, at being able to play a true note on a dead slack string. This year my friend John Jordan, who was about to bring out a magazine called *Poetry Ireland*, asked me for a stave and from my redoubt in Monaghan I sent this message to my peoples:

> *I am here in a garage in Monaghan.*
> *It is June and the weather is warm,*
> *Just a little bit cloudy. There's the sun again*
> *Lifting to importance my sixteen-acre farm.*
> *There are three swallows' nests in the rafters above me*
> *And the first clutches are already flying.*

Spread this news widely, tell all if you love me,
You who knew that when sick I was never dying
(Nae gane, nae gane, nae frae us torn
But taking a rest like John Jordan).

And so on. One wiseacre said that a garage in Monaghan couldn't be poetry and another of the same mental ilk said that I was going back to me roots and that I was good at the country stuff. Well, there's where it was. Courage is nearly everything. Our pure impulses are always right.

In the Name of The Father
The Son and The Mother
We explode
Ridiculously, uncode
A habit and find therein
A successful human being.

(Text of a television programme transmitted by RTÉ on 30 October 1962; published by The Dolmen Press, Dublin, 1964)

Bibliography

Essays, articles and reviews by Patrick Kavanagh are listed in *The Garden of the Golden Apples: A Bibliography of Patrick Kavanagh*, compiled and researched by Peter Kavanagh (The Peter Kavanagh Hand Press, New York, 1972), and in John Nemo, 'Patrick Kavanagh: A Bibliography of Materials by and about Patrick Kavanagh', *The Irish University Review*, Spring 1973.

COLUMNS

'City Commentary', *Irish Press*, 14 September 1942 to 18 February 1944, under the pen-name Piers Plowman (twice weekly).

'The Literary Scene', *The Standard*, 26 February to 11 June 1943 (weekly).

Film reviewing under various headings, *The Standard*, 22 February 1946 to 8 July 1949 (weekly).

'Diary', *Envoy*, December 1949 to July 1951 (monthly).

Creation, June 1957 to December 1957 (monthly).

Irish Farmers' Journal, 14 June 1958 to 9 March 1963 (weekly).

National Observer, July 1959 to January 1960 (monthly).

RTV Guide, 17 January 1964 to 30 June 1967 (weekly).

WEEKLY PAPER

Kavanagh's Weekly, with Peter Kavanagh, 12 April to 5 July 1952.

PAMPHLET

Self-Portrait, The Dolmen Press (Dublin, 1964) and Dufour Publishers (Pennsylvania, 1964).

BIBLIOGRAPHY

INTRODUCTIONS

Author's Note, *Collected Poems*, MacGibbon & Kee (London, 1964) and Devin-Adair (New York, 1964).

Introduction to W. Steuart Trench, *Realities of Irish Life*, MacGibbon & Kee (London, 1966).

Preface to *The Autobiography of William Carleton*, MacGibbon & Kee (London, 1968).

BOOKS CONTAINING PROSE WORKS

Patrick Kavanagh, *Collected Pruse*, MacGibbon & Kee (London, 1967).

Peter Kavanagh, ed., *November Haggard: Uncollected Prose and Verse of Patrick Kavanagh*, The Peter Kavanagh Hand Press (New York, 1971).

The Journal of Irish Literature, 'A Patrick Kavanagh Number', edited by John Nemo, January 1977.

Peter Kavanagh (ed.), *Patrick Kavanagh: Man and Poet*, Goldsmith Press (The Curragh, Ireland, 1987).

TYPESCRIPTS

The typescripts of 'The Stir' and of the unpublished collections *Some Evocations of No Importance* and *The Forgiven Plough* are in the Kavanagh Archive, Library of University College Dublin.

MAGAZINES TO WHICH KAVANAGH CONTRIBUTED (SELECTED)

The Bell. Monthly 1940 to 1954. Suspended after April 1948, resumed November 1950. Edited by Sean O'Faoláin 1940–6; thereafter by Peadar O'Donnell. Subtitled, variously, 'A Survey of Irish Life', 'A Magazine for Creative Fiction', and 'A Magazine of Ireland Today'.

Creation, 'A Journal of Fashion and Décor'. Monthly 1956–66.

Envoy. A monthly review of literature and art, founded and edited by John Ryan. December 1949 to July 1951.

The Family Doctor. British Medical Association journal. Monthly 1951–66.

Ireland of the Welcomes. Bi-monthly magazine published by the Irish Tourist Association from 1952.

Irish Writing, 'The Magazine of Contemporary Irish Literature', founded in 1946 by David Marcus and Tristram Smith.

Kavanagh's Weekly, 'A Journal of Literature and Politics', 12 April to 5 July 1952.

The Kilkenny Magazine, 'An All-Ireland Literary Review'. Edited by James Delehanty for The Kilkenny Literary Society. Irregularly 1960–70.

The National Observer, 'A Journal of Current Affairs', edited by Declan Costello and Alexis Fitzgerald and published monthly from July 1958 to October/December 1960 (the final issues appeared irregularly). It was a Fine Gael-sponsored publication but did not state this.

Nimbus. 'A Magazine of New Writing', London. Quarterly 1951–6.

Nonplus. Literary magazine founded and edited by Patricia Murphy in October 1959 and published by The Dolmen Press, Dublin. Three issues only.

RTV Guide. Guide to entertainment on radio and television and feature articles. Weekly, 1 December 1961 to 24 June 1966. Renamed *RTÉ Guide* on 1 July 1966.

St Stephen's. University College Dublin students' literary magazine. Eamon Grennan was Editor of the Trinity Term 1962 issue in the 1960–71 series.

Studies. Irish quarterly review of letters, philosophy and science, published by the Society of Jesus. Founded 1922.

The Word. Catholic pictorial monthly magazine, published by the Divine Word Missionaries.

X. Quarterly review of art and literature, edited by David Wright and Patrick Swift, 1959–62.

Editor's Acknowledgments

I should like to express my gratitude to the following:

Brendan Barrington, editor at The Lilliput Press, for his attention to text.

Jonathan Williams, my agent, for his continued advice and support.

Anthony Cronin for information on Kavanagh's lost prose collection of 1951.

John Dillon, Regius Professor of Greek in the Classics Department, Trinity College Dublin, who kindly sourced the quotation from Philip of Thessalonika.

Uinseann MacEoin for his helpful response to my letter seeking information on *Creation*.

Frank McEvoy for drawing my attention to the Report on Kavanagh in the Presidential files of 1943 in Áras an Uachtaráin.

Cormac Walsh of the Arts Council for his prompt response to my request to consult Arts Council documents. Consultation of these documents in the National Archives, Dublin, was by kind permission of the Arts Council.

Caitriona Crowe and Tom Quinlan for guidance with Arts Council sources and Áras an Uachtaráin files in the National Archives.

Mrs Norma Jessop, librarian in charge of Special Collections, University College Dublin Library at Belfield, which houses the Kavanagh Archive, and the librarians at the National Archives, National Library, Royal Irish Academy and Trinity College, Dublin, for help in tracing Kavanagh's prose.

The writings of Patrick Kavanagh are printed by kind permission of the Trustees of the Estate of the late Katherine B. Kavanagh, through the Jonathan Williams Literary Agency.